Palgrave Insights into Apocalypse Economics

Series Editor
Richard Westra
Graduate School of Law
Nagoya University
Nagoya-shi, Aichi, Japan

This series is set to become the lodestone for critical Marxist and related Left scholarship on the raft of apocalyptic tendencies enveloping the global economy and society. Its working premise is that neoliberal policies from the 1980s not only failed to rejuvenate capitalist prosperity lost with the demise of the post-Second World War 'golden age' economy but in fact have generated a widening spectrum of pathologies that threaten humanity itself. At the most fundamental level the series cultivates state of the art critical political economic analysis of the crises, recessionary, deflationary and austerity conditions that have beset the world economy since the global meltdown of 2008–2009. However, though centered on work that critically explores global propensities for devastating financial convulsions, ever-widening inequalities and economic marginalisation due to information technologies, robotised production and low wage outsourcing, it seeks to draw on exacerbating factors such as climate change and global environmental despoliation, corrupted food systems and land-grabbing, rampant militarism, cyber crime and terrorism, all together which defy mainstream economics and conventional political policy solutions.

For critical Marxist and related Left scholars the series offers a non-sectarian outlet for academic work that is hard-hitting, inter/trans-disciplinary and multiperspectival. Its readership draws in academics, researchers, students, progressive governmental and non-governmental actors and the academically-informed public.

More information about this series at
http://www.palgrave.com/gp/series/15867

Joel Magnuson

Financing the Apocalypse

Drivers for Economic and Political Instability

palgrave
macmillan

Joel Magnuson
Independent Researcher
Tualatin, OR, USA

ISSN 2523-8108 ISSN 2523-8116 (electronic)
Palgrave Insights into Apocalypse Economics
ISBN 978-3-030-04719-1 ISBN 978-3-030-04720-7 (eBook)
https://doi.org/10.1007/978-3-030-04720-7

Library of Congress Control Number: 2018962763

This Palgrave Macmillan imprint is published by the registered company Springer Nature Switzerland AG
The registered company address is: Gewerbestrasse 11, 6330 Cham, Switzerland

Contents

List of Figures

List of Tables

1 Introduction

As we tour the four-hundred-year history of capitalism through its various phases of development, we see that financial system instability is always there lurking in the shadows. For at least four centuries the historical record is littered with periodic events of wild swings in financial markets, massive debt defaults, bank failures, and general economic instability. Historically, booms, busts, crises, and bailouts have run through familiar patterns of repetition, though they are becoming more frequent now and more severe. The major stock market crash and banking crisis that occurred in 1929 seemed to be a once-in-a-lifetime event, but similar patterns of instability are occurring at least once every decade now and are happening simultaneously around the world with growing magnitude. This is particularly noticeable in the last thirty-plus, or what we will be referring to as the Greenspan Era: from 1987 when the stock market took a serious tumble and Alan Greenspan assumed the chair position at the Federal Reserve to the Banking Crisis of 2007–2009 and on.

Like all financial crises, the ones that have occurred during this period have multiple causes. Arguably the most significant during the Greenspan Era is the phenomenon of financialization. Since the

J. Magnuson, *Financing the Apocalypse*,
Palgrave Insights into Apocalypse Economics,
https://doi.org/10.1007/978-3-030-04720-7_1

banking crisis, there has been much discussion in heterodox circles about the economics of financialization, though it is largely ignored in the mainstream. Financialization is a process in which financial institutions and markets systematically gain influence and control over increasingly large segments of the economy. The process has roots that go back to the beginning of capitalism, but has risen to a very high profile during the Greenspan Era. It is a reflection of a broader systemic crisis that has been erupting in this period in which companies in significant numbers are finding it increasingly difficult to generate profits through traditional means of actual producing things for sale in markets.

Built into the core logic of capitalism is the need to generate returns for investors and to plow back a portion of those returns to fuel expansion. The imperative to generate investor income drives businesses to continuously seek out or fabricate markets and opportunities for investment. Eventually, this exploration reaches limitations, sales slow to a trickle, and economic activity gets stuck in the mud. Authors John Bellamy Foster and Robert McChesney describe this process as capitalism's long-run tendency toward an "endless crisis," which relies on injections of "external stimuli" to keep it going such as government spending programs or new technological innovations or the discovery of new markets.[1]

The financial system has served to extend this process of innovation. As the hunt for profitable opportunities becomes more desperate, companies are scurrying into profitable opportunities as quickly as possible and jump out just as quickly when profits disappear. This requires a facile investment ecosystem in which capital is liquid enough to be moved anywhere swiftly, then settles in an investment fund, then briskly turn to cash and move to yet another location, like bees going from one flower to another searching for nectar. The more rapidly this takes place, the more pressure there is on the financial system to mobilize investment funds, and to underwrite and continually recreate new instruments: securities, commodities, derivatives. This drives the securitization, commodification, and financialization of every possible thing imaginable. Financial services are indeed becoming an increasingly significant sector. In the mid-twentieth century, financial services constituted about 2.5% of national output, then it grew to about

4% in 1980, then soared to 8.3% by 2006 right before the banking crisis began.[2] This goes a long way to explaining how and why our economies are becoming increasingly unstable; for in the historical view, there is always boom-bust instability that follows.

There are other causes of economic undulations during the Greenspan Era including the policies of the Federal Reserve. Among the most outstanding characteristics of the Greenspan Fed is its commitment to flooding the financial system with generous amounts of cheap credit, which stimulated a massive debt bubble. Household debt was 56% of national output in 1987, then it steadily rose to reach 63% in 2000, and then soared to 98% by the first quarter of 2008 on the eve of the banking crisis.[3] Household debt has been trimmed back to 78.7% yet remains persistently high by historical comparison.[4]

Public debt as a percentage of GDP has also increased during the Greenspan Era. It was 48% in 1987, hit a 65% peak in 1995, then tapered off temporarily. When the George W. Bush tax cuts for the wealthy were put into effect in 2001, public debt resumed its upward climb, and then soared during the Great Recession and continued to climb after the recession was over to hit 105% of GDP by 2016.[5] The Trump tax cuts have pushed public deficits and debts to new highs. Cheap and abundant credit flowing out of the Fed also served to keep interest rates on Treasury bonds at rock bottom. Pension fund managers could not meet the expectation of their retirees' financial plans and became compelled to seek out other securities for investment. As they did, they and other fund managers ventured further and further into the higher risk territories of corporate bonds that are rated in a range from sterling triple A to junk.

Among the biggest concerns regarding the debt bubble is the high amount of corporate debt and the concern that the low-interest rates on this debt do not accurately reflect risk. To give some perspective on this, the total dollar amount of capital traded in the US stock markets sums to about $30 trillion the ups and downs of which we hear about throughout each working day. The corporate bond market is much larger—about $41 trillion as of this writing. To help facilitate this expansion of debt, the Federal Reserve has jumped from holding about $800 billion in bonds, to over $4 trillion, which is about a

400% increase (see Appendix). Incentivized by low rates and available credit, corporations have charged up their debt over the last decade from 16% of national output to about 25%.[6] As the profile of corporate debt increases, so does the element of risk making the financial system increasingly vulnerable.

Another aspect is technology and the constant push for financial innovation. As the financial sector grew to be the glistening centerpiece of the economy during the Greenspan Era, Wall Street was the most seductive place to pursue a career in ways that traditional banking could never be. People with real talent, particularly those gifted with skills in creating mathematical algorithms, gravitated toward the steel and glass towers in the financial district of New York. Math models and computer models for trading became more complex and sophisticated and the cult of technological wizardry gave the illusion that the more complex the instruments created by investment banks, the more investors could speculate without risk. Innovation thus became the justification for the creation of new generations of securities and derivatives and new markets for trading. This combined with a growing digital infrastructure heightened the process of financialization. Financial engineers on Wall Street have been continuously contriving new ways to aggregate massive amounts of cash for multinational corporations and to make speculative trades in staggering amounts on computer screens. Wall Street corporations were at the center of financial world and the people there knew it. Their careers have been centered on a mandate to score profits for themselves and for their clients, even if this meant running the risk of destabilizing economies everywhere, which is precisely what they did. All of this carries on under the banner of anti-government, pro-market neoliberal propaganda. But there is a deeper institutional aspect to both the phenomenon of financialization and the instabilities it has engendered.

The aim of *Financing the Apocalypse* is to add this dimension to the discourse. The core narrative in the story presented here is that financialization and the fragilities that come with it are the outward manifestations of deep institutional pathologies that have been building in the system for over a century. Specifically, we are referring to system conditions that are associated with the ascent of corporate hegemony that came into its full maturity during the Greenspan Era.

Several decades before the Greenspan Era began this institutional perspective on the evolution of corporate hegemony originated with the long-term vision held by economist and grandfather of institutional economics, Thorstein Veblen.

Veblen's Secular Trend

A century ago, Thorstein Veblen looked to the future and didn't like what he saw. In one of the very last pieces of writing toward the end of his life, he outlined what he called "The Secular Trend."[7] He examined past trends, present conditions, and extrapolated to the future of economic society in America that seems certain to tear itself apart into an almost biblical state of antagonistic dichotomy among economic institutions. For Veblen economic institutions are simply habituated ways that humans behave in society economically or "action-patterns induced by the run of past habituation."[8] What he saw for our future was a deep schism opening between healthy, well-adjusted institutions and those that are pathological and maladjusted.

On the well-adjusted side, Veblen identified habitual ways of behaving that are grounded in science, problem-solving, creativity, and are useful to the human life process. They guide our work in ways that are more useful to people, not because there are fortunes to be made, but because of the historically rich craft traditions in which humans are fascinated with the idea of doing things better. These stand on the side of progress, appropriately implemented technology, stability, and the provision for the general wellbeing of the population.

On the other side are maladjusted institutions that exist to accumulate ostentatious fortunes, status, and conquests for a small class of the wealthy and powerful "absentee owners." Rather than contribute to progress, they smother the economy with greed, corruption, and stagnation. They do not create, they own and extract it. For Veblen, the large publicly traded corporation emerged on this side of the rift and came to dominate the economic scene completely. Veblen attested to the rise of the corporation, not as a business model, but as a dominant institution that he called, "the Interests." By its own mandate, it is fashioned to be indifferent to social provisioning, and is governed by the narrowest of objectives—to make money for vested owners, "The effective control of the economic situation, in business, industry, and civil life, rests on the on the control of credit. Therefore, the effectual exercise of initiative, discretion, and authority is perforce vested in those massive aggregations of absentee ownership that make the Interests."[9] What was most troubling for Veblen was that he saw a future in which the corporate world would push all else aside and the entire economic system would cease to be concerned about providing for the needs of people and only about financial gain—a pathological end game.

A century before they became household names, Thorstein Veblen warned of the formidable power of Wall Street and giant corporations. He looked to the future and saw that if our society allows corporate entities to become the size of Jupiter, all else will become its moons and satellites, with a gravitational bind among them that is so strong that, "the rest of the community, the industrial system and the underlying population are at the disposal of the Interests."[10] For Veblen, the Interests represents the principal shareholders and the corporate class of professionals that work at the top of the hierarchy. He sees the members of this class positioning themselves to take control of the economy with a patent indifference to economic stability, industrial progress, or anything else that might contribute to social wellbeing beyond financial gain. In his view, the corporation is a legal-financial institution that is structured around securities trades for capitalization and commodity trades for profits. It is an institution that is programmed such that its stakeholders are not required to accomplish anything, or even care what the business does, except generate returns for owners. Rather the "ways and means of business, to be managed in a temperate spirit of *usufruct* for the continued and cumulative benefit of the major Interests and their absentee owners."[11]

Usufruct, in Veblen's somewhat arcane terminology, means to exploit the economic system for the aggrandizement of individuals who are already wealthy and powerful. To that end, the corporate sector became "the main controlling factor in the established order of things" (ibid., 4).[12] He attested to an evolutionary drift toward corporate hegemony in which all other major institutions were becoming increasingly rendered under the boot of corporate power. He described the formation of an emergent system as, "One Big Union made up of partners, auxiliaries, subsidiaries, extensions and purveyors of traffic."[13] In other words, what Veblen was describing was an evolutionary trend toward corporate hegemony, which like so many other creations of capitalism, it has developed a kind of mind of its own.

Veblen's Secular Trend inspired institutionalist economist William Dugger, who decades later to produced his comprehensive work on corporate power titled, *Corporate Hegemony* (1989). Dugger introduces his work,

> [The] capitalist corporate is an inherently narrow and short-sighted organization. It has not evolved to serve the public purpose. It has not evolved to monitor and coordinate economic activity for the benefit of society at large. The corporation has evolved to serve the interests of whoever controls it, at the expense of whoever does not. This is a simple but profound truth. The corporation, not the market, is the dominant economic institution in the industrialized West.[14]

By the time Dugger conveyed this message, the Greenspan Era was already underway. For a good century and more, corporate evolution was given free passage to stitch together a network of behemoths that collectively brought government and central bank institutions everywhere into its sphere of influence. This became among the most powerful club of wealth and influence in modern history. The dominant institution controls the markets in retail, auto, pharmaceuticals, media finance, and every other industry either through oligopoly, virtual monopolies, or joint ventures—which are basically legalized cartels—though nonetheless still largely viewed in economic and business theory as mere business models.

And all of this is sugar-coated for mass consumption with neoliberalism propaganda. Politically captured, policymakers are lulled into complacency and dismissiveness toward the most pressing dangers that have been building in the system for decades, not least of which are instabilities on gargantuan scale, the punishment of climate change, and a chasm of economic inequality.

The rider of the black horse of the apocalypse is said to have come carrying a set of scales surrounded by a voice claiming, "A measure of wheat for a penny, and three measures of barley for a penny; and see thou hurt not the oil and the wine,"[15] which could reasonably be interpreted as a warning to maintain some kind of balance or stability in commerce and in relation to available resources. The consequences for ignoring this follow in the form of a ghostly "pale horse: and his name that sate on him was Death, and Hell followed with him."[16]

However, one chooses to interpret such a passage, it is not hard to see that we are being held accountable in some way or another when we allow things to warp out of balance. The indications of profound imbalance are overwhelming. Foremost among the many concerns raised in *Financing the Apocalypse* is that these institutional and ideological developments are deepening the crisis conditions our financial system at a time when societies everywhere are already being rendered vulnerable by the ravages of climate change, reactionary political movements, and a dwindling resource base. Moreover, these trends appear to be on a path to converge into a perfect storm of collapse.

Collapse and Apocalypse: It's All Anthropogenic

Taking a quick view of the pathological system conditions, we can see that they are all on the ascent (see the Appendix for charts) and on a path to converge feed into one another. In addition to mounting debts in every sector, stocks and housing markets are also in bubble condition. The Case Shiller U.S. Housing Market Index representing 20 major metropolitan areas, shows housing prices significantly above the long-term trend. If the markets were to return to trend with a correction, this would mean the markets would tank showing a fall in the index from its current level of 204 to collapse to about 160, or roughly 22%. The Standard & Poors Index representing a broad segment of the corporate sphere shows stocks inflated significantly above the long-term trend. If the markets were to return to trend, which is popularly referred to as a correction, this would mean a collapse—about a 1000-point drop or roughly 39%. One thing we know for sure about financial market bubbles is that they always pop. When these do, the economic fallout will be astronomical.

To rescue Wall Street from its troubles, the Federal Reserve embarked on a buying spree of Mortgage-backed securities, government debt, and other securities and created an asset bubble. Its holdings of assets soared from about $800 billion in 2007 to nearly $4.5 trillion a decade later. To do this it created about $3.5 trillion dollars out of thin air. If the Fed were to try to unwind its holdings of these assets and return to trend, it would have to reverse that process and dump about $3 trillion of these back on the markets. Such a move would crash the market and precipitate a global financial meltdown.

The way the US economic system works is that when crises unfold, it is those who are most economically vulnerable bear the bulk of the damage. Measured in terms of inequality, such vulnerability is building in the system with an "inequality bubble." The Gini Index is a measurement of income distribution (see Chapter 6). The higher the index number, the more unequal the distribution of income becomes for the population. The long-term trend is for an increasingly wide chasm of separating the wealthy from the rest of the population. Given the current political climate, the trend will continue and shows no sign of ever returning to a condition of equitable income distribution. This trend is certain to cause social instability at some point.

The ravages of climate change are upon us as is the "carbon dioxide bubble" grows larger each year. According to scientist James Hansen, it is estimated that the world can limit the worst effects of climate change by bringing the concentration of atmospheric carbon dioxide to below 350 parts per million from its current levels of over 400. This number was considered the key to avoiding the climate change "tipping point" beyond which the global climate condition moves from stable to unstable. Humans have already past that point and there is no turning back. Together these developments are pointing to instability in one shape or another—financial and economic instability, political instability, and climate instability—as they would have to because bubbles are inherently unstable structures, and they are all anthropogenic.

As we say that these conditions are anthropogenic, we are saying that these condition are caused by human activity. In the view presented here, when we say human activity we are saying human behavior as it is shaped and conditioned by institutions, and when way talk of institutions in our contemporary society we are talking about corporations. And when talk of corporations, William Dugger's conception of "organized irresponsibility" comes to mind, "the corporation is organized in such a way that the humans who stand to gain from its actions are not responsible for those actions should they go awry." Dugger notes that by the nineteenth century, limited liability for shareholders was firmly established in corporate institutions, executives are mere employees, and directors are agents of shareholders. No humans are accountable or culpable, "Thus the organized irresponsibility of corporate life was institutionalized."[17] In other words, it's just business.

Financing the Apocalypse

The word anthropogenic is finally being largely accepted in climate change discourse and it means that these are conditions we have created for ourselves. All these pathological conditions are anthropogenic as they originate from our economic system and institutions. In the hope of helping to better our understanding how we got here, *Financing the Apocalypse* begins with building a systems institutional framework of economic analysis. Unlike mainstream theory that views economic activity as nothing more than individualistic choice-making, this approach holds that these choices are structured within a hierarchy of institutional forces. People make choices obviously, but the choices are heavily institutionalized. This framework is also holistic in the sense that economic institutions themselves are structured within a broader systemic context. The central theme, therefore, is that human economic behavior is inescapably bound to a broader nexus of institutions.

Chapter 3 takes a closer at the largest and most dominant institutions that have fused capital and risen beyond dominance to supreme levels of concentration. These are Fortune 500 and Wall Street corporations that stand astride the economic landscape. A handful of these companies combine to an amount of annual revenue that is larger than national output of most countries. It is this fact, sheer size, and scale, that make them the corporate alpha dogs. Moreover, they have the ability to amass unprecedented amounts of financial wealth and play reckless games reckless and speculative games with tens or hundreds of billions in cash, much of which is borrowed. They are social and political entities as much as they are economic, and together they form a structure of corporate hegemony that is beyond the reach of democratic accountability.

The message of Chapter 4 is that such a hegemonic structure could not hold together for long without a mutual support network of institutions including the Federal Reserve, the U.S. Treasury and other government establishments, media, think tanks, and academia. Collectively, this support network performs a variety of functions that serve the interests of the core such as laying down financial safety nets, offering up vast amounts of cheap credit, passing favorable legislation and court rulings, marginalizing opposition, and providing ideological justification. These institutions set the rules for how financial activity is to be carried out and for whom. They set normative boundaries for economic discourse and policy priorities.

Chapters 5 and 6 point to neoliberalism that is the ideological support system for corporate hegemony. sublimates economic individualism and questions the roles played by other institutions. Contemporary neoliberalism distinguishes itself from traditional laissez-faire liberalism in an important sense in that it views government institutions as necessary economic players, but it may not seem so from what we hear in the media from conservative pundits. But most pop anti-government rhetoric is targeted at aspects of government intrusion that interferes with business profit-making such as progressive taxation, social security provisions, or environmental regulations. Also, during the Greenspan Era, the allure of gaining easy money has developed into a pervasive sense of entitlement. This sense of entitlement is part of a cultural trend that political analyst, Thomas Frank, identified as "market populism" that began in the late 1980s, and has molded public opinion into a kind of cheerleading squad for corporate hegemony.

Chapters 7, 8 and 9 tell the stories of instabilities that fire directly out the double barrels of corporate hegemony and neoliberal ideology. During the Greenspan Era, these institutional and ideological developments have created the conditions for having extremely large funds concentrated and handled by a super team of institutional giants. The danger, as we have experienced, is cyclonic instability on a terrible scale. Nothing of substance has changed since the last major crisis except that the conditions for instability intensified. The patterns revealed here give us a reasonably clear indication that another cyclone of trouble is building in the system, which is substantiated by data (see Appendix) showing that highly inflated bubble markets are on their way to burst.

The crises that derive from financial market instability and systemic risk in banking are dramas that are replayed over and again. *Financing the Apocalypse* addresses this as a system condition that remains deeply embedded in our financial system's neoliberal institutional and ideological structure. As this continues, more meltdowns and breakdowns will follow.

In the decade that has passed since the crisis of 2008, the banking and financial sectors have become more concentrated than ever before, economies are more debt-dependent than ever before, bubble markets have ballooned massively again, and the regulatory climate is now more staunchly neoliberal than ever before. It seems fair to say, therefore, that the next crises could very well eclipse them all.

Naturally many progressive-minded people are looking for solutions. The last three chapters examine what many to consider to be alternatives to business as usual, but are nonetheless captured by the same corporate hegemony and neoliberal ideology, and hence stand as non-solutions. These stories attest to the formidable grip neoliberalism has on the popular imagination. The common element among them is mission drift stemming from an untenable belief in win-win scenarios in which people and communities can get wealth while working against pathological systems conditions. What makes the untenable is that they are fashioned within the same institutions that created the pathological conditions in the first place, and were therefore doomed to fail from the outset. Chapter 10 tells the story of microfinance that was once held in high esteem as an innovative alternative to loan sharking and as a strategy for poverty reduction in the developing world. It was embraced globally as an effort for the world's poor to save themselves from predatory loan sharks, and unsustainable debt traps, but eventually pushed to a neoliberal model. As such, it reverted to the same loan sharking environment it was designed to work against.

Chapter 11 highlights peer-to-peer (P-2-P) and crowdfunding models of source funding have gone through a similar process. Once celebrated as grassroots financial models and alternatives to Wall Street, they have become variations on the same theme. P-2-P has risen to prominence as one of the next great new things to help the poor through internet portals. But just beneath the glossy imagery on portal websites lies gimmickry designed to attract donors. This has created a backlash of suspicion and even cynicism that the P-2-P programs serve to ameliorate the guilt of wealthy donors, while leaving the actual causes of poverty unaddressed. Like microfinance lenders, surrounding the hype and buzz of equity, crowdfunding are entrepreneurs who are aggressively pushing this model in hopes of garnering lucrative consulting fees at the expense of small business. Evidence of mission drift is surfacing as the models are hustled away from small-is-beautiful to a professional services bonanza.

Chapter 12 highlights how the neoliberal wagon train has rolled out an abundance of proposals to integrate social and environmental impacts into the profit-making system. The list is exhaustive: Socially Responsible Investment funds (SRIs), The Natural Step, Triple Bottom Line accounting or the Three Es (equity, economy, ecology), a host of impact entrepreneurship models, and so on not least of which is the oxymoron, green capitalism.

Both in institutional form and ideological belief, these are all products of the Greenspan Era. They are systems conditions. Three decades into the Greenspan Era, we are bearing witness to the effects of climate change in real time, extreme polarization of wealth distribution, the ascent of reactionary politics, resource depletion, and grand episodes of instability. It is a matter of choice as to which of these represents the deathly pale horse of the apocalypse—one proving to be just as dangerous as the other. And it would be fair to say now, at long last, that neoliberal win-win scenarios are not working. They cannot work because they are, like oxymorons, inherently contradictory. To believe that our contemporary crises be resolved with very same neoliberal institutions and belief systems that are causing these crises is like believing that a slave system can somehow be made humanistic using racism and chattel labor. Slavery was an institutional condition and so is corporate hegemony, and to remain captured will be our will be our undoing.

Notes

1. John Bellamy Foster and Robert McChesney, *The Endless Crisis: How Monopoly-Finance Capital Produces Stagnation and Upheaval from the USA to China* (New York, NY: Monthly Review Press, 2012), p. 12.
2. Ibid. See also Thomas Phillippon, "The Future of the Financial Industry," New York University, Leonard N. Stern School of Business, http://w4.stern.nyu.edu/blogs/sternonfinance/2008/11/the-future-of-the-financial-in.html.
3. Household Debt to GDP for the United States, Federal Reserve Bank of St. Louis, https://fred.stlouisfed.org/series/HDTGPDUSQ163N.
4. See Trading Economics website at https://tradingeconomics.com/united-states/households-debt-to-gdp.
5. Ibid.
6. Niel Irwin, "What Will Cause the Next Recession? A Look at the 3 Most Likely Possibilities," *The New York Times*, August 2, 2018.
7. Thorstein Veblen, *Absentee Ownership: Business Enterprise in Recent Times: The Case of America* [1923] (New Brunswick, NJ: Transaction Publishers, 1997), pp. 398–445.
8. Ibid., p. 398.
9. Ibid., pp. 398–399.
10. Veblen, 1997, p. 399.
11. Ibid.
12. Ibid., p. 4.
13. Ibid., p. 399.
14. William H. Dugger, *Corporate Hegemony* (New York, NY: Greenwood Press, 1989), p. xiii.
15. *The Holy Bible*, The Revelation, Chapter 6, Verses 5 and 6.
16. Ibid., Verse 8.
17. Dugger, 1989, p. 12.

References

Dugger, William H. *Corporate Hegemony* (Westport, CT: Greenwood Press, 1989), p. xiii.

Foster, John Bellamy, and Robert McChesney. *The Endless Crisis: How Monopoly-Finance Capital Produces Stagnation and Upheaval from the USA to China* (New York, NY: Monthly Review Press, 2012), p. 12.

"Household Debt to GDP for the United States," April 2017. https://fred.stlouisfed.org/series/HDTGPDUSQ163N.

Irwin, Neil. "What Will Cause the Next Recession? A Look at the 3 Most Likely Possibilities," *The New York Times*, August 2, 2018.

Phillippon, Thomas. "The Future of the Financial Industry," New York University, Leonard N. Stern School of Business (2008). http://w4.stern.nyu.edu/blogs/sternonfinance/2008/11/the-future-of-the-financial-in.html.

"Trading Economics: United States Households Debt to GDP: 1952–2018," 2018. https://tradingeconomics.com/united-states/households-debt-to-gdp.

The Holy Bible, "The Revelation," Chapter 6, Verses 5 and 6.

Veblen, Thorstein. *Absentee Ownership: Business Enterprise in Recent Times: The Case of America* [1923] (New Brunswick, NJ: Transaction Publishers, 1997), pp. 398–445.

2
Taking the Long View

Late in the year 2000, something relatively minor happened that set off an extraordinary chain reaction of events that eventually brought the global economy to its knees. Texas Republican Senator Phil Gramm surreptitiously slipped a provision into the Commodity Futures Modernizations Act just a few days before President Bill Clinton signed the 262-page bill into law on December 21, 2000.[1] The provision exempted certain over-the-counter derivative transactions, including oil futures and mortgage derivatives, from the regulatory jurisdiction of the Commodity Futures Trading Commission (CFTC). It was designed by Gramm's wife, Wendy Gramm, who was formerly the chair of the CFTC and later became one of the directors for the infamous Houston-based energy company, Enron.

The provision eventually came to be as the "Enron Loophole" as it allowed energy trading companies like Enron to form their own derivative exchanges off the radar of government regulators. Oil futures, among other things, were set free to be traded in the dark and this triggered a frenzy of speculation. When an unregulated market is targeted for speculation where traders buy and sell hoping to pocket short-term

J. Magnuson, *Financing the Apocalypse*,
Palgrave Insights into Apocalypse Economics,
https://doi.org/10.1007/978-3-030-04720-7_2

gains, it has the potential to become volatile—a roller coaster ride of price upswings and downswings. The Gramm deregulation maneuver sent speculators jumping into oil.

After a brief interlude during which energy traders set up their exchanges, oil prices began to soar. On the New York Mercantile Exchange, oil went from about $30 per barrel in late 2002 to a peak of over $140 per barrel in 2008.[2] Analysts and media pundits at the time ignored the speculative frenzy and rather pointed to higher demand for oil coming from the growing economies of China and India as the main cause. Although it is true that economic growth can put upward pressure on energy prices, such an effect is more gradual and parallels overall economic growth. This was 350–400% spike in just a few years caused by speculative trading in an unregulated market.

During this speculative boom, oil prices vaulted over $50 per barrel in global markets. That was a turning point. Gasoline price rose along with oil and the US auto industry took a beating because its main business was producing large, fuel hungry SUVs while consumers were looking for smaller, more efficient cars. The Federal Reserve was closely monitoring all of this as it typically becomes concerned about general price inflation when energy costs rise. The Fed—under the leadership of Alan Greenspan who enthusiastically endorsed derivative deregulation—took its usual stand against inflation and began raising benchmark interest rates. As the Fed began raising rates, this prompted banks to raise the prime rate for large corporate borrowers, and with a hike in the prime rate, interest rates on virtually all forms of credit, including mortgages, began to rise.

Rate hikes affect everything. Anywhere where people and businesses are borrowing money, which is everywhere, higher rates will have an impact. This is particularly true in the housing industry, which depends heavily on a steady flow of available credit. Once that flow slowed down with the higher cost of borrowing, another link in the chain reaction launched into full swing. Variable interest rates on mortgages pushed up the monthly payments for borrowers and this caused a wave defaults, particularly for those in the subprime category. All the Gramm-deregulated mortgage derivatives that were tied to the streams of mortgage payments began to lose value as the streams dried up. The market for these derivatives, like the oil futures, were volatile and quickly collapsed. The major banks and hedge funds that took large positions on these derivatives started losing asset values and cash flow. Banks became suspicious of each other as, one by one, they ran out of cash and eventually stopped lending to each other in short-term credit markets.

This was another turning point. Short-term credit and cash flow are vital in the corporate system. Giant corporations rely heavily on being able to borrow to shore up cash flow. Commercial banks make high interest, long-term loans by cobbling together money from low-interest short-term loans, then roll these over from one month to the next. When access to this short-term credit is blocked, everything starts to go haywire. The machinery of the corporate capitalist system starts to grind down. It is like shutting off all the electricity in a building. Everything goes dark and silent.

A full-blown economic crisis began to unfold as the malaise in the financial sector spread to every other sector in the economy. Every month in 2009, the Bureau of Labor Statistics reported hundreds of thousands jobs lost.[3] Mass corporate layoffs led to another round of mortgage defaults, and the economy plunged into the worst recession in decades—the Great Recession. In an effort to contain the multiple cascading crises, the Fed, the U.S. Treasury, and central banks everywhere tossed trillions of dollars in bailout money around their financial sectors like they were delivering newspapers. Government debt skyrocketed. Everything changed.

When economic crises like this occur, the knee-jerk response of the political establishment and the corporate media is to look for a culprit or some kind of technical glitch. Either some heads need to roll or someone needs to quickly come up with a patch so that everything can go back to business as usual.

But Phil and Wendy Gramm's little bit of political mischief alone could not have created a crisis of such magnitude. Nor could have Alan Greenspan's monetary policies, or derivative speculators, or subprime borrowers. No person or thing in isolation can cause the global economy to crumble on itself. The Banking Crisis of 2007–2009 and the Great Recession that followed are systemic crises. The system conditions for these crises were already in place, all they needed was to set in motion, like a butterfly effect. In other words, these crises are the exterior manifestations of conditions that are deeply embedded within our corporate system. They are institutional problems.

Most of us think of a corporation as a kind of business model. In school, we learn that there are sole proprietorships, partnerships, LLCs, S corporations, C corporations, and so forth. Although it is true that these are categories of business ownership models, the corporation is much more than that. It is an *institution.* It is a legal-financial entity that is structured around securities trades for capitalization and commodity trades for profits. It is an institution that is programmed such that its owners—shareholders—are not required to accomplish anything or even care what the business does except generate returns. The large, publicly traded corporation is a fictitious person without eyes, ears, brain, or heart. It is driven by a single imperative to compound returns, and to that end it stops at nothing. The planet and everything on it are either marketable instruments to be exploited for profit or are obstacles to be removed. People are either consumers, shareholders, or are irrelevant. Communities and entire countries are either markets or "emerging" markets. And governments are its domesticated pets.

The corporation transforms everything in its path accordingly. And if the path leads to a dead end and stagnates, it turns to devour its competitors in a wave of mergers. When the competition vanishes and it hits more dead ends, the corporation turns inward to create illusions of prosperity by creating over-inflated asset prices, which lead to crises and real economic ruin.

Moreover, the corporation is at the center of a vast network of powerful commercial, financial, government, media, and monetary institutions—a corporate hegemony. And within that hegemony, the largest Fortune 500 corporations and leviathan bank holding companies are the dominant, alpha institutions. This corporate hegemony has been evolving for well over a century and stands astride nations everywhere. It has quietly and perniciously taken quasi-sovereign powers as it holds virtually all other institutions in its thrall. People everywhere are divided into either the privileged corporate class of jet setters or the class of little people living in a constant state of uncertainty and insecurity.

The corporation has also enshrouded itself in its own ideology: *neoliberalism.* Neoliberalism is the cement that holds the hegemony together by continuously reinforcing a belief that a specific version of a corporate-friendly, deregulated, open market system is not only the strongest system ever, it is the *only* system possible, despite the troubled conditions it has created for people the world over. Part of this ideology is a convenient pretense that social structures of power like a corporate hegemony do not even exist. There are only individual consumers and entrepreneurs making rational choices in an open field of markets.

A Neoliberal Society Without a Society

Former British Prime Minister Margaret Thatcher in a 1987 interview famously declared that, "There is no such thing as society. There is a living tapestry of men and women and people and the beauty of that tapestry and the quality of our lives will depend-upon how much each of us is prepared to take responsibility for ourselves…"[4] Her individualistic worldview has a certain appeal, particularly for Americans. Most of us prefer not to think that the practicalities of daily economic life—making a living, buying things, investing in the future—are controlled by something other than our own will and choices. Rather, we tend to see ourselves as free-range workers and shoppers in an open and unrestrained marketplace where everyone is liberated from social coercion and are always free to choose according to our individual preferences. "It's a free country," people like to say as if there are no actual rules that restrict our actions. To say there is no such thing as society makes it easier to believe that all that happens in the economy stems from individual choice-making behavior. This is a central tenet of neoliberalism.

It was also in 1987 that Alan Greenspan, a staunch neoliberalist, became chair of the Federal Reserve System. Greenspan shared Thatcher's view of economic individualism as did many other key figures in the financial-political establishment, including then American president Ronald Reagan. During what I am calling the Greenspan Era—from 1987 onward—political and corporate leaders sold a vision to the country and to the world. Their vision was of perfect economic freedom in which prosperity naturally flows from individuals living in a society unrestrained by anything but self-interest and market forces. Their vision turned into a movement, the main thrust of which was/is to pull government rules and regulations as far from corporate enterprise as possible. The neoliberal mantra was for "small government," lower taxes, less regulation, and to get the government off the backs of business. All of which was heralded under the banner of freedom for the individual consumer and entrepreneur.

As we will see in the pages that follow, neoliberalism during the Greenspan Era was never actually about smaller government or even deregulation. It has always been about shifting economic control from the state to the corporation. it served to create a global economic system in which corporate institutions were empowered to assert their will and further their agenda of building a global hegemony. The movement has proven to be a reckless experiment in institutional change, particularly in the banking and financial sectors. It has been part of a broader hegemonic movement to refashion all of society in ways that suit corporate interests and the interests of social classes that reside at the top of its citadels.

Thatcher's proclamation that there is no such thing as society could not be further from the truth. To say that there is no such thing as society is like saying there is no such thing as language. Social institutions not only exist, they are ubiquitous and are the substance that makes up every aspect of a rule-structured society. All economic systems, present and past, stand as the composite whole of a network of institutions. It might be helpful, therefore, to have a few reality checks about institutions, their power they have over how we act and think, and how to function in economic society. The renowned institutionalist economist, Clarence Ayres, observed this succinctly, "Some sort of division of the social whole into parts is inevitable, and for this the familiar 'institutions' stand ready to hand."[5]

Institutions Matter

Institutions are instruments of social control. They are both undeniable and necessary. Without institutions we would not be able to protect ourselves from the violence of others or educate our children, nor would we be able to organize even the most basic economic activities. They are fundamental to how we establish order out of chaos and to how we coordinate our livelihoods purposefully. Institutions regulate society and provide a means through which society is understood. They are the social structures surround us like a magnetic field encompassing an array of rules, norms, or codes. All of which provide order, purpose and a sense of obligation as we interact with one another. Some institutions have "or else" consequences as with the state and its rule of law, and others are simple shared strategies followed by a community of like-minded people. They shape our actions by establishing the do and don't guidelines of social behavior, give individuals a sense of obligation, and enlist compliance. Institutions matter primarily because they abound. Our lives revolve around structured interactions at home, at work, at the shopping mall, in the courtroom, and in school.

According to Nobel laureate, Elinor Ostrom, "[social institutions] organize all forms of repetitive and structured interactions including those within families, neighborhoods, markets, firms, sports leagues, churches, private associations, and governments at all scales… Thus, understanding institutions is a serious endeavor."[6]

Economic institutions are a subset of social institutions. They structure how we buy and sell things and how market exchanges work; the establish the bylaws and charters of corporations, set the rules for banking practices, codify industry standards, formalize labor contract negotiations, place restrictions on trade; and media institutions mold the tastes and preferences of the consuming public. Whether we like it or not, our economic behavior is heavily institutionalized, and it has always been. By learning how to set rules for dividing and systematically coordinating work tasks, our ancestors became effective hunters, gatherers, farmers, manufacturers, engineers, craftspeople, musicians, and scientists. The ability to do so is key to how the human species has adapted and thrived in vastly different climates and landscapes through the ages. So commonplace are institutional forces that they are mostly taken for granted—invisible.

Money, for example, is a pretty basic thing. But when see it through an institutional lens, it is a marvel of complexity. Most of us don't give it a second thought when we drop coins in a vending machine, throw some paper money on the table at a restaurant, swipe a debit card, or use a cell phone app at Starbucks. The physical form that money takes is unimportant. What is important is that underlying the use of money is a nexus institutional interactions involving retail businesses, merchant services, commercial banks, central banks, credit card networks, the internet, and government treasuries. All these institutions are working in conjunction in a complex and evolving system. When these institutions become dysfunctional, which they often do, the economic system starts to fail.

Our daily economic lives are structured within these systems of institutions. It is true that we as individuals exercise free will and make choices, but we do so within the parameters of a network of institutions. The issue I would like to raise here is not about whether we should or should not try to exist on an institutional grid. This is a necessity. Rather, the issue is to identify the function and structure of such a grid and to ask what is it shaping us into: What are its rules for behavior in economic society? How did those rules come into being? How can we change this grid? In this sense, institutions matter enormously. Perhaps even more so than the individual choices we make.

Much of what we experience is institutionalized behavior. The idea of institutionalization typically carries a negative connotation as we associate it with prisons or archaic mental hospitals, but institutionalization does not necessarily imply that. It is merely the process by which human behavior is structured, orderly, and purposeful, which can be positive and healthy or negative and destructive. In any case, they establish the rules governing the actions of people and for that reason institutions are structures of power.

Economic Institutions as Social Structures of Power

As institutions abound, so do social structures of power and authority. This sounds undemocratic, but that is not always the case. There is a range of possibilities. Some institutions are coercive and authoritarian, and some are democratic and consensual depending on the broader milieu. In the context of capitalist systems, the prevailing economic institutions are centered around property rights and the private ownership of the means of production. Despite neoliberal platitudes about free markets, business owners are endowed with the full autonomy to command production and sales targets, enforce the mission of the company, and to hire and fire employees. This is real, palpable authoritarian power embedded in the social relations of business enterprise. And if workers do not do as the business owners dictate, they risk getting sacked, losing their livelihoods, possibly suffering long-term unemployment, becoming vulnerable to loan default, and having their credit standing ruined. So, people by and large follow the rules.

This acquiescence stems in part from the fact that corporate society has created its own systems for modulating social behavior. Throughout the corporate system, there are mechanisms of self-surveillance and self-censorship through human resource department rules and corporate culture. They exist to enforce the corporate agenda and legitimize the actions of those in power.

The market system, too, is layered with institutional rules of the game. Markets are seldom free in the libertarian sense, despite the claims that they are somehow democratic in the sense that people "vote with their pocketbooks." Markets gravitate toward those with the richest pocketbooks. They are also most likely to be saturated with things like industry codes, specifications, guidelines, minimum wage laws, government oversight, price supports, and tariffs. Moreover, market is subject to the raw power of businesses that have monopoly (dominant producer) and monopsony (dominant buyer) control over production, prices, and access. In the market system, there has always been a continuous tug-of-war between people and businesses over prices, quality, wages, and working conditions. But this struggle has never been balanced as businesses nearly always have an advantage on both sides of the market system. The exception being the case in which there are strong labor institutions and consumer protection advocacy.

Even so, it is not enough to recognize structures of power in corporate capitalism. To get the full picture, we need to take another step back to get a more holistic vision; for economic institutions, like human being, do not exist in isolation.

The Unbroken Web of Economic Institutions

Zooming out to take the long view of economic systems, we see that economic institutions themselves are bundled within a nexus of mutually interdependent institutions. Corporations depend on financial markets for capitalization, financial markets depend on stable monetary institutions provided by central banks, and all these institutions depend on the state for the rule of law. Everything is connected to everything else.

Going back to the story of Phil and Wendy Gramm, they set in motion a series of institutional changes by tweaking the structure of derivative regulations. This triggered higher oil prices, which triggered higher rate policy by the Fed, which triggered mortgage defaults and so on. When one aspect of the system changes, everything changes—sometimes imperceptibly and sometimes dramatically. Walton Hamilton, an early twentieth-century scholar who coined the term "institutional economics," describes an institution and its connection to the broader system in this way,

> Institution is a verbal symbol which for want of a better term describes a cluster of social usages. It connotes a way of thought or action of some prevalence and permanence which is imbedded in the habits of a group or the customs of a people… it is another word for procedure, convention, or arrangement; it is the singular of which the mores or folkways are the plural. Institutions fix the confines of and impose form upon the activities of human beings. … The world of [economic activity], to which imperfectly we accommodate our lives, is a tangled unbroken web of institutions.[7]

In other words, the unbroken web is a system of institutions linked together as one. Each economic institution—the household, the state, the central bank, the market system, the corporation—is collectively integrated into a total structure in which all the elements in the economic landscape are defined: industrial relations, collective bargaining processes, corporate governance, accounting standards, market structures, legal and juridical concepts, government policies, and consumer behavior.

Such a systems view, however, is not the way of conventional economics. Economics in the mainstream is trapped in the mechanistic worldview from the eighteenth and nineteenth centuries. It clings slavishly to neoliberal ideology and is intentionally blind to social structures of power. It is the analog to Thatcher's society without a society.

Mainstream Economics—An Economy Without a Society

Around the turn of the twentieth century, a major paradigm shift occurred in scientific disciplines across the board. Prior to this shift, sciences had been captured by a mechanistic worldview. In this worldview, all structures and events were understood in terms of material particles in empty space where cultures and institutions do not exist. Everything in the universe, from celestial bodies to the tiniest molecules, was conceptualized as comprised from something like inert billiard balls moving around in vacuous Euclidean three-dimensional space. Change and movement occur only when the particles are bumped into motion by external stimuli, and the motion is governed by the Newtonian laws gravity. Physicist Frijof Capra describes, "There was no purpose, life, or spirituality in matter. Nature worked according to mechanical laws, and everything in the material world could be explained in terms of the arrangement and movement of its parts."[8]

Mainstream economics—neoclassical economics—was fashioned wholly out this mechanistic worldview. Individual consumers and producers are treated mathematically like moving parts in empty space, completely removed from social context. Humans are considered to be passive and are only prompted into action by external pleasure or pain stimuli. Pleasure for the consumer is derived in consumption and pain comes from parting with money to buy the consumer goods. Pleasure for the producer is profit gained in selling the goods and pain comes from the irksomeness of having to perform work to produce them. In this paradigm, humans are driven by fixed, motor impulses to have and consume; to seek out pleasure or avoid pain. We are seen as cultureless things compelled into motion only by way of enticements and punishments presented by the idealized principles of supply and demand of the market.

In this mechanistic worldview, societies do not exist—an economy without a society—only individuals behaving atomistically in a social void. An economy without a society in which institutions are either completely ignored or taken for granted as something largely external to economic behavior. A pioneer of ecological economics Nicholas Georgescu-Roegen describes the mechanistic portrayal of human behavior in mainstream economics,

> …strips man's behavior of every cultural propensity, which is tantamount to saying that in his economic life man acts mechanically…. The whole truth is that economics, in the way this discipline is now generally professed, is mechanistic in the same strong sense in which we generally believe only classical mechanics to be.[9]

To be fair, there is a modicum of truth in this approach to economic as there is with all forms of mythology. To some degree, people and companies do behave like rational automatons, but this is trivial compared to the institutional forces that set the parameters of those choices. But depicting reality is not really the purpose of standard economics. If we purge social institutions from our purview, we eliminate social structures of power from the discourse and thereby avoid discussing social change altogether. Social criticism is pushed aside to make room for apocryphal stories of how human selfishness in an unfettered market environment leads to social progress.

The question begs as to how a social science could sustain such a socially alienating and irrelevant approach to human behavior. When pressed with this question, economists generally answer a tautology, "we do it this way because this is the way it is done."

Conventional economics remains trapped in a framework of mathematical formalisms that are largely incomprehensible to anyone outside certain academic circles. The password for being accepted into these circles is the mastery of mathematical sophistry that serves to intimidate anyone who is not an ardent devotee. Conventional economists use arcane mathematics to keep potential critics outside the margins of discourse. Very few people will bother spending years developing their math skills and analytical abilities only to be able to state a fact, which is obvious to most people anyway, that standard economic models are essentially bullshit. According to notable scholar and critic E.K. Hunt,

> From the 1870s until today, many economists in the neoclassical tradition have abandoned any real concerns with existing economic institutions and problems. Instead, many of them have retired to the rarefied stratosphere of mathematical model building, constructing endless variations on esoteric trivia.[10]

We take a different approach and draw concepts from various heterodox economic sources, but mainly from institutionalism. The nature of interbeing in the world of economics begs for a more systems or ecological frame of reference. In that sense, the institutionalist approach—with its emphasis on holism, evolution, social provisioning, and pragmatism—proves helpful.

Institutional Economics and Holism

Institutional economics began to take shape in the United States during the paradigm shift in science that occurred around the turn of the twentieth century. By then, the mechanistic approach to science had begun to fade as a flurry of new ways of understanding the world came alive. James Clerk Maxwell saw that electromagnetic fields were more important for understanding physical reality than particles rolling around in empty space. Albert Einstein created a radically different view of space and time. Marie Curie and Antoine Becquerel found that the penetrating power of radioactivity could not be explained using a mechanistic paradigm. Karl Marx and Charles Darwin created entirely new frameworks of human existence in which static, mechanistic inertia was replaced progressive and cumulative change in the social and biological worlds. In his "process philosophy," Alfred North Whitehead asserted that the interactions between things are important to understanding reality than things themselves.

With these intellectual developments, the vision of ourselves and everything around us changing—process replaced structure, dynamic change replaced static inertia, and holism replaced reductionism. Everything was changing, with the exception of conventional economics which continues to serve out its life sentence in a Newtonian box.

Holism in science generally traces back to the work of the South African scholar, Jan Christian Smuts as he was inspired by these intellectual developments at the turn of the twentieth century and the work of Darwin.[11] The term 'holistic' is rooted in the classical Greek word *holos*, which means 'whole.' For social and scientific analysis, holism takes the physical, social, and environmental universes as evolving, dynamic wholes or syntheses. A key premise is the notion of emergent properties. As things interact with other things, certain characteristics emerge that are distinct from the things themselves. It is the idea that the whole is greater than the sum of the parts such that the whole has properties that cannot be found in the parts.

The properties of water, for example, cannot be understood by examining a hydrogen atom in isolation. It is only when two parts hydrogen and one part oxygen integrate to form a molecule that the properties of water emerge: buoyancy, freezing temperature, ability to sustain life. In the holistic view, all physical, social, and ecological phenomena are whole entities or emergent structures that transcend the basic elements from which they are made.

Institutionalism takes a holistic view in this sense. The specific behavior of producers and consumers has little meaning apart from the larger social context in which takes place. Our behavior is conditioned by social institutions, and institutions themselves are emergent as they arise when people interact with each other economically through production and exchange. Through social interaction, human behavior begins to form into discernable patterns. These patterns of behavior become habituated, and eventually emerge as social institutions. These institutions are formations that eventually take root and take on a life of their own. Institutional economist Russel Dixon writes,

> [A human being] is not engaged at one time in the gaining of a livelihood to the exclusion of his political, social, or religious activities. Instead, his efforts to make a living are directed and conditioned by his whole round of life—his attitudes toward the political organization of his state, toward the other members of his family or club, and toward the church in which he worships. All these in turn are conditioned by his economic activities... To understand modern economic activity, which has become the dominant and directive force in our industrialized world, one must appreciate its place in the social entity called culture.[12]

This is the dual life of economic institutions. They control human behavior and at the same time created by human behavior. And as institutions emerge as distinct structures, they interact with others to form networks of institutions that cohere into systems. These, in turn, are embedded within broader cultural and ideological formations. The way we act in the world and the way we think about the world are habituated over time as a result of our activity. These habits reify into institutions that confine and impose form upon on our behavior. These institutions cohere with one another to form a web of interconnectedness.[13] And so the complexity of our world goes, like an endless series of Russian dolls and each level has its own unique emergent properties locked into a complex, unbroken web of interconnectedness.

Whether we take holism as a metaphor or a scientific framework, it illuminates the interbeing of ourselves and our surrounding institutions. Amidst this unbroken web, however, is a corporate structure of power that has evolved over centuries do a position of dominance. We will return to this in the next chapter as we tell the story of how the corporation has evolved and captured other institutions in its web of influence. As we reflect on the existence of these powerful social structures, we must also reflect on their purpose. Does the corporate hegemony exist to secure the wellbeing of all members of its society, or is it to enrich a small and privileged class? For institutional economists, economic systems are always permeated with normative purpose. Is it wealth accumulation for the Interests that Veblen saw, or is it a process social provisioning to secure the wellbeing of the population.

Institutional Economics, Pragmatism, and Social Provisioning

In a general way, every approach to economics must settle on a strategy for meeting the needs of people. Through a process that institutional economist, Alan Gruchy, refers to as "social provisioning" economic systems mobilize resources to provide food, housing, health care, education, security in retirement, and all the other things required to sustain the population.[14] In conventional economics this is process would happen as a result of individualistic, self-interested consumers and producers expressing their desires in the marketplace. But institutional economists see things in a broader sense that there are a variety of ways for the economy to meet these needs. Using the market is only one limited possibility. Regardless, social provisioning will be based on the prevailing institutions of society at a given time. If people seek to have a society that provides for the wellbeing of the population, there must be an established set of institutions that set the rules for doing so and hold provisioning as a priority. The implication is that there is a certain level of activism involved in the institutionalization process and social structure building. For Gruchy, the pragmatic philosophy of John Dewey is valuable in this regard as "This philosophy leads to social activism in the service of humanity."[15]

In the early1930s, John Dewey began to explore human behavior as emerging from a deeper activist self rather than simply responders to market prices. Dewey writes, "The idea of a thing intrinsically wholly inert in the sense of absolutely passive is expelled from physics and has taken refuge in the psychology of current economics."[16] In his philosophy, he sees people as motivated to act as an existential drive to be proactive, "In truth man acts anyway, he can't help acting. In every fundamental sense it is false that a man requires a motive to make him do something. To a healthy man inaction is the greatest of woes."[17] But Dewey also saw that the form this action would take will be largely structured by social or institutional forces.

Dewey makes a case for human social behavior that springs from an existential drive to shape the world around them. As people follow this instinct and become engaged in social development, they can create better institutions that advance social intelligence and foster the development of education, art, health, technology, and purposeful economic activity. By doing so, communities pursue a pragmatic path toward creating opportunities for individuals to develop their own unique powers and capabilities. These powers and capabilities, in turn, will allow a person to become an effective participant in the life of the community, and can advance the project of building institutions that provide for their wellbeing. In this way, communities and the individuals who live in them can coevolve. But Dewey also asserts that specific behavior is entirely a product of social conditioning. Humans are programmed to act in the world, but the extent to which their actions contribute to social provisioning are contingent on the social situation.

Veblen was a contemporary of Dewey and sympathetic to philosophical pragmatism. Like Dewey, Veblen also sees human action in a proactive way and challenges the neoclassical assertion that people are passive responders to external stimuli. He looks deeper into the volitional aspects of human behavior as something that stems from certain tendencies and is directed toward certain pragmatic goals. Such tendencies, or propensities, are habitual aspects of society's cultural fabric. Veblen explains,

> According to this conception it is the characteristic of man to do something, not simply to suffer pleasures and pains through the impact of suitable forces. He is not simply a bundle of desires that are to be saturated by being placed on the path of the forces of the environment, but rather a coherent structure of propensities and habits which seeks realization and expression in unfolding activity. According to this view, human activity, and economic activity among the rest, is not apprehended as something incidental to the process of saturating given desires.[18]

In other words, Veblen sees human economic behavior as willful and directed from within. For Veblen the will to act in the world is universal to all people, but, like Dewey, holds that the specific actions people structured socially. Social institutions are not the by-product of human instinctive behavior, but rather are what determine the specific nature of human behavior in which the instinct to act becomes manifest.

Another important institutionalist economist, John Commons, refers to these social structures as "working rules."[19] Commons shares with Veblen this vision that at the core of the human self is a volitional will to "do something" but still directed by the institutional rules of the game. For institutionalists, therefore, the nature of the individual self is to be an active agent—to act in the world outwardly in some way. The specific nature of the action is contingent on whether the individual is conditioned by patterns established with the social milieu. Commons takes a holistic view of social environment as a total constellation of all the material elements of culture that include physical capital, resources, and technology, along with social elements that include values, ideology, worldviews, and the social institutions that convey rules of economic activity. The dual life of our institutional nature is that we both creating these elements of our cultural complex and are formed by them. For Veblen, the individual is subject to "permanent alteration by a cumulative series of actions. In fact, the actor becomes the product of the cumulative series."[20]

We are all in continuous state of dynamic interplay between our individual selves and the social milieu, and both are in state of flux and change. Economic historian, Allan Gruchy summarizes that, "The assumptions of the holistic economists relating to the nature of human behavior are in conformity with their view of the economic system as an evolving cultural complex."[21] The questions that follow are, What kind of social environment are we being formed within? Which direction is it evolving? Does it serve the pragmatic goal of social provisioning for the population?

Institutional Economics and Evolution

For the institutionalists, the whole of culture is not something that is static or fixed in nature, but is subject to change and transformation. Human behavior, as it is formed within culture, is also subject to cumulative change. As we act in the world, we change the world; as the world changes, it changes how we act in it in a series of cumulative changes and adaptations time. Economic historian, David Hamilton, summarizes that, "To the institutionalist, the individual acting in economic society is subject to permanent alteration by a cumulative series of actions. In fact the actor becomes the product of the cumulative series."[22] We act in a world we inherited, and through a kind of karmic volition, we pass it along with our particular brand of changes to subsequent generations. For the institutionalists, there is not a teleological aim or grand design in this evolutionary process. Economic systems, in an open-ended process of continuous and cumulative state of evolution and change. For John Commons, such perpetual change is "the uncertain world of institutional economics."[23] Social evolution is a mere drift in which the system will evolve in one direction or another where human society can achieve progress in how we go about social provisioning or make things worse for itself. As Marx noted, "Men make their own history, but they do not make it just as they please; they do not make it under circumstances chosen by themselves, but under given circumstances directly encountered and inherited from the past. The tradition of all the generations of the dead weighs like a nightmare on the brain of the living."[24]

But the institutionalists share with Dewey the idea of progress, which is linked to technological development and improvements in the means of production.[25] Veblen identified an underlying mechanism for change that points our cultural evolution in one direction or another—for better or worse. This mechanism is what he calls "invention and diffusion."[26] As people act in the world, they invent and change things. This could be a new form of technology, a new word, a policy, or a business model. The internet or the creation of the Federal Reserve System, for example, are inventions that have had significant impact on our economic system. But others could be as small as a new recipe for bread. However large or small the invention, it results in a shift in how people act and relate to each other. These new things and actions become diffused through social interaction and eventually new habits are formed around them. Eventually, these new things become part of the evolving cultural complex while the old habits fade in a continuous process of renewal and change.

Each incremental change, for institutionalists, is either seen as adaptive or maladaptive. If the invention and diffusion of something results in improvements in the means of production, it is adaptive and leads toward real progress in social provisioning. But the character of the invention depends on the prevailing instincts at the time it was developed. If it blooms from a prevalent instinct to creatively advance the wellbeing of the population, it is adaptive. A new medicine, more efficient use of energy, or policies for eliminating poverty stem from a pragmatic desire to create something that can be put into service of humanity. They lead to real progress.

If, however, the invention was developed out of prevailing instinct of predation, then it leads to a kind of cultural de-evolution. Inventions that foster predatory conquests, amassing fortunes in speculation for ego-aggrandizement are distinct from real creative or productive work. Their purpose is to sublimate the activities of individuals who give the outward appearance of heroic feats of cunning, mystery, or conquest. In this situation, there is little or no progress in terms of wellbeing or social provisioning.

For institutionalists, the creative instincts and predatory instincts are trapped in a state of antagonism. Both are potentialities that exist like seeds in the human spirit. Which seeds that get watered and are allowed to grow depend on the prevailing institutions. What circumstances are we currently creating and passing on? Each of us is born into a world surrounded by cultural signs and symbols with their particular meanings. These include institutionalized forms of social organization accompanied with symbols of status and prestige—the symbol of the dollar or the pound, or the title of CEO—and most of these are just taken for granted as they have stood the test of time and as such require no explanation or justification.[27] Over the centuries of modern corporate development, our culture has evolved into a massive structure that is saturated with the idolatry of financial wealth. This is not hard to see if we pay attention to its ubiquity: continuously updated stock market indexes, corporate logos plastered on nearly every surface, television commercials blasting at high volumes in every possible nook, and the falling cultural avalanche of all the other symbols of sought-after lifestyles. From one generation to the next, we habitually and unquestioningly pass on what is collectively exalted as success as if the accoutrements of affluence no matter how they were accumulated are synonymous with wellbeing.

Thorstein Veblen, asserted that the creative and transformative work of economic production derives in part from a parental instinct to see that our offspring have a fair chance at a better life. Driven by this instinct, he argues that each generation seeks to make its material standard of living better than the last by seeking higher and higher levels of production for a given community of people. But, if Veblen's assertions are true, this productive instinct is limited to the extent that it can be sustained only by the carrying capacity of the natural environment. If production systems grow beyond this capacity, then, ironically, the productive capacity of our children's and grandchildren's generations will be jeopardized and our duty as a parent is compromised. Very few individuals would argue that advances in technology and productivity have not brought about substantial improvements in people's lives, but as our economic system demands more and more from our planet, these same advances could eventually bring about a speedy decline in human welfare.

For institutionalists, such a cultural complex is an institutionalized web of delusions that equate high material standards of what it means to live a good life. In this state, people seek to obtain all the trappings of affluent lifestyles, which they believe are the only ways to become happy. Veblen identified this kind of delusion using the now famous term, "conspicuous consumption."[28] Conspicuous consumption has become ubiquitous consumption, and the result is a nearly universal acceptance of greed in the collective mindset. Through habituation, such a culture conditions our way of thinking, which in turn further conditions our habitual ways of acting in society. We become trapped and such a trap is a root cause of human suffering—pathos. But under the rubric of neoliberalism, this ego-driven situation in which everyone is pitted against everyone else the open market is the best of all possible worlds.

Cultures in which capitalism is the dominant social system of production are permeated with a normative sense of the rightness or correctness of capitalist profit making and accumulation. It is seen as the source of material progress and higher standards of living. Under this rubric, the logic of capitalism becomes the mechanism for selecting which technics or practices will survive and which will become extinct.

As such, cultures and social systems of production evolve toward higher and higher levels of accumulation and growth. This normative formation gives direction to the development of specific institutions, including educational institutions and economics departments at universities, and directs the economic activities of people.

An economy is a complex and evolving system of institutions. It is like an ecosystem of institutions that is evolving. As we will see in the pages ahead, the premier characteristic of the US economy as a whole is that it is a hegemony of institutions, the centerpiece of which is the large corporation. Along with this hegemonic structure is a deeply embedded instinct to accumulate wealth and a general disinterest in the wellbeing of the population or the planet. This system as a whole disappears from the purview of standard economics that chooses instead to ignore it or take it for granted. Instead, the focus is on choice-making behavior as if institutions did not impinge on our behavior at all. But in this systems institutional approach we take a different view. Institutions are key to understanding the way economies work as well as their troubling aspects.

In the institutionalists' holistic framework of analysis, individual behavior is patterned by a combination of an innate drive to act in the world and the institutions that direct those actions. These institutions are habituated usages of material and nonmaterial technics that and recombine over time to solidify into social structures. These structures provide work rules, social norms, and mores that guide human social behavior, and, in an economic sense, economic behavior. Through this process of coherence, institutions combine with one another to form more complex, higher-order structures or social systems of production. Social systems of production constitute a web of institutional interconnectedness, or a whole of culture, serving specific purposes that transcend the individual institutions that comprise them. The mechanism for selecting which institutions are to survive and which are to be selected for extinction is, for institutionalists, a biological Darwinian concept of evolution. Evolution, for institutionalists, is nonteleological and measured by material progress and technology, but with no predetermined end to which technology is advancing beyond Dewey's pragmatic optimism of human wellbeing. The argument presented here is to take this holistic view a step further and assert that the logic of capitalism—the dominant social system of production—places the highest emphasis on capital accumulation. In the corporate-dominated world, this has come to be the supreme cultural measure of progress.

As we seek alternatives that will help us cope with problems of recurring financial system instability, we have to survey these problems within the broader context of the economic system. But at the center of that system is the large, publicly traded corporation. In the next chapter, we'll explore in more detail how the corporate institution has evolved to become such a formidable economic, political, and cultural force in the world.

Notes

1. Antonia Juhacz, *The Tyranny of Oil: The World's Most Powerful Industry—And What We Must Do to Stop It* (New York, NY: HarperCollins, 2008), pp. 147–148.
2. http://quotes.ino.com/exchanges/exchange.html?e=NYMEX.
3. https://data.bls.gov/timeseries/CES0000000001?output_view=net_1mth.
4. Interview September 23, 1987, as quoted by Douglas Keay in the magazine, *Woman's Own*, October 31, 1987, pp. 8–10.
5. Clarence E. Ayres, *The Theory of Economic Progress* (Kalamazoo, MI: New Issues Press, 3rd ed., 1978), p. 178.
6. Elinor Ostrom, *Understanding Institutional Diversity* (Princeton University Press, 2005), p. 3.
7. Quoted in David Hamilton, *Evolutionary Economics: A Study of Change in Economic Thought* (University of New Mexico Press, 1978), p. 77.
8. Fritjof Capra, *The Turning Point: Science, Society, and the Rising Culture* (New York, NY: Simon and Schuster, 1982), 60.
9. Nicholas Georgescu Roegen, *The Entropy Law and the Economic Process* (Cambridge, MA: Cambridge University Press, 1971) p. 1.
10. E.K. Hunt, *Property and Prophets: The Evolution of Economic Institutions and Ideologies* (New York, NY: ME Sharpe, 2003) p. 126.
11. Allan Gruchy, *Modern Economic Thought: The American Contribution* (New York, NY: Prentice-Hall, 1947), p. viii.

12. Russel Dixon, *Economic Institutions and Cultural Change* (New York, NY: McGraw-Hill, 1941), p. 5.
13. J. Rogers Hollingsworth and Robert Boyer, *Contemporary Capitalism: The Embeddedness of Institutions* (Cambridge, UK: Cambridge University Press, 1997), p. 2.
14. Gruchy, 1947, p. xii.
15. Allan Gruchy, *Contemporary Economic Thought: The Contribution of Neo-Institutional Economics* (Clifton, NJ: Augustus M. Kelley, 1972), p. 127.
16. John Dewey, *Human Nature and Conduct* (New York, NY: Modern Library, 1930), pp. 118–119.
17. Ibid.
18. Thorstein Veblen, *The Instinct of Workmanship and the State of Industrial Arts* (New York, NY: W.B. Huebsch, 1922), p. 88.
19. John Commons, *Institutional Economics* (New York, NY: Macmilan, 1934), pp. 23–26.
20. Veblen, 1922, pp. 55–56.
21. Gruchy, 1947, pp. 560–565.
22. Hamilton, 1977, pp. 55–56.
23. Commons, 1934, p. 58.
24. See collection of essays Karl Marx, "Eighteen Brumaire of Louis Bonaparte," prepared for the internet by David J. Romagnolo, http://www.marx2mao.com/M&E/EBLB52.html.
25. Veblen, 1922, p. 231.
26. Ibid., pp. 112–113.
27. Alfred Schutz, *On Phenomenology and Social Relations* (University of Chicago, 1970), p. 80.
28. Thorstein Veblen, *The Theory of the Leisure Class* (New York, NY: The Viking Press, 1899), p. 68.

References

Ayres, Clarence E. *The Theory of Economic Progress* (Kalamazoo, MI: New Issues Press, 3rd ed., 1978).

Bureau of Labor Statistics. https://data.bls.gov/timeseries/CES0000000001?output_view=net_1mth.

Capra, Fritjof. *The Turning Point: Science, Society, and the Rising Culture* (New York, NY: Simon and Schuster, 1982).

Commons, John. *Institutional Economics* (New York, NY: Macmillan, 1934).
Dewey, John. *Human Nature and Conduct* (New York, NY: Modern Library, 1930).
Dixon, Russel. *Economic Institutions and Cultural Change* (New York, NY: McGraw-Hill, 1941).
Georgescu-Roegen, Nicholas. *The Entropy Law and the Economic Process* (Cambridge, MA: Cambridge University Press, 1971).
Gruchy, Allan. *Modern Economic Thought: The American Contribution* (New York, NY: Prentice-Hall, 1947).
Gruchy, Allan. *Contemporary Economic Thought: The Contribution of Neo-Institutional Economics* (Clifton, NJ: Augustus M. Kelley, 1972).
Hamilton, David. *Evolutionary Economics: A Study of Change in Economic Thought* (New York, NY: University of New Mexico Press, 1978).
Hollingsworth, J. Rogers, and Robert Boyer. *Contemporary Capitalism: The Embeddedness of Institutions* (Cambridge, UK: Cambridge University Press, 1997), p. 2.
Hunt, E.K. *Property and Prophets: The Evolution of Economic Institutions and Ideologies* (New York, NY: ME Sharpe, 2003).
INO.COM. http://quotes.ino.com/exchanges/exchange.html?e=NYMEX.
Juhacz, Antonia. *The Tyranny of Oil: The World's Most Powerful Industry—And What We Must Do to Stop It* (New York, NY: HarperCollins, 2008).
Keay, Douglas. *Woman's Own*, October 31, 1987.
Marx, Karl. "Eighteen Brumaire of Louis Bonaparte," 1852. https://www.marxists.org/archive/marx/works/1852/18th-brumaire/ch01.htm.
Ostrom, Elinor. *Understanding Institutional Diversity* (New York, NY: Princeton University Press, 2005).
Schutz, Alfred. *On Phenomenology and Social Relations* (New York, NY: University of Chicago, 1970).
Veblen, Thorstein. *The Theory of the Leisure Class* (New York, NY: The Viking Press, 1899).
Veblen, Thorstein. *The Instinct of Workmanship and the State of Industrial Arts* (New York, NY: W.B. Huebsch, 1922).

3

Fortune 500 and Wall Street Leviathans

As one of the founders of institutional economics Thorstein Veblen had an evolutionary view. He observed that the corporate sphere, "has visibly come be to be the main controlling factor in the established order of things."[1] He attested to an evolutionary drift toward corporate hegemony in which all other major institutions were becoming increasingly rendered under the boot of corporate power. He described the beginnings of what came to be a corporate hegemony as, "One Big Union made up of partners, auxiliaries, subsidiaries, extensions and purveyors of traffic."[2] A kind of wolf pack of institutions, the alpha members of which evolved into today's Fortune 500 enterprises and Wall Street leviathan bank holding companies. In this system, the rules of the corporation become the rules of the whole of society—corporate articles of incorporation, bylaws, and mission statements became the working rules for everyone.

Others at the time were standing alongside Veblen chronicling the ascent of corporate power. Adolph Berle and Gardiner Means published their classic, *The Modern Corporation and Private Property* in 1934. Their seminal work was the first comprehensive examination of the corporation as not just a model of business enterprise, but as an

J. Magnuson, *Financing the Apocalypse*,
Palgrave Insights into Apocalypse Economics,
https://doi.org/10.1007/978-3-030-04720-7_3

institution of social governance that rivaled the state. They concluded that there has, "evolved a 'corporate system' as there was once a feudal system—which has attracted to itself a combination of attributes and powers, and has attained a degree of prominence entitling it to be dealt with as a major social institution."[3] In the early twentieth century these scholars were warning that the economic system in America was a corporate-dominated hegemony in the making.

Almost a century later, author Joel Bakan reflects on what Veblen, Berle, Means and others in the early twentieth warned would come to pass, "Over the last 150 years, the corporation has risen from relative obscurity to become the world's dominant economic institution. Today, corporations govern our lives. They determine what we eat, what we watch, what we wear, where we work, and what we do."[4] As they control markets, banks, employment, and media, people everywhere are inundated with corporate culture. The corporation has institutionally moved beyond being just an economic force in the world. Bakan further notes that, "like the church and the monarchy in other times, they posture as infallible and omnipotent, glorifying themselves in imposing buildings and elaborate displays. Increasingly, corporations dictate the decisions of their supposed overseers in government and control domains of society once firmly embedded within the public sphere."[5] Under corporate dominance, the endless accumulation of financial wealth, endless economic growth, and the idolatry of money have all become unassailable societal norms and virtually all other concerns of social provisioning or wellbeing have been drowned out and forgotten.[6] Before we trace some of the history of the rise of corporate hegemony, we should first get a look at some numbers that give scale to the corporate behemoth as it stands today.

Corporate Alpha Dogs

In 2018, Fortune magazine published its 64th edition of its list of five hundred largest corporations in the United States. The collective revenue for the Fortune 500 businesses totals $12.8 trillion, which makes this list the third largest economy in the world behind the United States and China, and is about 63% of the nominal gross domestic product (GDP) of the United States From their revenues, these companies amassed about $1.0 trillion in profits, which helped them harvest $21.6 trillion in wealth measured by the market value of their publicly traded stocks. The wealthiest are well known: Apple, Amazon, Alphabet, Microsoft, Berkshire Hathaway, Facebook, J.P. Morgan Chase, Johnson & Johnson, Exxon Mobil, and Bank of America. To amass such wealth for shareholders, these companies put to work about 28.2 million people around the globe.[7] In the summer of 2018, Apple became the first corporation to have a market capitalization (share price multiplied by the number of shares outstanding) to surpass the $1 trillion mark. Amazon followed a couple of months later.[8] To put this in perspective, if we took one trillion one-dollar bills and placed them end to end, they would form a tether that would reach 96.7 million miles, which is a distance longer than that between the Earth and the Sun.

Looking at the numbers in another way, the top 15 companies on the Fortune 500 list have a combined revenue of over $2.8 trillion. If we translate that number to something comparable to GDP, such as gross corporate product, these fifteen companies together would rank fifth rank in the world (Table 3.1).

From the sheer size reflected in these numbers, the economic power of large corporations is unquestionable. Again, these are not just businesses, they are massive bureaucratic institutions that have the power to

Table 3.1 Top 15 companies compared to ten national GDPs by country

Rank	Country	2018 Nominal GDP (x billions)
1	United States	$20,199.96
2	China	$12,118.69
3	Japan	$5063.13
4	Germany	$3934.81
5	Top 15 companies	$2823.90
6	France	$2765.60
7	United Kingdom	$2661.23
8	India	$2654.17
9	Brazil	$2199.72
10	Italy	$2048.99

Source "World Economic Outlook Database". International Monetary Fund. 17 April 2018 and *Wikipedia* company profiles

direct what we buy, to shape our opinions, and control the machinery of national governments. They determine what is or is not appropriate cultural and media production, what is health care and who should have access to it, and what we eat. The own and operate public utilities, control access to information technology and the internet, control access to credit, determine the interest rates on that credit, own vast tracts of land, own all the data centers and server farms, and have virtually all the world's resources at their command. And in terms of institutional governance, all this control is concentrated within a social structure that is fundamentally nondemocratic.

Warnings of the nondemocratic power of corporations abounds. Journalist Marjorie Kelly warns us in *The Divine Right of Capital* (2001) that a corporate aristocracy is unnatural, irrational, and something that the population should not allow to stand in a legitimately democratic society.[9] David Korten, in his classic *When Corporations Rule the World* (1995, 2004) takes a similar position as he describes corporate dominance as a crisis of governance. For Korten, the political power of corporations has given rise to a Washington-Wall Street establishment that has resulted in "shifting power away from governments responsible for the public good and toward a handful of corporations and financial institutions driven by a single imperative, the quest for short-term financial gain."[10]

Playwright and former President of the Czech Republic, Vaclav Havel describes this structure as something mirroring a totalitarian socialist state,

> Enormous private multinational corporations are curiously like socialist states, with industrialization, centralization, specialization, monopolization. Finally, with automation and computerization, the elements of depersonalization and the loss of meaning in work become more and more profound everywhere. Along with that goes the general manipulation of people's lives by the system (no matter how inconspicuous such manipulation may be), comparable with that of the totalitarian state.[11]

These critics are describing a complex system and like all complex systems, it is continually evolving. Taking the holistic and evolutionary approach of institutional economics, we can trace the evolution of this system through a series of successive stages. In each stage, the corporation develops emergent properties as a social institution such that it becomes more powerful and seemingly more indifferent to social provisioning. And in the shadows of all this, Thatcherism and the mainstream economics position that there are only individual consumers and entrepreneurs and that social structures do not exist, appear quite removed from reality.

With a bit of reflection, inevitably the question arises as to how could a country that presumably cherishes democratic values find itself under the boot of such a nondemocratic political-economic system. At least a partial answer to that question is that it was a long time in the making. The rise of a corporate-dominated system in the United States, as well as many parts of the world, is the product of what Veblen identified as evolutionary drift. It is a system that emerged from the womb of the capitalist mode of production, but it matured into a life of its own. It is the outcome of a long process during which the corporation and its surrounding support network evolved through a series of developmental stages toward hegemony. Throughout this process, though the corporation was challenged in the courts and political arena, its rise to dominance seemed inevitable. Arguably the most salient ingredient and ultimate source of the corporation's power is its remarkable capacity to aggregate vast amounts of capital.

The Centralization of Capital and the Decentralization of Risk

Centuries ago, the earliest incarnation of a corporation as an institution was created as an extension of the nation-state. The prototype of the modern corporation—the joint stock company—was formed as an adjunct to the power of European monarchs that sought to build modernized countries. Typically, these companies were created when a king or queen would grant special charters that gave companies the exclusive rights to trade in spices, tea, textiles and other commodities in a particular area. These were private enterprises, but the charters were controlled by the sovereigns with the objective of using these companies to amass financial wealth. Money was increasingly coveted as something that could easily be translated into weapons, mercenaries, and power.

The principal advantage of the joint stock company was that finance could be gathered and centralized by selling shares to a broad section of the population, which included virtually anyone with some money and the willingness to take a risk. When a king or queen or business tycoon imagined of doing something on a fantastic scale such as conquering an entire subcontinent or building a transcontinental railroad, there was always the question of how to finance such an undertaking—how to raise enough capital to do something really big. Forming corporations that can pull together vast amounts of capital from widely dispersed sources was the most expedient answer. This became the first and perhaps most significant emergent property of the corporate institution—its ability to aggregate capital.

Though it may seem mundane now, this institutional development was a profound development in the history of capitalism. Labor historian Harry Braverman tells us, "The scale of capitalist enterprise, prior to the development of the modern corporation, was limited by both the availability of capital and the management capacities of the capitalist or group of partners.... Huge aggregates of capital may be assembled that far transcend the sum of the wealth of those immediately associate with the enterprise."[12] Through the process of capital aggregation, the corporate whole emerged to become greater than the sum of its parts and an institutional entity was born. Capitalism as a system carried on with wealth accumulation as usual, but now it was enhanced with the added capacity to assemble and use the capital from a multitude of investors, and to harness the ability to undertake tasks that were of a scale far beyond the financial reach of any individual entrepreneur.

To centralize capital in this way, new market institutions needed to be developed. In tandem with the rise of the corporation, securities exchanges, commodities markets, and trading systems sprang up in cities everywhere. As the corporation has risen to commanding heights, it stands to reason that the instruments created and trade in its sphere would also increase in trading volume. Speculative manias—widespread and irrational trading in securities markets—broke out like epidemics. A speculator pulls out cash to buy a security such as a stock or bond, watch the value of the security grow, then sell it for a profit without having to exert labor or actually create something of value. With the expanded wealth, the speculator could perform the same transaction again and again. By so doing, one could amass a fortune, and with the right luck perhaps do so over a very short period of time. A fascination with "easy money" takes hold in the popular imagination as people got word that fortunes were to be made betting on the markets. The more drawn to get-rich-schemes in speculative markets, the larger and more widespread became the crisis that followed.

Speculation, of course, comes with risk. Speculators could just as easily watch their investments collapse and they could watch them expand. If these markets are left uncontrolled or unregulated, they tend to undulate though boom and bust patterns of instability. Prices can move up or down as market conditions change—sometimes overnight and sometimes by the minute. Capital was drawn together and centralized, and risk was spread outward and decentralized. The result of widespread risk is a *system condition* and this condition is a basis for endemic instability. Securities markets are particularly vulnerable to such instability as they are designed to be liquid or easily converted to cash. As such they are subject to constantly changing conditions and uncertainty and speculators move their cash in and out often on a whim or rumors. One this is also certain from the historical record, speculative booms are almost always followed by busts, leaving behind a wide patch of financial ruin.

A discernable pattern developed early on: the corporation created a need for securities exchanges, securities exchanges gave rise to speculation, and speculation noted that whenever these speculative booms attracted money from a broad base of the population.

Speculative manias occur not coincidentally, where corporate institutions have become an integral part of economic life. This system condition has been magnified by modern financial institutions.

Another characteristic that became a distinguishing mark of a corporation as an institution is the limited liability status of shareholders. Limited liability extends from the legal separation of the corporation as separate entity from its shareholders as well as managers. As a legal entity, it protects those who supply capital by limiting their liability to the amount of their original investment. Unlike individual proprietors or partners stockholders are not responsible to creditors to repay debts of the corporation in which they invest, nor are they typically accountable for other legal liabilities of the companies. In the most practical sense, the only liability for corporate shareholders is the dollar amount of their original investments they stand to lose if the company fails.

On the earnings side, however, there are no limits. The shared profits and equity growth distributed to stockholders are virtually boundless. This asymmetry between unlimited earnings potential and limited liability proved to be a winning combination and a lure to drawn out investors. As money pours from absentee owners eager to make fortunes, the corporation became a supreme capital-raising machine, became an economic force to be reckoned with, and as its power grew proportionally with its size, it eventually tore itself away from the institution of the state that was originally its sponsor.

The monarchs who created the corporations and controlled their charters were often at cross-purposes with the members of the entrepreneurial class who financed them. The monarchs were less interested in capitalism and more interested in building nation-states and augmenting their political power, but the investor class was interested in private wealth accumulation. With the ascent of capitalism came the belief that investors should rightfully accumulate money, profits and wealth for themselves and not for the monarch. This conflict was ultimately resolved in bloody violence. The conflict between the sovereigns and emerging class of capitalist entrepreneurs was at the very heart of the American and French Revolutions that began in the late eighteenth century. The capitalists emerged triumphant, and as the power of Europe's ruling monarchies began to decline, so did their ability to maintain control over the corporate charters.

For many historians the American Civil War (1861–1865) is seen as the last of a series of capitalist revolutions that spanned nearly 350 years. The Civil War brought the quasi-feudal slave system in the American South to an end, and this allowed capitalism to expand and consolidate throughout a broader, unified nation. The United States became a kind of testing ground for a pure form of capitalism with giant corporate monopolies in a central position. The corporate personhood movement in the post-Civil War period helped solidify its position by redefining the corporate entity—through a series of dubious supreme court rulings—to have standing as a *person* under the rule of constitutional law.[13]

Armed with the constitutional protections intended for actual persons, corporations began their legacy of dominance decades before women won the right to vote. Between 1898 and 1904, about 1800 formerly independent corporations were consolidated into 157 monopolies in the United States.[14] As it liberated itself from the meddlesome institution of the state, the corporation was becoming strong enough to defy its sovereignty, though throughout the twentieth century there was pushback from the state as it retained the authority to ratify and enforce antitrust laws to uphold the rights of labor to collectively bargain, and to set in place a vast structure of regulatory agencies designed to curb the excesses of corporate power. Nonetheless, the corporation was largely set free to maximize returns for shareholders, take control of markets, buy out competitors and attain monopoly control of entire industries, and it was able to do these things with little regard or sense of responsibility for the interests of real people affected by their actions.

Karl Marx attested to a historical process of monopolization as the natural outcropping of the capitalist system's drive for wealth accumulation and the inevitable drift toward industry concentration. Marx saw that capitalism was becoming monopolized as competing firms fused capital by either violently annexing one another in the wilds of the open market where "certain capitals become such preponderant centers of attraction for others that they shatter the individual cohesion… then draw the separate fragments to themselves…" Or, less violently through mergers in which there is a "fusion of a number of capitals already formed or in process of formation takes place by the smoother process of organizing joint-stock companies."[15] In other words, merger waves.

Early Corporate Mergers and the Fusion of Capital

In the last century of corporate capitalism, there have been several waves of merger activity in the United States. In the early twentieth century, most were horizontal mergers, which is a fusion of formerly competing companies from the same industry into one. The drive to fuse capital picked up speed after the establishment of corporate personhood. After the massive merger wave that ended in 1904, others followed. For about a decade prior to the stock market crash of 1929, a wave of horizontal mergers—swept across various sectors including banking, chemicals, food products, and retailing.[16] Part of the impulse to merge was speculation as speculators are particularly interested in putting bets on stocks of companies that are about to merge. Companies that are targeted for a merger or takeover by another tend to see a rise in stock prices. Investment pool operators, banks that were lending to speculators on margin, and corporate insiders together placed speculative bets on the stocks of a company that was the target of a takeover. But overall, the main strategy of mergers at that time was simply to eliminate competition to create monopolies or oligopolies that work together as a cartel and collectively act like a monopoly.[17]

Even though antitrust laws were part of the legal code of the United States, they were not strictly enforced in the courts. The landmark Sherman Antitrust Act of 1890 was vaguely worded and did not unequivocally prohibit monopolies or try to prevent them from forming. Rather, the law focused on the actions businesses took once they achieved such power. Standard Oil Company had a near total monopoly in oil production and distribution and was in flagrant violation of the law. It widely was expected that the court would force the company to break into smaller, more competitive bits, which it did. But after the Supreme Court finally ordered the dismantling of Standard Oil's empire in the *Standard Oil Co. of New Jersey v. United States* (1911), the court's position on antitrust became weaker.

As corporations became progressively more influential in the political arena, courts were less inclined to enforce antitrust. Until the mid-twentieth century, the court's philosophy, known as "the rule of reason," interpreted corporate mergers and monopolization of industries generally lawful unless it could be proven that the companies involved explicitly used their power to restrain trade and drive out competitors. During this period, US Steel Corporation controlled over half of all steel production in America. Under the president Woodrow Wilson Administration, the government sought to take similar action as it did against Standard Oil. But the Supreme Court instead decided in the *United States v. U.S. Steel Corp.* (1920) that, "[T]he law does not make mere size an offense, or the existence of unexerted power an offense."[18] The court's interpretation of exerted power implied deliberate attempts to eliminate competition by unfair business practices, and that such attempts would have to be proven in court before any action of justice would be taken. This opened the door to endless and expensive litigation, which for gigantic companies is a mere cost of doing business.

It was around the time of this Supreme Court case that Veblen was formulating his long-term vision of a future completely dominated by corporate institutions as they could extend their influence far beyond the world of business.

The Institutionalization of Capital

In *Modern Corporation*, Berle and Means chronicled the meteoric rise of the corporation, and they focused particularly on the fact that had secured financial independence. Corporations were making money for shareholders and the corporate class with monopoly profits, dividends, bonuses, executive salaries, and so on. But they were also stockpiling fortunes in their own coffers. These fortunes fell under the control of a bureaucracy of professional managers. This independence gave rise to a new emergent property characterized by a separation of ownership from governance. This drew the attention of Berle and Means as they pondered whether this was fragmenting the structure of property relations of capitalism, and possibly lead to the end of capitalism. They assert that, "In its new aspect the corporation is a means whereby the wealth of innumerable individuals has been concentrated into huge aggregates and whereby control over this wealth has been surrendered to a unified direction."[19] But this did not impede capitalism from expansion and accumulation. Shareholders remained as the ultimate claimants to the assets and earnings of the corporation and the essential characteristic of the capitalist mode of production—the private ownership of the means of production—remained unchanged. Rather than fragmenting the capitalist system as Berle and Means feared, the ascent of the corporation actually allowed it to become more entrenched, centralized, and the processes of financialization followed like an aura.

In their classic, *Monopoly Capital*, economists Paul Baran and Paul Sweezy argue that, "…the big corporation, if not more profit-oriented than the individual entrepreneur … is at any rate better equipped to pursue a policy of profit maximization."[20] Also taking a broader systems perspective they see that under corporate capitalism, "The result is much the same: the economy of large corporations is more, not less, dominated by the logic of profitmaking than the economy of small entrepreneurs ever was" (ibid.).[21] Capitalism was not changing its essential character, it was becoming more complex socially compared to sole-entrepreneurial capitalism.

Otherwise the sociological structure of capitalism remained fundamentally unaltered by the rise of the corporation. Rather creating problems in the social relations of production, they expanded them. The sociology of capitalism extended into a class of business professionals who were largely cut from the same cloth as the principal shareholders. Shareholders were never entirely removed from management and management was never entirely removed from ownership. Nonetheless, as Braverman points out, "…in each enterprise the direct and personal unity between the two is ruptured. Capital has now transcended its limited and limiting personal form and has entered into an institutional form."[22]

In this way, corporate capitalism became more diffused among multifaceted group of stakeholders, though chief among them are the owners. Like all other forms of business enterprise within capitalism, governance rests with the ownership. For the typical publicly traded corporate enterprise, this is the privilege common shareholders. To achieve a coherent management structure from a diffusion of independent shareholders, corporations typically employ an electoral process in which owners of common stock are endowed with one voting right for each share owned. Common shareholders are sent a ballot on which they cast votes for board of director nominees and other election items that have a bearing on the status of their ownership. They will elect members of the board of directors with the expectation that the directors will then oversee that the decisions and actions of executive management will be the benefit and satisfaction of owners.

The corporate system was coming into its full power by the mid-twentieth century. By the 1960s, another massive corporate merger wave swept across the American economic landscape. Companies trying to diversify, with mergers that created conglomerates such as General Electric, which had businesses ranging from manufacturing equipment, to television, and even financial services. Single corporate enterprises stretched across state lines and their political power and influence grew accordingly This time it was a conglomerate wave in which businesses that are more or less unrelated were merging.[23]

Institutional economists John K. Galbraith and Clarence Ayres, and sociologist C. Wright Mills observed all of this with keen interest. Galbraith emphasizes that there is an inconsistency between the corporation's idealized definition and its actual existence. The general textbookish presentation of a corporation is normative as it tends to be defined as something it should be, "an association of persons into an autonomous legal unit with a distinct legal personality that enables it to carry on business, own property and contract debts."[24] But Galbraith contrasts this with what it actually is as a market powerhouse that is, "influential in the markets in which it buys materials, components and labor and in which it sells its finished products… disenfranchises stockholders, becomes gargantuan, expands into wholly unrelated activities, has the powers of a monopsony where it buys and of a monopoly where it sells."[25] The contrast illuminating what the corporation is said to be and what it actually is suggests that there is something abnormal or anomalous about what kind of institution was evolving into. Galbraith concludes that the economics profession largely ignores all of this discord and instead rests on the viewpoint of an economy without a society.

Galbraith goes on to show another emergent property of the corporation as it evolved into a de facto institution of national economic planning. To the extent that economists talk about planning at all, the discussion usually falls under the category of industrial policies or incomes policies set by the government. Galbraith notes that the corporation has become a policy-making institution in its own right, although it has never been recognized as such officially or in mainstream academia. By virtue of size and market power it sets forth plans for production schedules on what to produce and how much, it decides consumer trends and fashions, it creates its own technological infrastructure, decides what should be available for people to buy and what should is no longer available, it molds preferences through advertising, controls the flow of credit and capital, and it does all this for the entire national economy.[26] The corporation, in other words, is like a shadow national economic planning commission chartered to serve the interests of the corporate class. As such, it has the capacity to pull other social institutions under its umbrella including organized labor, systems of higher education, and government agencies and form what he calls a technostructure.[27] Within this structure, however, Galbraith also saw the possibility of these institutions—particularly labor—standing as "countervailing" powers that would balance the power dynamics otherwise skewed toward the corporation.[28] He outlined the possibility of an emergent system of checks and balances in which the excesses of corporate aggression could be tempered with worker activism and legislation.

C. Wright Mills shared some of Galbraith's concerns but took a different view regarding countervailing powers. He sees the expansion and interweaving of corporations and various other associations that exist to further their interests both within and among industries.[29] Organizations such as the Chamber of Commerce, the National Association of Manufacturers, and the army of corporate lobbyists in Washington represent not only business interests, but also those of a sophisticated class of elites led by the corporate class. The corporate class, together with their government sponsors and allies in academia, represent a superstructure attending to corporate power. Mills rejected Galbraith's notion of countervailing power as not convincing and as an "odd view of the powerful."[30] In a hegemonic system, countervailing institutions are either coopted or pushed aside. Mills launched a powerful indictment of the totalitarian nature of the corporate hegemony as more like "states within states than simply private business."[31] Though Mills was writing in the fifties, his words seem even more relevant today and deserve fullest expression,

> The economy of America has been largely incorporated, and within their incorporation the corporate chiefs have captured the technological innovation, accumulated the existing great fortunes as well as much lesser, scattered wealth, and capitalized the future... Corporations command raw materials, and the patents on inventions with which to turn them into finished products. They command the most expensive, and therefore what must be the finest, legal minds in the world, to invent and to refine their defenses and their strategies. They employ man as producer and they make that which he buys as consumer. They clothe him and feed him and invest his money. They make that with which he fights the wars and they finance the ballyhoo of advertisement and the obscurantist bunk of public relations that surround him during the wars and between them... If they do not reign, they do govern at many of the vital points of everyday life in America and no powers effectively and consistently countervail against them.[32]

Mills documented the rise to iconic status of the corporate executive class. As the corporate agenda became society's agenda, corporate executives were sublimated in the popular mindset as sophisticated, competent leaders and heroic figures. Mills writes, "Within the free, private, enterprising system, it is said, there has arisen a set of executives who are quite distinct from the 'crude old-fashioned entrepreneurs' out for themselves in the ruthless ways of capitalism now long dead."[33] The corporation had to be recreated as something civilized and its leaders had come to be, "responsible trustees, impartial umpires, and expert brokers for a plurality of economic interests, including those of all the millions of small property holders who hold stock in the great American enterprises, but also the wage workers and the consumers who benefit from the great flow of goods and services."[34] Corporate leaders assumed the role of the stewards of the process of social provisioning. But for Mills, this was a fiction and "mere kindergarten chatter for the economic illiterates."[35]

In light of all this, Mills went on to illustrate a profound irony in American culture. The United States, always the vanguard of "freedom" and "democracy" for the world, yet allowing an authoritarian, nondemocratic institution rise to dominance. Mills illustration was direct and biting, "Americans like to think of themselves as the most individualistic people in the world, but among them the impersonal corporation has proceeded the farthest and now reaches into every area and detail of daily life."[36] Though it is an institution that has a kind of mythical identity as an individual or person that is no different from a flesh and blood human being. Mills, like institutionalist economists, saw the ascent of the corporation as an evolutionary process that had been underway for over a century, "The story of the American economy since the Civil War is thus the story of the creation and consolidation of this corporate world of centralized property."[37]

A contemporary of Galbraith and Mills, institutional economist Clarence Ayres also observed the evolutionary rise of corporate power with concern. In the traditions established by Veblen and Dewey, Ayres held the normative position that the broadest aim of any economic system should be social provisioning. He saw that the projects of provisioning could make real progress with technological advancement and economic development. But he was concerned that the provisioning aspects of economic development were being marginalized and in its place grew what he called "ceremonialism" in corporate society. By this Ayres means that the overriding function of a corporate-dominated economy drifts away from what is socially helpful in order to maintain something more symbolic: the status, wealth, and power of the elite.[38] Corporate empire building and the aggrandizement of the executive class was overtaking all else. For Ayres, this was "the moral crisis of the twentieth century."[39] The ability of society to use systematic knowledge for solving problems in the "general life process" was constrained by the growing corporate structure that was functioning to serve the social, political, and economic domination of the powerful and wealthy.

Also taking this institutionalist view, William Dugger emphasized the rawness of corporate power perhaps more than any other economists. Like Galbraith, Dugger had once envisioned a balanced countervailing system with corporations one side of the scale and organized labor on the other. Perhaps at one time in history it might have been possible to see this happening, but organized labor and other countervailing institutions have faded while the Fortune 500 corporations and Wall Street banks moved to take possession of the national economy and everything in it. Dugger saw this development and buried any hope of a system of checks and balances in the American political economy. He expresses the lopsidedness of corporate power succinctly as it came to be endowed with "the ability to tell other people what to do with some degree of certainty that they will do it."[40] Other people, in this case, are government officials, central bankers, and others eager to be acknowledged as members of the corporate class. In the next chapter we will explore in more detail Dugger's as he defined contours of American corporate hegemony at the beginning of the Greenspan Era.

The loss of the countervailing power of organized labor is today perhaps even more evident than it was in the time of Galbraith and Mills. See organized labor sinking in the quicksand created by hostile institutions, Jared Bernstein an economist and senior fellow at the Center on Budget and Priorities informs us that working conditions for Americans have been stagnating over the long term even though 2018 was a banner year for low unemployment and strong economic growth. Theoretically such conditions should lead to higher wages for working people, but they have not. Bernstein writes, "…bargaining power is feeble, the weakest I've seen in decades. Hostile institutions—the Trump administration, the courts, the corporate sector—are limiting their avenues for demanding higher pay."[41] There is no other cogent explanation why the courts and executive branch of the government would take a hostile position to labor during boom times other than they are doing what corporate leaders tell them to do.

Accordingly, in the political mainstream, there is a one-dimensional litmus test for corporate power: the perception of market competition. The ostensible watchdog government agency on corporate power, the Federal Trade Commission, only raises questions about such power only when there is an apparent threat to competition in markets. Otherwise the concerns raised by Galbraith, Mills, Ayres, Dugger are consistently ignored. The consolidation of corporate power was turbocharged during the Greenspan Era and radical push toward neoliberalism that allowed for another remarkable series of corporate mega-mergers.

Greenspan Era Mergers and the Ascent of Leviathan Banks

The 1980s was once dubbed the decade of the "merger mania," but this was shallow compared to the merger phenomena that occurred in the 1990s as a result of deregulation. The ten largest merger and acquisition deals in the world during the eighties averaged $20.3 billion per deal.[42] Nine of these ten deals were in the United States. The two largest were Kohlberg Kravis Roberts buyout of RJF Nabisco $52 billion and Standard Oil of California buyout of Gulf Oil for $31 billion. By the 1990s, the average of the ten largest mergers deals jumped to $116.3 billion, six times larger than those of the 1980s.[43] Seven of these ten deals were in the United States. The two largest were Vodafone of the UK purchase of the German company Mannesmann for $202 billion and in the US Pfizer's purchase of Lambert for $111.8 billion.[44] Corporate mergers became larger, deeper, and more globally expansive during the Greenspan Era, particularly in banking.

A hallmark of the Greenspan Era was spate of deregulation initiatives resulting in a series of bank mergers that profoundly changed the structure of banking and finance. A major deregulation bill pushed through during the first Clinton administration was the Riegle-Neal Interstate Banking and Branching Efficiency Act (1994). In the early nineties, large Wall Street banks sought to merge with other banks with charters in other states. Such mergers were blocked by the Bank Holding Act (1956). The idea behind the Bank Holding Act was a common sense attempt to keep Wall Street banks from becoming *too big to fail*. Riegle-Neal repealed this provision and set the stage for a massive upsurge of bank mergers across state. During this wave, there were over 3500 bank mergers between 1994 and 2003 in which the acquiring banks gobbled up about $3 trillion in assets and took over about $2 trillion in deposits.[45]

Regional banks became national giants. Chemical Bank and Manufacturers Hanover, which had merged a few years earlier, was able to merge with Chase Manhattan in 1995, then later merged with J.P. Morgan to become J.P. Morgan Chase in 1998. Bank of America bought Fleet-Boston, which was the merged combination of the three largest banks in New England. Nations Bank acquired Barnett in 1997 and then this merged giant was taken over by Bank of America in 1998 in a $62 billion merger deal. Wells Fargo bought First Interstate and Norwest in 1998 for $34 billion. Wachovia merged with First Union, CoreStates, and then eventually merged with Citicorp to form Citigroup. Citigroup and Traveler's Insurance was a high profile $70 billion merger deal in 1998. That merger should have been more controversial than it was because Glass Steagall had not yet been repealed and the merger was technically illegal (Johnson, 85).[46] And so the story of banking industry consolidation goes.

At the dawn of the Greenspan Era, the ten largest banks in the US controlled less than 30% of all deposits. After these mergers, the ten largest banks seized control of over 60%, and by 2010, three banks—J.P. Morgan Chase, Bank of America, and Wells Fargo—control a third of all deposits.

The extension of corporate power was no longer something to be anticipated, it was clearly being demonstrated. Riegle-Neal was supported by a cheerleading crowd of academic economists, libertarian think tanks, Treasury officials, and Fed governors. One of their arguments was that the interstate bank mergers could make banks larger and theoretically more efficient through "economies of scale" which is a euphemism for having the ability to dominate markets by virtue of sheer giantism. Another argument in support of Riegle-Neal was that larger banks would eventually have a better shot at penetrating international markets than smaller ones, and therefore the economy overall would become competitive. Wall Street giants have always meddled in the financial sectors of other countries. The deregulation move would heighten their ability to do this and there is no evidence that the countries involved have gained anything from this domination. Though after the crises that started in 2007, it became quite evident that countries everywhere had become devastated by the massive debacles originating on Wall Street.

Corporate-friendly economists also tried to justify Riegle-Neal arguing that by limiting the scope of interstate mergers this would limit market access, create regional banking monopolies, and hinder competition. This argument, however, is not defensible as a multitudes of smaller competing banks still operated in each of the local markets; that is, before they were taken over by the larger banks after Riegle-Neal was passed. These questionable arguments aside, the main priority behind unleashing was not about becoming more competitive. It was to give large banks what they really wanted: the ability to cannibalize the market share and technologies that had already been established by other banks.

Riegle-Neal cleared the way for a massive wave of interstate mergers and the banking industry became extremely concentrated in a short period of time. And once these merger processes are underway, they take on their own momentum. Small or moderate sized banks watch other banks get gobbled up by larger banks, and larger banks merge with other large banks to form leviathan banks. Suddenly smaller banks become aware of their ant-like position in the industry and their survival starts to seem tentative. They are compelled to draw the conclusion that if their competitors are merging, they better do it as well or be driven to extinction.

Meanwhile the political clout of the largest banks has grown proportionally to their market share. With their interstate profile, megabanks gained influence in Congress as they began to have a business presence in more than one state. Thus empowered, large banks pushed for even more banking deregulation and sought to dismantle other anti-merger regulations, particularly the Glass Steagall Act of 1933.

Glass Steagall, sponsored by Senator Carter Glass of Virginia and Henry Steagall of Alabama, was created as a measure to cope with the massive bank failures that occurred in the early years of the Great Depression. After the stock market crash of 1929 and the wave of banking and business failures that followed, it had become obvious to political leaders that banking and financial market stability is crucial for overall economic stability. At the same time, however, legislators recognized that banks were too reckless and unstable and needed to be more tightly regulated. It was in this context that the Glass Steagall Act of 1933 was passed.

The passage of this bill was arguably the most important piece of banking legislation in US history as it contained two hugely significant provisions. One was to establish the Federal Deposit Insurance Corporation (FDIC) that was chartered to federally insure people's deposits up to a certain amount to prevent bank panics. The FDIC gave people assurances that their money was safe even if the banks were in trouble and was a milestone in establishing banking stability.

The other provision prohibited depository institutions like commercial banks merging with investment banks and insurance companies. Glass Steagall put a firewall between commercial banks that provide basic banking services like taking people's deposits for savings or checking accounts and making loans; investment banks that are involved in underwriting securities, capitalizing new businesses, handling mergers, and other activities that involve much risk; and insurance companies that collect premium payments and make large-scale financial investments. The justification for this legislation was that lawmakers saw that it was too risky to have so many aspects of the financial industry held in the hands of large banks—too many eggs in a basket. More specifically it was seen as too risky to allow investment banks garner access to people's deposits and insurance premiums, or to use deposits as collateral to underwrite risky securities. Under Glass Steagall, depository institutions, investment banks, and insurance companies would operate in separate markets and be regulated by separate authorities. By doing so, when instabilities arise, they could be more effectively contained and less likely to spread from one sector to another.

The push to repeal Glass Steagall came from key figures at the top of the Washington-Wall Street power structure. Large banks like Citibank wanted to merge with large insurance companies like Travelers, and large commercial banks like Chase Manhattan wanted to merge with large investment banks like J.P. Morgan. On behalf of these companies, Robert Rubin and Lawrence Summers in the Clinton Treasury Department and Alan Greenspan and Janet Yellen at the Fed were relentless in their call for Congress to repeal Glass Steagall (Johnson, 92–100).[47]

Together they were a chorus attuned to the standard arguments that deregulation was needed so these banks could become as big and diversified as possible to compete in global markets. They also argued that given a series of financial crises that exploded in East Asia at the time, larger banks would be more able to withstand an international financial meltdown. Large icebergs do not melt to water as quickly as small ones. But the banking crisis of 2007–2009 proved this wrong. Big companies not only go down faster, they leave a much wider swath of collateral damage along the way.

Notwithstanding the emerging leviathan banks were no longer recognizable as businesses. Rather, they became institutions that owned portfolios of businesses operating in multiple markets and created empires of financial services. In 2009, Federal Reserve Governor Daniel Tarullo summarized the character of the new financial system after wave upon wave of mergers, "The result was a financial services industry dominated by one set of very large holding companies centered on a large commercial bank and another set of very large financial institutions not subject to prudential regulation."[48]

The repeal legislation finally arrived with the Gramm-Leach-Bliley, partially sponsored by the same Phil Gramm who sponsored the Commodities Futures Modernization Act a year later. This set off another round of bank mergers. Bank of America went on a merging binge as it acquired Fleet Boston Financial for $49 billion, MBNA Corp for $36 billion, North American Holding for $21 billion, and later bought Merrill Lynch for $50 billion in a deal that was sealed with $200 billion government money and loan guarantees. Merrill Lynch itself had acquired First Republic Bank that controls over $100 billion in deposits. J.P. Morgan Chase acquired Bank One in 2004 for $59 billion. Wachovia acquired Golden West Financial for $26 billion in 2006 and then later was taken over by Wells Fargo.[49]

By 2000, the largest 5 banks controlled about 11% of all deposits and by 2009 the top 3 largest banks held over 10% of all deposits. By 2010, the 5 largest banks controlled as much as 40% of all deposits, and the top 3, J.P. Morgan Chase, Bank of America, and Wells Fargo, held about one-third of all deposits. With each merger wave the banks became more reckless because their mergers were stamped with the Treasury and the Federal Reserve's *too big to fail* seals of approval. As they transformed themselves into "universal banks" functioning as bank holding overlords with command over commercial banks, investment banks, hedge funds, and virtually all else that falls under the category of finance. They turned into financial institutions unlike anything seen before and far beyond their previous *too big to fail* status.

Although there are still many small community banks and credit unions in operation today, the deregulation and consolidation movement created an environment in which leviathan banks rose to the top of the pack and began a series of dogfights during which all banks tried to become as large and possible, to expand globally, and do all this as quickly as possible. Ostensibly this was a scramble for survival, but the upshot was that banking became a cartel. This kind of aggressive industry concentration was something that former Fed chairman and principal advocate of the original Bank Holding Act, William McChesney Martin, Jr., warned us about decades ago, "To my mind, the greatest risk is in the concentration of economic power. If we combine a holding company with a typical business firm… we run the risk of cartelizing our economy."[50] By the Greenspan Era, no one in any real positions of power seemed to be heeding Martin's warning.

The fusion of capital continues unabated. The years 2015 and 2018 were outstanding years for high-profile corporate mergers. 2015 was a record year during which about $4.7 trillion in merger deals were announced, with the highest percentage ever derived from companies valued at more than $5 billion.[51] Slow growth in some industries has played a key role in facilitating these mergers as giant corporations that find it hard to grow start looking at taking over other companies and their markets as a way to expand their own. The Federal Reserve has kept interest rates quite low for several years and this had made financing large merger deals nearly cost free. Shareholders helped pressure companies to open mega merger deals as they see this as a quick and easy way to have their share prices jump in the markets.

As of this writing, 2018 is on track to break the 2015 record. More than $2.5 trillion mergers were announced in the first half of 2018. Of course, low Fed rates again played a key role, but the companies announced that the main reason for the mergers was that they were the only ways the companies could stay alive given an aggressive competitive threat coming from the tech sector. Corporate earnings were growing thanks to the Trump tax cuts and stock prices soared to historic highs, nonetheless corporations were seeking more aggressive ways to find market expansion. As companies like Amazon, which just acquired retail grocery giant Whole Foods in a $13.7 billion deal, other companies in media and health care feared the tech sector ability to push into their markets.[52] Chemical giants Dow Chemical and DuPont merged into a $130 billion gargantua, and in beverages Anheuser-Busch and InBev combined in $104 billion deal.[53] In media, merger deals totaled $323 billion in the first half of 2018.

Compared to 2017, the merger wave of 2018 showed substantially higher volume in every industry (Table 3.2).

That year media giants AT&T and Time Warner we given the green light by a federal judge to merge, but the Justice Department expressed resistance on account of the merger could give the company too much control over online streaming services. During this time Comcast and Disney rammed heads as they preyed on bits and pieces of Fox's entertainment assets. Disney eventually gobbled up the largest chunks of Fox in a $52 billion deal and left the scraps for Comcast and Time Warner. Disney's acquisition of Fox also gave it majority control of Hulu and other media firms in the Fox empire. A federal judge signaled approval for AT&T and Time Warner to merge in a staggering $85.4 billion deal. And as Amazon pushed into health care, it triggered a wave of fear-driven heavyweight mergers. CVS Health merged with Aetna for

Table 3.2 Dollar value of merger deals in 2017 and 2018 (x billions)

Industry	2017	2018	Percentage change (%)
Energy and power	$238.70	$388.70	63
Media and entertainment	$60.50	$323.40	435
Health care	$154.90	$315.70	104
Industrials	$159.00	$242.20	52
Financials	$148.20	$213.70	44
High technology	$135.60	$7.90	53
Real estate	$218.60	$200.40	−8
Consumer staples	$104.10	$178.50	71
Materials	$109.50	$156.20	43
Telecommunications	$50.30	$122.00	143
Consumer products and services	$109.40	$87.40	−20
Retail	$67.40	$77.70	15

Source Thomson Reuters/*New York Times*

$69 billion, Cigna merged with Express Scripts for $52 billion.[54] With the rise of Donald J. Trump as president, the processes of fusing capital and constructing business empires is accelerating at a dizzying pace. The corporation is being given more power to exert its influence everywhere, to make its presence felt in every industry, every state, and every community across the geographic domain.

In his "Secular Trend" Veblen saw the consolidation of corporate power as no less than a raw, myopic pursuit of wealth accumulation and strategic control of all the major industries, "through shrewd investments and coalitions with other business men" with disregard for the legitimate and pragmatic purposes for which the industries were originally created.[55] He saw a system emerging in which the entire economy would eventually succumb to predatory impulses in which taking and conquering becomes more important that actual productive work or social provisioning. Veblen's secular trend came to be a kind of structural drift in which the entire system was moving toward a system condition of maladjustment that Veblen described as "systematic retardation and derangement."[56] The economic order of things has drifted into a kind of dysfunctional structure that is indifferent to genuine well-being and has a tendency to grind down into a permanent state of crisis. Paper wealth accumulation became *the* economic priority and was pursued at all costs. The Deweyan project of social provisioning is irrelevant or, at best, of secondary importance.

Financialization and the instability that goes with it are symptoms of this maladjustment.

With its emphasis on aggregating financial capital, buying and selling and taking profits wherever they can be found, corporate financialization took the place of social provisioning. This process accelerated during the Greenspan Era in which the total assets controlled by financial companies grew from about 55% of the nation's GDP in 1980 to 95% by 2000.[57] Financial sector profits during this period also soared from an average of 13% of total US corporate profits to about 30%.[58] As our financial system drifts away from its original, legitimate purpose and toward speculation, bubbles and instability become a recurring feature. And with the corporation institutions that are larger than most countries around the world, the scale of instability is off the charts.

Financialization during the Greenspan Era encapsulates Veblen's conception of economic derangement. The corporation is programmed for endless accrual of financial wealth by any means possible. What is becoming increasingly clear, however, is that such growth is hitting the wall for a multitude of reasons. Stagnating returns on capital investment, intensified competition in global markets, and physical limits to growth are binding the process of expansion like a rope. As this is occurring, the system is thrown into a state of contradiction and crisis. On the one hand, it must continue to grow, but on the other hand, it cannot. In the popular mindset, most would rather illusions of growth rather than directly face and reconcile this contradiction, even if that means achieving growth in one sector by cannibalizing another, and even if that means creating financial market bubbles as an illusion of expanding prosperity.

The corporate system does not require brute force to do this. As we will see in the chapters that follow, it has captured all other major institutions in its net of influence, and the public has been culturally conditioned to accept the reality of this power without being aware of it as the population too is saturated with neoliberal ideology.

Notes

1. Thorstein Veblen, *The Theory of the Leisure Class* (New York, NY: The Viking Press, 1899), p. 4.
2. Ibid., p. 399.
3. Adolf A. Berle and Gardiner C. Means, *The Modern Corporation and Private Property* [1932] (New Brunswick: Transaction Publishers, 2010), p. 3.
4. Joel Bakan, *The Corporation: The Pathological Pursuit of Profit and Power* (New York, NY: Free Press, 2004), p. 5.
5. Ibid.
6. Dirk Philipsen, *The Little Big Number: How GDP Came to Rule the World and What to Do About It* (Princeton University Press, 2015), p. 44.
7. See *Fortune Magazine* at http://fortune.com/fortune500/list/.
8. David Streitfeld, "Amazon Hits $1,000,000,000,000 in Value, Following Apple," *The New York Times*, September 4, 2018.

9. Marjorie Kelly, *The Divine Right of Capital: Dethroning the Corporate Aristocracy* (San Francisco: Berrett-Koehler, 2001), pp. xi–xiii.
10. David Korten, *When Corporations Rule the World* (San Francisco, CA: Berrett-Koehler, 2nd ed., 2001), p. 22.
11. Vaclav Havel, *Disturbing the Peace: A Conversation with Karel Huizdala* (New York, NY: Vintage, 1991), p. 14.
12. Harry Braverman, *Labor and Monopoly Capital: The Degradation of Work in the Twentieth Century* (New York, NY: Monthly Review Press, 1974), pp. 257–258.
13. See Joel Magnuson, *Mindful Economics*, 2008, pp. 71–73.
14. Joel Bakan, *The Corporation: The Pathological Pursuit of Profit and Power* (New York, NY: Free Press, 2004), p. 14.
15. Karl Marx, *Capital* [1867] (Moscow: Progress Publishers, 1970), Vol. I, p. 588.
16. R.B. Du Boff and E.S. Herman, "Merger, Concentration, and the Erosion of Democracy," *Monthly Review*, May, 2001. https://monthlyreview.org/2001/05/01/mergers-concentration-and-the-erosion-of-democracy/.
17. R.B. Du Boff and E.S. Herman, "The Promotional-Financial Dynamic of Merger Movements: A Historical Perspective," *Journal of Economic Issues*, March 23, 1989.
18. Law Library-American Law and Legal Information: Antitrust, 2018. http://law.jrank.org/pages/22773/Monopolies-Antitrust-Law-Monopoly-Cases.html.
19. Berle and Means, 2010, p. 4.
20. Paul Baran and Paul Sweezy, *Monopoly Capital: An Essay on the American Economic and Social Order* (New York, NY: Monthly Review Press, 1966), pp. 27–28.
21. Ibid.
22. Braverman, 1974, p. 258.
23. Janet Lowe, *The Secret Empire: How 25 Multinationals Rule the World* (Burr Ridge, IL: Business One, Irwin, 1992), p. 65.
24. John K. Galbraith, *The New Industrial State* (Boston: Houghton Mifflin, 1967), p. 76.
25. Ibid.
26. Ibid., p. 81.
27. Ibid., p. 74.
28. John K. Galbraith, *American Capitalism: The Concept of Countervailing Power* (New York, NY: Houghton Mifflin, 1952), p. 126.

29. See also a critical assessment of Galbraith's view at the time in Earl Latham, "The Body Politic of the Corporation," in E.S. Mason, *The Corporation in Modern Society* (Cambridge: Harvard University Press, 1959).
30. C. Wright Mills, *The Power Elite* (New York, NY: Oxford University Press, 1959), p. 125.
31. Ibid., p. 124.
32. Ibid., pp. 124–125.
33. Ibid., p. 118.
34. Ibid.
35. Ibid., p. 119.
36. Ibid., p. 120.
37. Ibid.
38. Clarence E. Ayres, *Toward a Reasonable Society* (Austin: University of Texas Press, 1961), p. 28.
39. Ibid., p. 49.
40. William M. Dugger, "The Administered Labor Market: An Institutional Analysis," *Journal of Economic Issues*, June 15, 1981, pp. 397–407.
41. Jared Bernstein, "Why Real Wages Are Stuck," *The New York Times*, July 19, 2018.
42. The figures listed here are measured in terms inflation adjusted dollar values of assets acquired. See "M&A Statistics—Worldwide, Regions, Industries & Countries," IMAA-Institute. Retrieved 2017-09-06.
43. Ibid.
44. Ibid.
45. Steven J. Pilloff, "Bank Merger Activity in the United States, 1994–2003," Staff Study 176, Board of Governors of the Federal Reserve System, 2004.
46. Simon Johnson and James Kwak, *Thirteen Bankers: The Wall Street Takeover and the Next Financial Meltdown* (New York, NY: Pantheon, 2010), p. 85.
47. Johnson and Kwak, 2010, pp. 92–100. See also Ezra Klein, "Janet Yellen Backed the Repeal of Glass-Steagall in 1997," *Huffington Post*, September 17, 2013.
48. Daniel K. Tarullo, "Confronting Too Big to Fail," a lecture presented at the Exchequer Club in Washington, DC, October 21, 2009 posted on federalreserve.gov/newsevents/speech/tarullo20191021a.htm.

49. See "M&A Statistics—Worldwide, Regions, Industries & Countries," IMAA-Institute. Retrieved 2017-09-06.
50. Statement by William McChesney Martin, Jr. Chairman, Board of Governors of the Federal Reserve SystemBefore the Committee on Banking and Currency, House of Representatives, April 18, 1969 posted at https://fraser.stlouisfed.org/content/?item_id=7938&file-path=/files/docs/historical/martin/martin69_0418.pdf.
51. Thomson Reuters, June 30, 2018; see also *The New York Times*, July 4, 2018.
52. https://www.cnbc.com/2017/06/16/amazon-is-buying-whole-foods-in-a-deal-valued-at-13-point-7-billion.html.
53. Leslie Picker, "A Standout Year for Deals, in Volume and Complexity," *The New York Times*, January 3, 2016.
54. Stephen Grocer, "Fear of Silicon Valley Brings Merger Mania Back, with a Vengeance," *The New York Times*, July 4, 2018.
55. Thorstein Veblen, *The Theory of Business Enterprise* [1904] (Clifton, NJ: Augustus Kelly, 1975), p. 24.
56. Veblen, *Absentee Ownership* (1997), p. 421.
57. *Federal Reserve Flow of Funds*, *supra* note 13, Tables L. 109, L. 126., L. 129 and Bureau of Economic Analysis, *supra* note 8, Table 1.1.5.
58. Bureau of Economic Analysis, 2018 *supra* note 8, Table 6.16.

References

Ayres, Clarence E. *Toward a Reasonable Society* (Austin: University of Texas Press, 1961).

Bakan, Joel. *The Corporation: The Pathological Pursuit of Profit and Power* (New York, NY: Free Press, 2004).

Bernstein, Jared. "Why Real Wages Are Stuck," *The New York Times*, July 19, 2018.

Braverman, Harry. *Labor and Monopoly Capital: The Degradation of Work in the Twentieth Century* (New York, NY: Monthly Review Press, 1974).

Bureau of Economic Analysis, 2018. https://www.bea.gov/data/gdp/gross-domestic-product.

CNBC. "Whole Foods Stock Rockets 28% on $13.7 Billion Amazon Takeover Deal," June 2017. https://www.cnbc.com/2017/06/16/amazon-is-buying-whole-foods-in-a-deal-valued-at-13-point-7-billion.html.

Dugger, William M. "The Administered Labor Market: An Institutional Analysis," *Journal of Economic Issues*, Vol. 15, No. 2, June 15, 1981, pp. 397–407.

Fortune Magazine. http://fortune.com/fortune500/list/.

Galbraith, John K. *The New Industrial State* (Boston: Houghton Mifflin, 1967).

Grocer, Stephen. "Fear of Silicon Valley Brings Merger Mania Back, with a Vengeance," *The New York Times*, July 4, 2018.

Havel, Vaclav. *Disturbing the Peace: A Conversation with Karel Huizdala* (New York, NY: Vintage, 1991).

Johnson, Simon, and James Kwak. *Thirteen Bankers: The Wall Street Takeover and the Next Financial Meltdown* (New York, NY: Pantheon, 2010).

Kelly, Marjorie. *The Divine Right of Capital: Dethroning the Corporate Aristocracy* (San Francisco: Berrett-Koehler, 2001).

Korten, David. *When Corporations Rule the World* (San Francisco, CA: Berrett-Koehler, 2nd ed., 2001).

Lowe, Janet. *The Secret Empire: How 25 Multinationals Rule the World* (Burr Ridge, IL: Business One, Irwin, 1992).

Magnuson, Joel. *Mindful Economics: How the U.S. Economy Works, Why It Matters, and How It Could Be Different* (New York, NY: Seven Stories Press, 2008).

Martin, William McChesney, Jr., Chairman, Board of Governors of the Federal Reserve System Before the Committee on Banking and Currency, House of Representatives, April 18, 1969. https://fraser.stlouisfed.org/title/448/item/7938.

Mason, E.S. *The Corporation in Modern Society* (Cambridge: Harvard University Press), 1959.

Merger and Acquisition Institute, IMAA, M&A Stats. https://imaa-institute.org/m-and-a-statistics-countries/.

Mills, C. Wright. *The Power Elite* (New York, NY: Oxford University Press, 1959).

Philipsen, Dirk. *The Little Big Number: How GDP Came to Rule the World and What to Do About It* (Princeton, NJ: Princeton University Press, 2015).

Picker, Leslie. "A Standout Year for Deals, in Volume and Complexity," *The New York Times*, January 3, 2016.

Pilloff, Steven J. "Bank Merger Activity in the United States, 1994–2003," Staff Study 176, Board of Governors of the Federal Reserve System, 2004. https://ideas.repec.org/p/fip/fedgss/176.html.

Streitfeld, David. "Amazon Hits $1,000,000,000,000 in Value, Following Apple," *The New York Times*, September 4, 2018.

Tarullo, Daniel K. "Confronting Too Big to Fail," a Lecture Presented at the Exchequer Club in Washington, DC, October 21, 2009. https://ideas.repec.org/p/fip/fedgsq/482.html.

Veblen, Thorstein. *Absentee Ownership: Business Enterprise in Recent Times: The Case of America* [1923] (New Brunswick, NJ: Transaction Publishers, 1997).

Veblen, Thorstein. *The Theory of Business Enterprise* [1904] (Clifton, NJ: Augustus Kelly, 1975).

4

Corporate Hegemony and the Mutual Support Network

When the banking crisis of 2007–2009 began exploding around the world, an amazing spectacle unfolded in Washington. A group of executives from gigantic corporations in the financial sector descended on the nation's capital and presented the government with an ultimatum. The government was to either release billions in bailout money or face the consequences of sending the nation's economy into a cataclysm and sacking millions of jobs. What amounted to extortion by Wall Street executives was met with little resistance in the political establishment. Instead, White House officials and members of Congress went scurrying in all directions to comply with the demands of these companies. On a single day in October 2008, the U.S. Treasury Department was authorized to spend a staggering $120 billion of public funds to acquire preferred shares of six banking giants. Bank of America, Citigroup, Wells Fargo, and J.P. Morgan Chase each received $25 billion, and Goldman Sachs and Morgan Stanley received $10 billion each. The US federal budget deficit soared to $237 billion for the month of October alone.[1] And that was just the beginning.

A couple of months later, the Federal Reserve's monetary policy crew, the Federal Open Market Committee, convened for a special meeting.

J. Magnuson, *Financing the Apocalypse*,
Palgrave Insights into Apocalypse Economics,
https://doi.org/10.1007/978-3-030-04720-7_4

The agenda was to discuss dealing with a worldwide banking panic that was by then in full swing. At this meeting, the Fed officially adopted what came to be known as the "zero-bound" interest rate policy in the hopes that tossing shiploads of free money in short-term lending markets would keep troubled Wall Street banks from falling into insolvency. The Fed used every possible technique and created trillions of dollars out of vapor to bring investment banks, hedge funds, and bank holding companies back from the precipice of ruin. Wall Street bankers were thrilled. At a meeting between of major Wall Street firms and Treasury and Fed officials to discuss the terms of the October 2008 bailout, Vikram Pandit, then CEO of Citigroup, blurted out gleefully, "This is very cheap capital!"[2]

That the US government would comply with the demands of Wall Street in this way was not unusual. By 2008 there was an established pattern in which an industry is cut loose in the name of free-market capitalism and let the open market run its course. When that course leads to a crisis, which it invariably does, the public sector is enlisted to engineer rescue bailout packages. Leaders in Congress, the Treasury, and the Federal Reserve were compelled to take bailout action, though there were other options that did not involve blindly throwing bailout money at Wall Street. One course would have been to take the troubled banks into conservatorship—as is typically done by the Federal Deposit Insurance Corp (FDIC) for insolvent banks—and restructure the banks as public entities. This was widely considered as a viable option and was endorsed by Nobel laureate economists, Paul Krugman and Joseph Stiglitz. The economists argued that at the very least, the government could take over the banks temporarily and restructure them into smaller more manageable bits. From there the government could operate the banks as public entities while re-establishing regulatory control, or eventually return the banks to the private sector once things were stabilized.

Operating financial institutions as public entities has precedent. The Federal National Mortgage Association and the Federal Home Loan Corporation, also known as Fannie Mae and Freddy Mac, are government institutions that have been involved in developing a stable mortgage industry for over five decades. Their principal business was to securitize mortgages as a way to help banks access funds so that they could more easily expand home lending. The broader mission was to expand home ownership among the population; a clear goal of social provisioning. With the onset of the banking crisis of 2007–2009, the mortgage-backed security business fell into deep trouble, but was as we will see later the trouble only started when Wall Street companies got involved. Though Stiglitz acknowledged that "Nationalization is the only answer" operating banks in the public sector was never seriously considered in Washington.[3] To do so would have both diminished the role of the corporation as the alpha institution and elevated the federal government beyond its role of a standby functionary.

The same servile role is expected of the Federal Reserve. Since it was created in 1913, the Fed has always stood as a lender of last resort for private sector banks, but that was never intended to be interpreted as a bailout fund for banks that got themselves in trouble because of recklessness; that is at least not until the Greenspan Era. Section 13 of the Fed charter empowers it to take action during "unusual and exigent circumstances" and extend loans accordingly. This provision, however, applies only for crises that extend from "actual commercial transactions; that is, notes, drafts, and bills of exchange issued or drawn for agricultural, industrial, or commercial purposes."[4] The Fed's charter clearly states that it is not its responsibility to patch up insolvent Wall Street institutions and make them whole, though this is what it did. Former Goldman Sachs economist and current president of Federal Reserve Bank of New York, William Dudley, openly admitted this conflict and mission drift, "It is impossible to both achieve the central bank's mandate in managing the trade-off between growth and inflation over the near term and also limit asset bubbles."[5] The Fed, in other words, faced a dilemma. It could remain committed to traditional monetary policy for the good of the nation or get into the business of maintaining speculative bubbles in financial markets for the good of Wall Street, but it could not do both. It chose the latter.

Officials at the Treasury and Fed seemed compelled to rescue Wall Street banks primarily because the banks had become *too big to fail*, a condition the same government institutions worked hard to help create. The government had other options, but they chose to help these large banks with bailout money and cheap credit because it is what the banks wanted. They assisted Wall Street in cleaning up its messes so that the banks could go back to business as usual. Government officials are seen expressing their occasional indignation at Wall Street misbehavior on CSPAN cameras, but away from the cameras their approach to banking industry regulation is remarkably tepid. William Dudley recently commented that, "There is evidence of deep-seated cultural and ethical failures at many large financial institutions," as if he had just thought of this for the first time; and Thomas Curry, the Comptroller of the Currency—the main banking regulatory body within the US Treasury—demurred from taking a hard stance on regulating the banking industry because, "It is not going to work if we approach it from a lawyerly standpoint," he said while suggesting that the role of government, "is more a priest-penitent relationship."[6] Fed and Treasury regulators would prefer to be more like moral counselors to bankers rather than genuine regulators pressing hard for corporate accountability.

The sobering implication is that during the Greenspan Era and the massive corporate mergers, leviathan banks and other Fortune 500 corporations have risen to become the most powerful and wealthy institutions in history. They have captured the political establishment to such an extent that they have the ability to make demands of the very institutions that are supposed to be their regulators. The structure of institutional power has inverted from democratic accountability to corporate dominance. Accordingly, government institutions that are chartered to be their regulators have shown, as Veblen put it, "unreflecting deferential concession to the usages of corporate organization and control."[7]

Wall Street and Washington are institutionally bonded. A steady stream of campaign donation money flows from Wall Street's remarkably deep pockets and into campaign coffers of politicians. A continually revolving door through which executives pass to take key positions in the Federal Reserve and the Treasury, then return to Wall Street. On both sides of the door is a shared ideology of neoliberalism which emphasizes that unregulated markets and financial innovation no matter how it was conceived serve the interests of the country. The message is drummed out as propaganda and has helped create a virtual national consensus that Wall Street's interests equals the nation's interest.

The corporation's political capture of the public sphere is perhaps now more calcified today than ever. Piece by piece, the countervailing institutions of the twentieth century that provided a semblance of checks and balances against corporate power have either turned to putty or restructured themselves in the corporate image. To this process, we turn again to institutional economist William Dugger and his work on corporate hegemony.

Corporate Hegemony

The concept of hegemony traditionally applies to an imperial nation-state or political party that uses military force to dominate all of society. The classic example is the National Socialist Party in Nazi Germany but hegemony does not necessarily require such blunt instruments as tanks and cannons to maintain institutional dominance. The rise of the corporation over the last century involved an insidious wrestling match between the institutions of the state and the corporation that was mostly settled without warfare. The struggle has been carried out in the halls of Congress, in the courts, and in the realm of popular opinion as a contest over things like control of the corporate charter, establishing corporate personhood, government environmental regulations, antitrust, and businesses rights to influence political campaigns through political action committee (PAC) expenditures. The struggle is ongoing, though has largely settled on a structure of shared governance in which the corporation has assumed key positions of control.

Basic cronyism and corruption are part of the power structure, but the corporate exercise of power over other institutions is often more complex and subtle. On the surface of shared governance there exist layers of gloss and subtle ties expressed for public consumption as "public-private" cooperation. This is a kind of civil co-existence indicating a sensible structure for policy and planning in which all can in which corporations are given a "voice." For Dugger, however, there is a deeper bond that that holds institutions together in a kind of mutual support network that remains largely invisible for sake of politeness and practical concerns of not rocking the institutional boat. This bond forms in a process that Dugger calls "invaluation" that helps keep intact a wider structure of social control that extends beyond the limitations of a single corporate enterprise.[8] Invaluation cements a more permanent and effective system of control by making sure that the values and ideology consistent with corporate aspirations are shared within all other institutions that matter including government, media, and education. Dugger identifies the dimensions to this invaluation process as emulation, contamination and subordination, and mystification.

Emulation

Recent work in sociological research has fleshed out a process called institutional isomorphism in which institutions in a particular setting start to look and act like one another (Beckert, 150–166).[9] In the case of corporate hegemony, the Fortune 500 and Wall Street institutions set the mold in which public institutions shape themselves. This process of isomorphism involves creating an identity crises among government institutions such that the public sector takes on the role of the "bad guy" whereas corporations are glorified as creators of wealth and jobs and thus most worthy of emulation. The invaluation of this corporate prestige derives in part from its dominance in the social relations of production in modern capitalism, and from its ability to amass and conquer wealth, which was always the goal of nation-state empire building. In this political economy, it appears most prudent and common sense for federal, state, and local institutions to pattern their organizations after the corporation in order to best serve the interests society.[10] Running public institutions like a business creates an expectation that they will become more efficient because businesses are better trained to function this way as they have been hardened by the discipline of the market.

In the financial sector, emulation exacts corporate-style conformity from Treasury officials and Fed governors. Dugger notes that there is a certain social status awarded to those who standing out to resemble Wall Street jet-setters. The general perception is that by doing so a government professional is "...raising one's standing in a group of status-ranked strivers, all of whom are trying to inflate their own status while simultaneously deflating the status of their competitors."[11] Individuals are more likely to succeed in rising through the ranks of Treasury and Fed agencies if they have the same business school alma maters, and express a mindset that mirrors those in the corporate executive class, and, better yet, have resumes that are thick with Wall Street experience. Dugger concludes that, "emulation has touched every major American institution in a way that has always raised the status of the corporation… The result has been the strengthening of corporate hegemony."[12]

Contamination and Subordination

Such institutional isomorphism leads to corporate homogenization and erodes the balance of pluralism in the institutional milieu. When the corporate mission becomes the mission for all, government regulatory institutions drift away from their original mandate and become assimilated. They lose their will to challenge the single-mindedness of shareholder sovereignty or the idea that running successful companies is the only worthwhile mission. As government agencies are pushed onto the corporate rails, they become subordinated to serve as means to corporate ends.

As an example of how this can happen, economic historian Dirk Philipsen traces the development of the project of national income accounting and the rise of gross domestic product (GDP). He tells the story of how the goals of national income accounting were pulled far away from the goals of those who created it—a case of mission drift away from the goals of social provisioning to those of the corporate sector. National income accounting was initially conceived by institutional economists Wesley Mitchell and Simon Kuznets during the Great Depression. They wanted to make a system of national economic metrics that would serve to guide economic policy directed at helping people who were being trampled by economic crises.[13] The metric was to compile data on employment levels across industrial, geographic, and demographic sectors; disparities between labor income and property income, or between blue collar income and white income, and so on. But these metrics were ignored and instead the federal Commerce Department settled on measuring things that were most relevant to corporate capitalism under the principle that what is good for corporate capitalism is good for all. The system of national metrics was contaminated with bottom-line imperatives and social provisioning was subordinated.

GDP became a measurement of commodification: the market value of all finished goods and services produced and distributed in a country. Kuznets expressed exasperation that his work was contaminated used as an instrument in the service of nothing more than "an acquisitive society."[14] Its development followed the rise to dominance of corporate capitalism. Philipsen writes, "Anything that could not be turned into a commodity, to be sold at a profit, became a cultural orphan, living precariously on the outskirts of the market… neither good nor service, neither person nor skill, neither land nor resource, had value unless it was financialized in the market."[15] In other words, these other values are subordinated unless proven useful to corporate interests.

Swept along with the drive to commodify everything is the normative assumption that more money means more happiness. Philipsen continues, "Indeed, the very definition of happiness and misery was increasingly reduced [in economic theory] to a cost-benefit analysis. … The pursuit of happiness shriveled into the pursuit of purchasing power. The many flavors of life vanishing behind the stench of greed."[16] The accumulation of money and profits presides as the taskmaster that drives growth in real production and all else is marginalized.

As the corporate hegemony continues to assert its dominance, it contaminates everything in its path with its own agenda and creates mission drift. Government institutions lack the spine and resources to hold large corporations and banks democratically accountable. Media no longer concerns itself with information and culture unless these contribute substantially to advertising revenue. Educational institutions have turned into degree mills that sell credits for dollars and actual student learning is subordinated. And most important for our purposes here, financial institutions—including microfinance institutions—are drifting away from whatever social or public purpose they may have once had.

Mystification

Dugger points out that along with the mission drift comes "value drift."[17] That is, the corporate agenda becomes adorned with symbols that hold positive value in the popular imagination. As neoliberal policies were unleashed during the Greenspan Era, they were rolled out in the media with great pageantry. The titles of banking deregulation legislation were ornamented with politically charged language that connote cherished values such as "freedom," "modernization," "efficiency," "innovation," and of course "job creation."

On the day his Commodity Futures Modernizations Act passed, Phil Gramm gushed with excitement to an enthusiastic audience of Washington Consensus neoliberals,

> We are here today to repeal Glass-Steagall because we have learned that government is not the answer. We have learned that freedom and competition are the answers. We have learned that we promote economic growth, and we promote stability, by having competition and freedom. I am proud to be here because this is an important bill. It is a deregulatory bill. I believe that that is the wave of the future. And I am awfully proud to have been part of making it a reality. (Applause)[18]

Mystification is the form that glosses over the substance of what the policy actually intends. Its effectiveness lies with linking a negatively charged value to a positively charged value.[19] The subtext of "freedom and competition" is to allow big banks to cross state lines and take over the markets of smaller banks. By "synergy and technologies" they mean allowing these newly merged megabanks to appropriate the technologies developed by other businesses. Though it is hard to tell what Gramm meant by "stability" for it had not been that long before that the government was still struggling to get out from under the financial burdens dumped on it by the Savings and Loan crisis that exploded after its deregulation.

Rubin joined in and insisted that deregulation was part of the "new technology" of banking for the twenty-first century. Bill Clinton signed the bill while rolling old chestnuts about giving banks the "freedom to innovate," and "banking competitiveness." Their use of rhetoric aside, the deregulation enthusiasts failed to demonstrate exactly how deregulation was supposed to foster new technology. Neoliberalism is centered, after all, on the two-hundred-year-old superstition known as the "invisible hand" of self-regulating market. Mystification subverts the original meaning of these references into something else entirely as they are captured in the web of the corporate sphere. Serving corporate interests becomes a national priority and thus an act of patriotism. Dugger concludes by emphasizing how far value drift has taken us, "remember that at one time patriotism was the best refuge of a scoundrel. Wrapped in the flag, you could get away with anything."[20]

At the risk of overstating the obvious, these processes of invaluation are nonetheless eclipsed by the most raw element of corporate financial power. This is the central mechanism in institutional isomorphism.[21] Much of the sociological research on this is focused on cross-national institutional adaptations in the aftermath of a war where the defeated nation is forced to assimilate the institutions of the victor. But in corporate hegemony, coercion lies with conditionality or "or else" demands corporate leaders impose on everyone. With regularity Fortune 500 companies demand tax concessions, trade liberalization, and subsidies on the condition that if governments do not comply, it will be the government that takes the blame for job losses or recession that might follow. Even more directly, however, is the brute force wielded by campaign finance spending.

Campaign Finance Reform and Contempt of Court

In its long struggle against corporate power, the federal government made several attempts to crack down on the corrupting influence of corporate money in electoral politics. Starting as early as turn of the twentieth century, Congress passed the *Tillman Act* (1907) intending to prohibit corporations, banks particularly, from contributing money to federal campaigns.[22] In 1910 and 1911, Congress passed additional bills requiring disclosure on federal campaign contributions impacting elections in the House and the Senate. These bills were strengthened by *Federal Corrupt Practices Act* (1925), which provided additional support for the previous disclosures bill.[23] This was followed by the *Hatch Act* of 1939 and subsequent amendments in 1940, which were additional attempts to impose campaign contribution limitations.[24] These were followed by *Taft-Hartley Act* in 1947 that sought to ban corporate and union campaign spending entirely.[25] Yet none of these reforms had any real impact on limiting corporate spending in electoral politics because they did not contain provisions authorizing the enforcement of the legislation. Without some kind of central yet independent authority that could ban, fine or sue corporations for violations, the laws lacked teeth and corporate money continued to flow through lobbying organizations.

In the 1970s, the federal government tried to remedy this problem with additional attempts at campaign spending reform. In 1971, Congress passed the *Federal Elections Campaign Act* (FECA), which limited donations from organizations and placed limits on individual contributions. The legislation also allowed corporations to give money indirectly to campaigns through PACs, though still subject to disclosure requirements as specified in the earlier legislation. PACs are organizations formed by special interests—corporations, unions, or other groups—that raise money and then make donations to political campaigns and pay for political advertisements. In 1974, Congress passed another bill amending FECA by creating an independent watchdog agency, the Federal Elections Commission (FEC), which was authorized to ensure compliance of campaign laws.

In 1974, FECA was challenged in the courts by two senators and political candidates. Republican Senator, James Buckley, and Democratic Senator, Eugene McCarthy, challenged the constitutionality of FECA and filed a suit with the Secretary of the Senate, Francis Valeo. The lawsuit eventually made its way to the US Supreme Court and came to be known as the landmark, *Buckley v. Valeo 1976* case. In *Buckley* the Supreme Court made a distinction between "contributions" and "expenditures." Contributions were interpreted as direct donations to individual candidates whereas expenditures were interpreted as money spent on the candidate's cause, namely advertising. The court stated,

> It is clear that a primary effect of these expenditure limitations is to restrict the quantity of campaign speech by individuals, groups and candidates. The restrictions... limit political expression at the core of our electoral process and of the First Amendment freedoms... expenditure ceiling impose significantly more severe restrictions on protected freedom of political expression and association than do its limitations on financial contributions.[26]

In other words, the Supreme Court ruled in *Buckley* that special interest spending on political messages is protected as freedom of speech by the First Amendment of the Constitution and therefore cannot be subjected to any laws passed by the federal government to impose limitations. The scales of power tilted toward large corporations that have the capability of spending enormous amounts of money on a particular candidate or issue. The corporate lobbying machine gained tremendous momentum and pushed for a 1979 amendment to FECA that allows unlimited amounts of soft money—money spent indirectly on advertising and political messaging.

Immediately after the 1979 amendment to FECA was passed, then Republican Governor of California, Ronald Reagan, became President of the United States. The Republicans, with their strong ties to big business, constructed a formidable soft money/lobbying apparatus. From the 1980s forward, the political landscape in Washington changed dramatically. Corporate lobbyists became more like Congressional staffers and government agencies that were created to regulate and enforce laws like the Securities Exchange Commission, Environmental Protection Agency, the Department of Agriculture, and the U.S. Treasury became clients of the corporations they were supposed to be regulating. The two-hundred-year-old tradition of democratic pushback began to fade and the Democratic Party shifted from the opposition party to the compromise party and then to the now capitulation party.

In 2002, Congress made one last attempt to push for campaign finance reform with the *Bipartisan Campaign Reform Act*, also commonly known as the McCain-Feingold. The name is misleading, however, because the Senate version that was sponsored by Senators John McCain, and Russell Feingold is not the version that was signed into law, rather it was the House version known as Shays-Meehan. Nonetheless, the name McCain-Feingold stuck. The legislation contained the so-called "electioneering communications" provision which banned corporations, either for profit or nonprofit, and labor unions from broadcasting soft political messages within 30–60 days of primary or general election. Electioneering communications are soft and considered not direct endorsements, yet are defined in the legislation as susceptible to no reasonable interpretation other than as an appeal to vote for or against a specific candidate.

Most of these key provisions the McCain-Feingold were struck down in subsequent Supreme Court rulings between 2007 and 2010. In 2007, the Court ruled that the bill's ban on political messaging between 30 and 60 days before an election is unconstitutional as a violation of the First Amendment. In 2008, the Court also ruled that placing limits on campaign contribution based on the amount that an individual spends from their own wealth is discriminatory and unconstitutional. In January of 2010, however, the Supreme Court made its most significant ruling to turn back the clocks on campaign finance reform in the case of *Citizens United v. Federal Election Commission* (2010).

The case originated with a dispute between a conservative nonprofit organization, Citizens United, and the FEC. Citizens United produced a documentary titled, *Hilary: The Movie*, which was overtly created to undermine Hilary Clinton's credibility as a presidential candidate (*Citizens United v. Federal Election Commission*, 2010).[27] The film was released in 2008 while Clinton was running a campaign for the US presidency in primary election. The film was slated to air on television, but was then scuttled when the FEC charged that Citizens United use of the film was a violation the "electioneering communications" provision in McCain-Feingold. The case was brought before the US District Court of Washington, DC where the court ruled in favor of the FEC.

The *Citizens United* case eventually made its way to the US Supreme Court. In a five-to-four decision the court reversed the District Court's decision. The five majority justices are corporate friendly conservatives who waved the banner of free speech and argued that the ban on electioneering communications is in violation of the First Amendment to the Constitution. On behalf of the conservative majority in the court,

Justice Kennedy commented that "If the First Amendment has any force, it prohibits Congress from fining or jailing citizens, or associations of citizens, for simply engaging in free political speech." Kennedy went on to say, "Expenditure is political speech presented to the electorate… [and] disclosure permits citizens and shareholders to react to the speech of corporate entities in a proper way."[28]

The dissenting justices were stridently opposed to this view. Justice Bader-Ginsberg declared that, "A corporation, after all, is not endowed by its creator with inalienable rights." Justice Stevens drew a parallel between selling votes and selling access to the electorate's opinions, "The difference between selling a vote and selling access is a matter of degree, not kind… And selling access is not qualitatively different from giving special preference to those who spent money on one's behalf." In other words, spending on electioneering communications is a form of corruption. Stevens also warned that the decision not only threatened American democracy, but the very credibility of the Supreme Court itself.[29]

Frustration with the court's decision was also expressed in the other branches of the federal government and in the media. Republican Senator, John McCain, from Arizona and co-sponsor of the McCain-Feingold bill, asserted that he was troubled by the by the "extreme naïveté" of some of the justices. In a state of the union address, President Obama called the ruling "a major victory for big oil, Wall Street banks, health insurance companies and the other powerful interests that marshal their power every day in Washington to drown out the voices of everyday Americans." The *New York Times* reported that the court's decision was a "sharp doctrinal shift" and in an editorial the *Times* warned that, "…the court's conservative majority has paved the way for corporations to use their vast treasuries to overwhelm elections and intimidate elected officials into doing their bidding." These statements seem to imply that up to now corporate influence in politics was somehow of minor importance or under control.[30]

There has been no major shift in Washington's structure of power as a result of the Supreme Court's ruling in the *Citizens United*. The importance of this ruling is that it has confirmed and cemented the already dominant role that corporations, their lobbyists, and their business associations play in electoral politics. Indeed, the midterm election that followed in 2010 was the most "moneyed" in American history. When the court's decision was made public, President Obama noted, "The last thing we need to do is hand more influence to the lobbyists in Washington, or more power to the special interests to tip the outcome of elections." The Supreme Court has given the green light to what is, by any other name, corporate bribery and extortion, and with this ruling the court has made the problem of corruption in politics infinitely more intractable. If we assume that the justices are aware of the implications of their rulings, and there is no reason why we would not, then their decision can only be interpreted as one of contempt for real democracy.

The Supreme Court did not, however, change the limitations individuals can spend on campaigns. The Federal Election Commission continues to enforce limitations on the amount individuals and organizations may spend directly to candidates or committees: ranging between $2000 and $5000 to each candidate or candidate committee per election. However, large corporations and organizations have found ways around this rule by soliciting campaign funds from their employees, friends, or family members and then bundling them together as a package. For example, four Wall Street giants bundled together over nearly three million dollars for the 2008 election from their employees. Goldman Sachs pulled together close to $994,000, Citigroup bundled $701,290, J.P. Morgan Chase, $695,132, and Morgan Stanley, $514, 881.[31]

Wall Street lobbyists are a ubiquitous presence in Washington. With their considerable campaign donations, they were guaranteed sympathetic ears in government. Their lobbyists were well trained and armed with sophisticated presentations on financial innovation and the need to remove antiquated government rules and regulations. Those who questioned the lobbyists demands were quickly cut off of campaign funds and publicly humiliated as ignorant Luddites. With such enormous pressure coming from both Washington and Wall Street, the deregulation move was inevitable.

The Koch Machine

The Supreme Court's decision in of *Citizens United v. Federal Election Commission* (2010) is the waterloo in the long litigious struggle for campaign finance reform. Among the most prominent activists to benefit from the court's decision are billionaire neoliberal ideologues, Charles and David Koch. The Koch brothers made their fortune in a highly merged conglomerate that covers a range of industries from manufacturing and oil refining to finance and commodity trading. They have a religious passion for political activism and use their considerable bank account balances for PAC spending to support candidates who share their embrace of unfettered capitalism. In the 2016 election cycle, the Koch brother spent about a billion dollars to underwrite candidates running on an anti-government platform But their powers of spending and influence extend beyond the political agenda.

For years universities have been receiving donations from the Koch brothers and each donation comes with strings attached. Koch money is stipulated to fund research agendas, think tanks, and professorships that conform to their ideological acid test: to celebrate capitalism, free markets, and small government. According to the *New York Times*, George Mason University has gone from "…a little known commuter school to a major public university" after receiving millions in Koch largesse.[32] GMU houses the Mercatus Center, which like the Cato Institute and the American Enterprise Institute, underwrites work that is seen in academia as not so much legitimate research as it is propaganda. Recently they sponsored enters and professorships at Wake Forest, Montana State University, and the University of Utah with the condition that these promote neoliberalism. The Koch brothers have not disclosed the exact amount they donate to higher education around the country, but it is estimated to be around $150 million over the last ten years, and $50 million of that was concentrated at GMU where Charles Koch serves on the board.[33]

In 2016, in addition to $10 million from Koch brothers, GMU also received an anonymous gift of $20 million. The agent for the gift was the Federalist Society, an organization of lawyers who share the Koch brothers commitment to free market capitalism.[34] The gift went to the George Mason University Law School on the condition that it change the name of the school to honor former Supreme Court justice and archconservative, Antonin Scalia. The name of the school was changed to The Antonin Scalia School of Law, but was immediately ridiculed for its unfortunate acronym, ASSoL. GMU quickly changed the name again to The Antonin Scalia Law School.

Housed within the law school is the Center for the Study of administrative State, founded by associate professor, Neomi Rao. The center also pursues a neoliberal agenda that specifically targets government regulatory agencies. Rao, a staunch supporter of Scalia, went on to head the Office of Information and Regulatory Affairs (OIRA) for the Trump Administration's Office of Management and Budget. OIRA reviews regulatory initiatives from federal agencies such as the Environmental Protections Agency, then decides whether the executive branch will enforce the regulations based on their own cost-benefit analyses.

According to the Center for Progressive Reform, OIRA analyses are mostly done under the supervision of corporations affected by the regulations under review, and has altered about 84% of agency proposals accordingly.[35] Time will tell the legacy of OIRA under Rao's watch, but from her words, the future of protecting our population, environment, and natural resources are is in trouble,

> The way I think it will work in practice is that agencies will identify regulations to eliminate. And those regulations might be ineffective ones or excessively burdensome. And those regulations will have to meet a cost-benefit analysis for deregulation before they're going to impose any new regulatory burdens.[36]

The ascension of Donald Trump to the White House should erase any questions about where the center of power lies in the American political-economic establishment. Trump is unpredictable, woefully uninformed, and politically inexperienced. His administration has been fraught with high turnover and colossal foreign policy blunders. But what will be the defining legacy of his administration will be the tax legislation that he and fellow Republicans rammed through in his first year in office. The bill radically changed the tax code in such a way that it created an unprecedented windfall for the largest corporations in the world and the already wealthy members of the corporate class, like Trump himself.

As the Greenspan Era transitions into the Trump Era, America will become even more class divided and debt ridden, while the corporate class celebrates the fact that its unassailable position of power is permanent. There was perhaps a time when it would have been possible to bring the corporate sector to some measure of democratic accountability, but not now. To the degree that there were structures in place representing democratic pluralism or countervailing checks and balances, those structures have been washed out by the corporation and there is no coming back from this.

Crossing the Rubicon

On Friday December 22, 2017, President Donald Trump ducked into an empty Oval Office, to ratify what has proven to be the most stunning piece of tax legislation in modern history. In the months leading up to the final votes on the *Tax Cuts and Jobs Act of 2017* (TCJA), the corporate media's press coverage was mostly limited to giddy speculation on who is going to get the biggest stocking stuffer from the new tax math. By then it had been well established that the changes in the tax structure would be a bonanza for the corporate class. But the ramifications of the Republican's legislation extend far beyond sorting out the winners and losers as it was tailored to score another milestone victory for the corporate hegemony. The TCJA stands as a salient example of Dugger's concept of mystification that served as one of the final steps toward consolidation of corporate hegemony.

Title Mystification

Lawmakers during the Greenspan Era developed the technique of word-smithing legislation titles by infusing positively charged words into the titles such as "modernization," "freedom," and "jobs." The bill was first introduced with the title Tax Cuts and Jobs Act by Texas Republican, Kevin Brady, in early November, 2017 and promised to "deliver more jobs, fairer taxes, bigger paychecks."[37] Although the tax cutting provisions in the bill were obvious, there were no provisions for job creation or wage increases. Like similar tax tax-cutting bills from the George W. Bush and Ronald Reagan administrations, this one was engineered to make the already wealthy wealthier, while projecting the illusion that by doing so it will trigger a magical and mysterious process that creates new and better jobs for everyone. There has never been conclusive evidence that connects tax cuts for the wealthy to job growth or wage growth for the general population. There is a trove of evidence, however, connecting them to income and wealth polarization. Nonetheless, by mystifying the bill by inserting "jobs" into the title, the sponsors put opponents on the defensive as seeming to oppose creating job opportunities for Americans. The project of mystification went far beyond wordsmithing the title.

Budget Projection Mystification

When reporting on the budget impact of the tax bill, mainstream media exclusively cited the reports from the Congressional Budget Office (CBO) and Joint Committee on Taxation (JCT). According to these agencies' projections, the changes in tax law will add about $1.45 trillion to the national debt over the next decade, and when the so-called macroeconomic feedback effects are taken into account, the figure is closer to $1 trillion.[38] These numbers turned out to be incorrect, and the government agencies did not correct the projections until after the bill passed both chambers of Congress and just a few hours before the president signed the bill. The effect of understating the budget impact of the tax cuts, served to reduce resistance by Congress and made it less likely to draw controversy in the media.

The CBO's baseline projection $1.45 trillion in additional deficits was based on an assumption that the top marginal tax rate—the highest tax bracket for top income earners—was going to fall from

39.6 to 38.5% as a result of the new law.[39] When it was finally ratified by the president, the top tax rate fell from 39.6 to 37%, not 38.5. On the surface, that difference may not seem like much but that 1.5 percentage point difference on incomes of $600,000 and over amounts to minimally about $9000 per person in that top bracket. This renders the CBO projection significantly underestimated. A correction to the forecast was eventually made, which inflated the amount additional national debt bubble out to over $1.9 trillion.[40] But since the correct figure was not unveiled until after Congress already voted for the bill, accuracy was rendered irrelevant. Lawmakers were given just days to vote on this five-hundred-page piece of legislation which was buried under false budget projections. It probably could have been easily thrown out as it was a violation of due process, but mystification painted over truth, reality, and due process in order to accomplish anti-tax objective.

The problems with the projections go deeper. Even with the revised $1.9 trillion in additional debt, this was the CBOs baseline number and did not include macroeconomic feedback effects. These effects reflect changes in consumer and investment spending that result from the tax changes, which can spur production and income changes in the economy overall, and this eventually feeds back into tax revenue changes. The task of estimating these feedback changes was handed over to the JCT and was presented in its report titled, "Macroeconomic Analysis of the Tax Cut and Jobs Act as Ordered Reported by the Senate Committee on Finance on November 16, 2017."[41] The report specifies that the feedbacks will have a positive impact on the budget and will shave enough off hundreds of billions from the CBO's debt projection and should bring it down to just a touch over $1 trillion. The JCT projection was based on numerous flaws and questionable assertions.

The JCT model used the same incorrect top marginal tax rate of 38.5% as did the CBO for their baseline, so they did not adjust the CBO projection up to $1.9 trillion. From there the JCT contrived mathematical models based on whey they called a theoretical "neoclassical production framework," which does not include real-world data. Rather, their projections on feedback effects are derived from conjecture on consumer choice-making behavior predicated on assumptions that individuals, "make consumption and labor supply decisions to maximize their lifetime wellbeing given the resources they can foresee will be available to them. They are assumed to have complete information, or 'perfect foresight,' about economic conditions, such as wages, prices, interest rates, tax rates, and government spending, over their lifetimes."[42] The models assume that every person in the economy has a crystal ball giving perfect foresight about every possible thing that could affect their income over their entire lifetime. They also make the same assumptions about business investment decisions such that, "amount of capital available to the economy is determined by investors' predictions of after-tax returns to capital, which depend on anticipated gross receipts, costs of factor inputs, and tax rates that affect those factors."[43]

With these assumptions in place, the JCT casts out its forecast over decades of perfectly foreseen consumers and businesses income, and how they will stream up their spending accordingly. It forecasts that tax revenue would climb up by a half trillion to mitigate the revenue loss from the tax cut.

Also, in the Section 199A or the "pass through" part of the tax cut bill, provides a tax credit for limited liability partnerships, S corporations, and other business models that do not pay corporate income taxes, but rather pass the tax liability earnings through to the owners or partners. The bill made a 20% deduction on the taxable earnings as it passed from the LLC to the owners. The JCT projections, however, are based on a 17.4% pass through reduction, not the 20% that became the law. Even though critics pointed out the error, the JCT made no corrections to their figures.[44]

Finally, the JCT forecast ignores negative feedback effects from the millions of middle-income homeowners and itemizers who have experienced a substantial tax liability *increase* as a result of the eliminating the personal exemption and capping the state and local tax deductions. The middle class in high tax states like California is a huge cohort and the negative feedback effects stemming from a loss of disposable income will have major repercussions sending the debt profile well beyond $2 trillion.

Given that the JCT ignored these middle-class tax increases, uses incorrectly low tax rates for individuals and businesses, and bases all of their numbers on questionable economic theory, it is fair to say that their projection of $1 trillion is questionable. The New York Times reported at the time that "party leaders circulated two pages of 'response points' that declared 'the substance, timing and growth assumptions of J.C.T.'s 'dynamic' score are suspect.' Among their arguments was that the joint committee was using 'consistently wrong' growth models to assess the effect the tax cuts would have on hiring, wages and investment."[45] That the report notes that the JCT feedback estimates were identified as consistently wrong did nothing to slow down the rush to pass the tax cut bill.

Corporate Tax Liability Mystification

One of the principal arguments for the tax bill was that it promised to bring US corporate tax burdens down to be more in line with other countries the G20: an international forum for the governments and central bankers with which the United States has trade and investment ties. The argument is based on comparative corporate tax rates and a shift toward a territorial corporate tax model. The territorial tax system means that instead of offshore subsidiaries of US corporation paying the US corporate income tax rate, they pay the tax rate that prevails in the countries where they have their operations. At the same time the domestic corporate tax rate shifts from a basically progressive structure to a flat tax of 21% (Fig. 4.1).

In their international comparisons, sponsors of the bill referred to statutory tax rates, which mean the rates specified in the tax code enforced by the IRS. In the chart above produced by the CBO, it shows the United States. having a statutory rate at 39% makes it the highest compared to its trading partners. The argument is that the higher tax provides a disincentive for businesses to generate income in the United States. By lowering statutory dramatically down to 21% it will incentivize companies repatriate their business in the States and thereby create more jobs here.

A closer look at the tax structure changes the story. The corporate tax rates as of 2017 (see chart in Table 4.1) were based on a

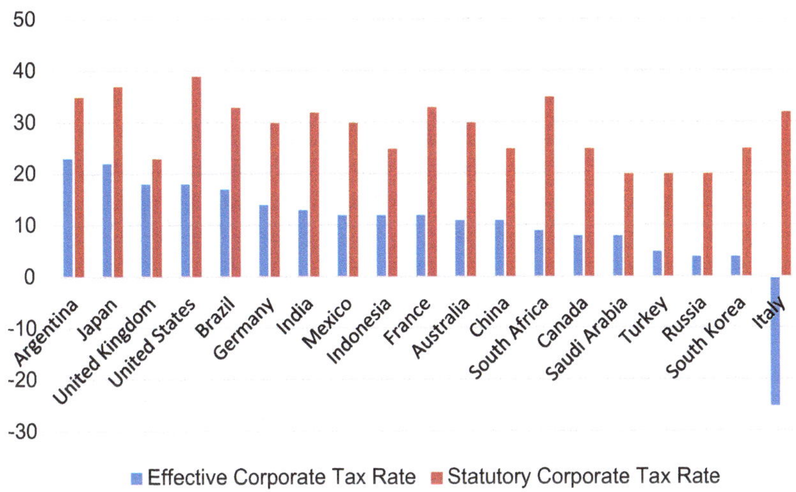

Fig. 4.1 Effective and statutory tax rates in G20 Countries, 2012 (*Source* Congressional Budget Office, the Organization for Economic Co-operation and Development, and the Oxford University Centre for Business Taxation)

Table 4.1 Corporate tax rate schedule, 2016

If taxable income in dollars (line 30, Form 1120) on page 1 is:			
Over	But not over	Tax is	Of amount over
0	50,000	15%	0
50,000	75,000	7500+25%	50,000
75,000	100,000	13,750+34%	75,000
100,000	335,000	22,250+39%	100,000
335,000	10,000,000	113,900+34%	335,000
10,000,000	15,000,000	3,400,000+35%	10,000,000
15,000,000	18,333,333	5,150,000+38%	15,000,000
18,333,333	–	35%	0

Source Department of the Treasury, Internal Revenue Service, Publication 542, revised 2016

strange progressive-regressive structure starting at 15% then through a few bracket steps up to 39%, but the 39% only applies to corporate incomes between $100,000 and $335,000, which is meaningless bracket for the giant companies that are the primary beneficiaries of the tax cut. The marginal rate then strangely falls to 34, rises to 35 and 38, then falls to 35 again at higher income levels.

Even the 35% rate on the highest income levels, the United States still appears to be at the higher end compared to international trading partners. But these are statutory rates and have little meaning for international comparisons because what actually matters to businesses when making a decision whether or not to repatriate their businesses are the effective tax rates. The effective rate is the rate businesses actually pay after they take all their write offs. Corporate tax write offs in the United States are significant compared to other countries, and the effective rate is closer to 18%, which brings it more in line with the rest of the world.[46] As a result of the tax cut, however, by arbitrarily lowering the statutory rate to 21% and keeping the write offs intact, the corporate taxation will prove to be significantly less than its trading partners (Table 4.1).

There is a host of other ways the tax bill is going to reduce revenues for the government with reduced estate taxes, elimination of the corporate alternative minimum tax, and removing excise taxes on alcoholic beverages. With all these changes in total it is difficult to get an accurate estimate of how much less the IRS will collect, but it would not be a surprise to see the additional debt figures climbing far beyond the revised $1.9 figure.

As of this writing, less than a year after the bill was passed, the CBO website shows a remarkable budget situation over the decade between 2018 and 2028. Starting in 2020, the projection puts federal government deficits and additional debt over $1 trillion annually and climbs every year after (Table 4.2).

These are deficit numbers that we have only seen between 2009 and 2012—the worst years of the Great Recession. Deficits rise during recessions because an economic slowdown reduces income tax revenues, but this is not the case in 2018. Though it is impossible to say exactly how much of these deficits will be caused by the tax cuts, we can say that there have not been deficits of this magnitude since the last recession and the CBO cites the tax cuts as the main reason.[47] Debt is projected to continue to rise as a percentage of GDP throughout the next decade.

Generally, such a dramatic tax cut policy would only be considered as a countercyclical policy measure to pull the economy out of a severe

Table 4.2 Congressional budget office projected deficits, 2018–2028

Year	CBO projected deficits (x billions)
2018	804
2019	981
2020	1008
2021	1123
2022	1276
2023	1273
2024	1244
2025	1352
2026	1320
2027	1316
2028	1526

Source Congressional Budget Office, 10-Year Budget Projection https://www.cbo.gov/about/products/budget-economic-data#3

recession characterized by contracting GDP, tanking corporate profits, and soaring unemployment. That that is far from the case here. At the time the tax cut bill was passed, the US economy had been out of a recession for almost a decade. Unemployment rate was about 4.1%, which was the lowest in decades.[48] Quarterly real GDP growth rates were robust, and each quarter was growing substantially from the quarter before. According to the Bureau of Economic Analysis data, corporate profits in third quarter, 2017 "… increased $91.6 billion in the third quarter, compared with an increase of $14.4 billion in the second quarter."[49] The US economic machine was running at full steam without the tax cuts.

Federal budget deficits generally rise and fall with business cycle booms and busts. Since the beginning of the Greenspan Era, much of that has changed. Budget deficits and rising debt are permanently fixed into our economy as a result of the series of tax cuts from the Reagan administration, to the George W. Bush administration, and to the Trump administration. Debates about the impact rising government debt is ongoing. On one side some argue that rising government debt does not matter because the United States is in a privileged position to be able to borrow at cheap rates from the rest of the world and just keep rolling it into the future. Others argue that there is a "crowding out effect" in which the more debt and interest on that debt accumulates, which means there will be less money for investment, infrastructure, education, or health. Paradoxically, key members of the Republican Party have used both arguments. In one instance against debt as a challenge to spending on social programs, and in another instance in support of tax cuts. But in both cases, the ramifications of their policies are the same: a widening socio-economic class separation.

Ultimately, the impact of rising debts depends on what the government does with the borrowed money and its intentions. According to the sponsors of the bill, the intention of TCJA was to cut taxes in order to stimulate investment in real capital which would raise productivity, boost output, create more jobs, and boost incomes for a broad base of the American population. Outside the world of mystification, reality tells a different story.

In May 2018, the US House of Representatives conducted a series of hearings on the measurable effects of the tax cuts so far. The most significant revelations to open up at these hearings was what most analysts had anticipated all along that the tax cuts have done nothing to stimulate investment, productivity, or working people's incomes. Instead, it did create a massive windfall for corporations that used the extra cash for stock buybacks in an effort to boost share values and boosted the fortunes of the wealthiest cohort in the United States.

The Economic Policy Institute (EPI) offered written testimony based on data it had gathered thus far. One of its findings is that about 83% of the extra after-tax income derived from the cut flowed into the bank accounts of the wealthiest 1% (Bivens 2018).[50] At the same time, wage growth remains trapped in stagnation as it has been before the cut. Corporations claimed that they were committed to using the tax cut windfall to fund bonuses and wage hikes. But there is no evidence of this other than large one-time bonuses for executives, and no discernable income change for anyone else.[51]

As for investment spending which is more long term, the EPI testified, "With regard to the corporate investment claim, there is no serious evidence that the TCJA spurred a notable pickup in business investment." According to the Bureau of Economic Analysis data, the first quarter of 2018 showed an actual decrease in capital investment.[52] Moreover, data shows that productivity rates are actually higher when corporate tax rates are higher.[53] In their testimony, the EPI attempted to cut through the mystification with candor, Claims that evidence is already showing large positive effects are based on data cherry-picking and are either innumerate or dishonest. The EPI is referring to Trump administration's Council of Economic Advisors boasting an economic boom already under way as a result of the cuts. The EPI goes on to emphasize that "the largest and only permanent cut in taxes stemming from the TCJA is a cut to corporate tax rates. Thus the best predictor of the likely effect of the TCJA is what happened after past episode when corporate tax rates were cut… evidence based on past experience with corporate rates cuts—either in the United States, in international peer countries, or in individual states—argues strongly that capital investment and pay for most American workers will no noticeably increase due to the TCJA."[54]

In the corporate hegemony, things like real investment, productivity, and fiscal stability are not that important. What is important is shareholder value. One easy way for a publicly traded corporation to prop up stock prices without having to go to the trouble of producing things for profit is to go to the open market and carry out stock buybacks. By doing so, the company can transmit buy commands to the market for its own stocks, which pushes up prices. Speculators seeing companies orchestrating their own stock buybacks, jump into the market on the anticipation that they buybacks will push help push up prices as intended. The only obstacle to buyback strategies is that they require a lot of cash. That obstacle was removed by TCJA. Corporations moved quickly to snap up their own stocks while prices were relatively low, then let the momentum of speculation let the share prices rise further.

As early as February 2018, American corporations had already stepped up with $171 billion in stock buybacks, which is a record high compared to the previous record of $76 billion in 2017. Cisco announced $25 billion in buybacks, Wells Fargo $22.6 billion, Pepsi $15.6 billion, Amgen $10 billion, AbbVie $10 billion, Alphabet $8.6 billion, and Visa announced $7.5 billion in buybacks.[55] This did not come as a surprise. A year earlier Bank of America-Merrill Lynch conducted a survey of over 300 executives at America's largest firms and ask them what they planned to do with the money after the tax cuts were put into effect. The top three answers were to pay down debt, finance more corporate mergers, and repurchase stocks, and Bank of America predicted that US multinational corporations would repatriate about $450 billion of foreign profits to buy back their stocks.[56] The markets loved them for this and stock prices vaulted. Since the wealthiest one percent of the population owns about 40% of these stocks traded in open markets, the corporate class hit the jackpot.

There is cumulative effect with these tax cuts. The wealthiest campaign donors who contributed substantial funds to political campaigns. The hundreds of billions in windfall for the giant corporations will unlock even more cash that will be used to gain even more political advantage in the next election cycle. The corporations and billionaire members of the corporate class that reaped millions of dollars in tax cuts are pumping some of that windfall in the Congressional Leadership Fund (CLF).[57] The CLF is a super PAC that has raised over $100 million as of this writing. The political messaging in the ads funded by the CLF are political attack ads aimed at Democrats running for office. The Washington Post reports that in all the ads it reviewed and found that "the Congressional Leadership Fund took a sliver of accurate information and spun it in a misleading way."[58] Money that could have once been used to fund education, environmental restoration, or health care instead have been redirected to fund attack ads that clog the airwaves with misinformation. Corporate hegemony becomes more deeply entrenched.

The revolving door between Washington and corporate boardrooms, industry insiders holding key positions on regulatory commissions, and the presence of legions of lobbyists swarming the US Capitol are now more palpable than at any time in recent history. Officials from both parties have rewritten laws on corporate mergers and have pushed through legislation to ratify multi-lateral trade policies that gave big business the opportunity to build empires internationally. They created tax advantages and subsidies for transnational corporations, revamped environmental regulations to make it easier for businesses to trash forests and blow up mountains, drill for oil, appointed industry insiders to serve as key members of federal regulatory commissions, lavished no-bid appropriations contracts for their friends in business, and both parties have shown an amazing eagerness to make enormous funds available for lavish corporate bailouts when things went sour at the bottom line, particularly the largest players on Wall Street.

It is now becoming clear that the economies of the world have been pulled together under the control of corporate hegemony. With the corporation as the alpha institution, others in government, media, education, and elsewhere are either refashioning themselves in a corporate image or obsequiously complying with corporate demands. Countervailing institutions have been largely dissolved, which opens the door even wider for corporations to stride in and dominate. On this, Dugger reflects,

> [T]he modern corporation is a unique legal entity that can everything a real person can do, and better. Not only can it grow and reproduce without limit, but it can divide like an amoeba. The corporation can also live forever. Powerful and real persons are equal to the rest of us in the end, for the grave gets us all. No so with powerful corporations. They can continue amassing power indefinitely.[59]

As been argued here throughout, the corporation is an institution more so than a business model. Recall also that in terms of economic governance, the DNA of an institution is the set of rules, norms and codes that structures behavior. As Marx, Veblen, and many other heterodox economists have identified, with the corporate hegemony of late capitalism, the rules, the mission, and the bylaws that define the activities of the corporation extend beyond its boundaries to become the rules, the mission, and the bylaws for all of society, including the public sector. The result is the formation of a nondemocratic, ever-expanding, system that is principally geared to benefit the jet-setting corporate class—the owners of capital and their cronies—*and all that is solid melts into air*. Such an outcome, of course, is something that is completely ignored in conventional economics because in their vision of things, social structures of power do not exist; only individuals, entrepreneurs, and markets.

As we will see in the chapters that follow, there remains the fundamental condition that financialization and all that goes with it would not have been possible on the current scale without corporate hegemony. The corporate institution is essentially a financial construct. It is a legal entity formed with the objectives of aggregating large amounts of capital through securities trades and accruing returns for investors. As the corporation hegemony expands, so do financial markets and securitization. Virtually everything is fair game for being transformed into an investment vehicle. The entire planet and everything in it becomes nothing more than an investment portfolio. From the portfolio comes the expectation of yields either through structured returns like interest payments or by speculation—buying low and selling high.

Herein lies the crux of the problem. The conditions of late capitalism, global resource depletion, and the intensity of cutthroat competition in markets are making economic production increasingly problematic. When the actual production of things for the market becomes too difficult or unprofitable, there is trouble in the corporate economy because the expectation of ongoing returns remains nonetheless. The economy turns to financial speculation as a surrogate for profit-making and replaces conventional trade. Like a starving snake that begins to eat its tail, finance stops being a means to an end and becomes an end in itself. At that point, the entire global economy can be expected to inflate and crash and soar and tumble because one thing we have learned from studying the four-hundred-year history of capitalism is that where there are financial markets, financial market instability follows like a gloomy shadow.

This problem worsens when the public institutions such as the Federal Reserve, which is supposed to be a stabilizing force, become enablers of instability. In August 2005 at their annual luxurious meeting in Jackson Hole, Wyoming, the Fed was boldly chastised for its mission drift by an IMF economist, Raghuram G. Rajan. The plan for the meeting was to give praise to Alan Greenspan for his prudent and effective leadership over the years. Rajan decided to give the Fed leadership a lashing instead. He pointed to their blind worship of innovation, deregulation, and institutional changes during the Greenspan Era that had made things much worse in the financial sector. Rajan raised uncomfortable issues of lavish salaries and bonuses for banking industry CEOs, their focus on short-term profits and gambling on derivatives that posed enormous dangers, and because of all this recklessness the interbank lending market could freeze up in such a way that banks would no longer lend out of distrust. He warned that the result could very well be a full-blown financial crisis and catastrophic meltdown. Rajan was spot on, of course, but no one at the meeting cared to listen.[60] Instead the Fed chose to congratulate themselves for their "risk management" approach to monetary policy.

Veblen saw the dangers of corporate hegemony and its penchant for financialization a century ago, as did Marx before him. This was troubling to Veblen, for he saw all that was good in modern economic situation had their roots in craft traditions—creativity, problem-solving, technology, or the passion for making the perfect mousetrap. As it rises to dominance, the corporation system transforms the economic landscape of society and turned the craft traditions to dust and the system loses its creativity and becomes imbecilic. For Marx, it was troubling because financialization represents something like late-stage cancer. It is part of a broader set of system conditions that lead to an endless round of crises that eventually kill the organic whole.

In either case, the basic institutional conditions have not substantively changed since the '07–'09 crisis. And as the conditions have not changed, sooner or later the crisis will be repeated. When it does it will bring about another round of trouble that will cause millions to lose their jobs, their homes, entire communities will be destroyed, governments will be compelled to pony up billions in bailout money, and they will sink deeper into unsustainable debt. This is financing the apocalypse.

Mystification plays a key role in all of this by whitewashing problems with conventional bromides and shrink wrapping the agenda of corporate hegemony with neoliberal ideology. There has been much discussion about institutional capture, but the final step in the completion of corporate hegemony is cultural hegemony; the capture of the collective mindset.

Notes

1. Padma Desai, *From Financial Crisis to Global Recovery* (New York, NY: Columbia University Press, 2011), p. 24.
2. David Wessel, *In Fed We Trust: Ben Bernanke's War on the Great Panic* (New York, NY: Crown Business, 2009), p. 239.

3. Joseph Stiglitz, "Nationalized Banks Are 'Only Answer,' Economist Stiglitz Says," Deutsche Welle, February 6, 2009, posted on www.dw-world.de/dw/article/0,4005355,00.html.
4. See https://www.federalreserve.gov/aboutthefed/section13.htm.
5. Danielle Booth, *Fed Up: An Insider's Take on Why the Federal Reserve Is Bad for America* (New York, NY: Penguin, 2017), p. 28.
6. Michael S. Derby, "Fed's Dudley: 'Deep Seated' Cultural, Ethical Lapses at Many Financial Firms," *Wall Street Journal*, November 7, 2013.
7. Thorstein Veblen, "The Higher Learning," in *The Portable Veblen* (New York, NY: Viking Press, 1948), p. 511.
8. Allan Gruchy, *Contemporary Economic Thought: The Contribution of Neo-Institutional Economics* (Clifton, NJ: Augustus M. Kelley, 1972), p. 133.
9. Jens Beckert, "Institutional Isomorphism Revisited: Convergence and Divergence in Institutional Change," *Sociological Theory*, Vol. 28, No. 2, June 2010, pp. 150–166.
10. See also Claus Offe, "Designing Institutions in East European Transitions," in R.E. Goodin (ed.), *The Theory of Institutional Design* (Cambridge, UK: Cambridge University Press, 1996), p. 210.
11. William M. Dugger, *Corporate Hegemony* (New York, NY: Greenwood Press, 1989), pp. 44–45.
12. Ibid., p. 144.
13. John P. Lewis and Robert C. Turner, *Business Conditions Analysis* (New York, NY: McGraw-Hill, 2nd ed., 1967 [1959]), p. 15.
14. Quoted in *The Little Big Number*, p. 105.
15. Philipsen, *The Little Big Number*, pp. 40–42.
16. Ibid., pp. 44–46.
17. Dugger, 1989, p. 157.
18. https://www.treasury.gov/press-center/press-releases/Pages/ls241.aspx.
19. Dugger, 1989, p. 46.
20. Ibid., p. 157.
21. Paul DiMaggio and Walter Powell, "The Iron Cage Revisited: Institutional Isomorphism and Collective Rationality in Organizational Fields," *American Sociological Review*, 1983, p. 150.
22. Middle Tennessee State University. https://mtsu.edu/first-amendment/article/1051/tillman-act-of-1907.
23. Cq Researcher. https://library.cqpress.com/cqresearcher/document.php?id=cqresrre1931070100#H2_2.

24. Britannica.com. https://www.britannica.com/topic/Hatch-Act-United-States-1939.
25. Federal Election Commission. https://transition.fec.gov/info/appfour.htm.
26. https://www.britannica.com/event/Buckley-v-Valeo.
27. http://law2.umkc.edu/faculty/projects/ftrials/conlaw/citizensunited2010.html.
28. Ibid.
29. https://www.npr.org/templates/story/story.php?storyId=112702586.
30. Adam Liptak, "Justices, 5-4, Reject Corporate Spending Limit," *The New York Times*, January 21, 2010.
31. David Gilson, "Hope and Spare Change: Obama vs. McCain in Campaign Cash," *Mother Jones*, 2010. https://www.motherjones.com/politics/2010/10/top-corporate-donors-in-2008-presidential-race/.
32. Erica L. Green and Stephanie Saul, "What Charles Koch and Other Donors to George Mason University Got for Their Money," *The New York Times*, May 5, 2018.
33. Ibid.
34. Steve Eder, "Neomi Rao, the Scholar Who Will Help Lead Trump's Regulatory Overhaul," *The New York Times*, July 9, 2017.
35. http://progressivereform.org/articles/Driesen_Testimony_HJudish_RegReformSub_070616.pdf.
36. Steve Eder, "Neomi Rao, the Scholar Who Will Help Lead Trump's Regulatory Overhaul," *New York Times*, July 9, 2017.
37. House of Representatives' Ways and Means Committee press release, "Legislation to Overhaul America's Tax Code for First Time in 31 Years Will Deliver More Jobs, Fairer Taxes, Bigger Paychecks," November 2, 2017. See https://waysandmeans.house.gov/chairman-brady-introduces-tax-cuts-jobs-act/.
38. See CBO November 13, 2017 report "Congressional Budget Office Cost Estimate" A bill to provide for reconciliation pursuant to titles II and V of the Concurrent Resolution on the Budget for Fiscal Year 2018 As ordered reported by the House Committee on Ways and Means on November 9, 2017. https://www.cbo.gov/system/files?file=115th-congress-2017-2018/costestimate/hr1.pdf, and the JCT November 30, 2017 report, *Macroeconomic Analysis of the "Tax Cut and Jobs Act" as Ordered Reported by the Senate Committee on Finance* on November 16, 2017, PDF downloaded from https://www.jct.gov/publications.html?id=5045&func=startdown.

39. CBO report, p. 3.
40. Niv Elis, "GOP Tax Law Will Add $1.9 Trillion to Debt: CBO," *The Hill*, April 9, 2018. See http://thehill.com/policy/finance/382319-gop-tax-law-will-add-19-trillion-to-debt-cbo.
41. Joint Committee on Taxation Report, downloadable at www.jct.gov/publications.html?id=5045&func=startdown.
42. Ibid., pp. 8–9.
43. Ibid.
44. JCT report, p. 3.
45. Jim Tankersley, "Republicans Sought to Undercut an Unfavorable Analysis of the Tax Plan," *The New York Times*, December 4, 2017.
46. Hunter Blair, "The Arguments Supporting Corporate Tax Cuts Are Wrong, and Territorial Taxation Will Make Things Worse," Economic Policy Institute, December 15, 2017. https://www.epi.org.
47. Jim Tankersley, "How the Trump Tax Cut Is Helping to Push the Federal Deficit to $1 Trillion," *The New York Times*, July 25, 2018.
48. Bureau of Labor Statistics. https://data.bls.gov/timeseries/LNS14000000.
49. Bureau of Economic Analysis, "National Income and Product Accounts Report," Third Quarter, 2017. https://www.bea.gov/newsreleases/national/gdp/2017/gdp3q17_2nd.htm.
50. "The Likely Economic Effects of the Tax Cuts and Jobs Act," Economic Policy Institute, February 25, 2018, p. 2.
51. Ibid., pp. 2–3.
52. BEA data reported in Akane Otani, Ben Eisen, and Chelsey Dulaney, "Capital Spending Boom Is No Great Boost to Capital Markets," *Wall Street Journal*, May 15, 2018.
53. Josh Bivens and Lawrence Mishel, "Understanding the Historic Divergence Between Productivity and Typical Workers' Pay: Why It Matters and Why It's Real," Economic Policy Institute, September 2, 2015. https://www.epi.org/publication/cutting-corporate-taxes-will-not-boost-american-wages/.
54. EPI, February 25, 2018, p. 1.
55. Matt Egan, "Tax Cut Scoreboard: Workers $6 Billions; Shareholders $171 Billion," CNN Money, February 16, 2018.
56. Heather Long, "'Why Aren't the Other Hands Up?' A Top Trump Adviser's Startling Response to CEOs Not Doing What Ee'd Expect," *Washington Post*, November 17, 2017.

57. Jim Tankersley and Michael Tackett, "Trump Tax Cut Pay Dividends for the GOP," *The New York Times*, August 19, 2018.
58. Salvador Rizzo, "Fact-Checking Republican Attack Ads in Tight House Races," *The Washington Post*, August 31, 2018.
59. Dugger, *Corporate Hegemony*, p. 12.
60. Booth, 2017, pp. 94–95.

References

Beckert, Jens. "Institutional Isomorphism Revisited: Convergence and Divergence in Institutional Change," *Sociological Theory*, Vol. 28, No. 2, June 2010, pp. 150–166.

Bivens, Josh, and Hunter Blair. "The Likely Economic Effects of the Tax Cuts and Jobs Act," Economic Policy Institute, February 25, 2018. https://www.epi.org/publication/the-likely-economic-effects-of-the-tax-cuts-and-jobs-act-tcja-higher-incomes-for-the-top-no-discernible-effect-on-wage-growth-for-typical-american-workers/.

Bivens, Josh, and Lawrence Mishel. "Understanding the Historic Divergence Between Productivity and Typical Workers' Pay: Why It Matters and Why It's Real," Economic Policy Institute, September 2, 2015.

Blair, Hunter. "The Arguments Supporting Corporate Tax Cuts Are Wrong, and Territorial Taxation Will Make Things Worse," Economic Policy Institute, December 15, 2017. https://www.epi.org/blog/page/4/?view=blogEconomic.

Booth, Danielle. *Fed Up: An Insider's Take On Why the Federal Reserve Is Bad for America* (New York, NY: Penguin, 2017).

Bureau of Economic Analysis. "National Income and Product Accounts Report," Third Quarter, 2017. https://www.bea.gov/newsreleases/national/gdp/2017/gdp3q17_2nd.htm.

Bureau of Labor Statistics. "Labor Force Statistics from the Current Population Survey," 2018. https://data.bls.gov/timeseries/LNS14000000.

Congressional Budget Office Report. "Congressional Budget Office Cost Estimate," November, 2017. https://www.cbo.gov/system/files?file=115th-congress-2017-2018/costestimate/hr1.pdf,%20and%20the%20JCT%20November%2030,%202017%20report,%20Macroeconomic%20Analysis%20of%20the%20%E2%80%9CTax%20Cut%20and%20Jobs%20Act%E2%80%9D%20As%20Ordered%20Reported%20by%20the%20Senate%20ommittee%20on%20Finance%20on%20

November%2016,%202017%20PDF%20downloaded%20from%20 https://www.jct.gov/publications.html?id = 5045&func = startdown.
CQ Researcher. library.cqpress.com/cqresearcher/document.php?id=cqresrre 1931070100#H2_2.
Derby, Michael S. "Fed's Dudley: 'Deep Seated' Cultural, Ethical Lapses at Many Financial Firms," *Wall Street Journal*, November 7, 2013.
Desai, Padma. *From Financial Crisis to Global Recovery* (New York, NY: Columbia University Press, 2011).
DiMaggio, Paul, and Walter Powell. "The Iron Cage Revisited: Institutional Isomorphism and Collective Rationality in Organizational Fields," *American Sociological Review*, Vol. 48, 1983, pp. 147–160.
Driesen, David. "Testimony Before House of Representatives," July 6, 2016. http://progressivereform.org/articles/Driesen_Testimony_HJudish_RegReformSub_070616.pdf.
Dugger, William M. *Corporate Hegemony* (Westport, CT: Greenwood Press, 1989), p. xiii.
Eder, Steve. "Neomi Rao, the Scholar Who Will Help Lead Trump's Regulatory Overhaul," *New York Times*, July 9, 2017.
Egan, Matt. "Tax Cut Scoreboard: Workers $6 Billions; Shareholders $171 Billion," CNN Money, February 16, 2018.
Federal Elections Commission. https://www.fec.gov/.
Federal Reserve. https://www.federalreserve.gov/aboutthefed/section13.htm.
Gilson, David. "Hope and Spare Change: Obama vs. McCain in Campaign Cash," *Mother Jones*, 2010.
Green, Erica L., and Stephanie Saul. "What Charles Koch and Other Donors to George Mason University Got for Their Money," *The New York Times*, May 5, 2018.
Gruchy, Allan. *Contemporary Economic Thought: The Contribution of Neo-Institutional Economics* (Clifton, NJ: Augustus M. Kelley, 1972).
House of Representatives' Ways and Means Committee Press Release. "Legislation to Overhaul America's Tax Code for First Time in 31 Years Will Deliver More Jobs, Fairer Taxes, Bigger Paychecks," November 2, 2017.
Joint Committee on Taxation Report, November, 2017. https://www.jct.gov/publications.html?id=5045&func=startdown.
Jones, Clifford. "Buckley v Valeo Law Case," *Encyclopedia Britannica*. https://www.britannica.com/event/Buckley-v-Valeo.
Lewis, John P., and Robert C. Turner. *Business Conditions Analysis* (New York, NY: McGraw-Hill, 2nd ed., 1967).

Liptak, Adam. "Justices, 5-4, Reject Corporate Spending Limit," *The New York Times*, January 21, 2010.

Long, Heather. "'Why Aren't the Other Hands Up?' A Top Trump Adviser's Startling Response to CEOs not Doing What We'd Expect," *Washington Post*, November 17, 2017.

Offe, Claus. "Designing Institutions in East European Transitions," in R.E. Goodin (ed.), *The Theory of Institutional Design* (Cambridge, UK: Cambridge University Press, 1996).

Otani, Akane, Ben Eisen, and Chelsey Dulaney. "Capital Spending Boom Is No Great Boost to Capital Markets," *Wall Street Journal*, May 15, 2018.

Philipsen, Dirk. *The Little Big Number: How GDP Came to Rule the World and What to Do About It* (Princeton, NJ: Princeton University Press, 2015).

Rizzo, Salvador. "Fact-Checking Republican Attack Ads in Tight House Races," *The Washington Post*, August 31, 2018.

Stiglitz, Joseph. "Nationalized Banks Are 'Only Answer,' Economist Stiglitz Says," Deutsche Welle, February 6, 2009, posted on www.dw-world.de/dw/article/0,4005355,00.html.

Tankersley, Jim. "Republicans Sought to Undercut an Unfavorable Analysis of the Tax Plan," *The New York Times*, December 4, 2017.

Tankersley, Jim. "How the Trump Tax Cut Is Helping to Push the Federal Deficit to $1 Trillion," *The New York Times*, July 25, 2018.

Tankersley, Jim, and Michael Tackett. "Trump Tax Cut Pay Dividends for the GOP," *The New York Times*, August 19, 2018.

Totenberg, Nina, "Supreme Hears Campaign Finance Case," *NPR Morning Edition*, September 10, 2009.

U.S. Treasury Press Release. https://home.treasury.gov/.

Veblen, Thorstein. "The Higher Learning," in *The Portable Veblen* (New York, NY: Viking Press, 1948), p. 511.

Wessel, David. *In Fed We Trust: Ben Bernanke's War on the Great Panic* (New York, NY: Crown Business, 2009).

5

Contemporary Neoliberalism

Within a few years, Donald Trump and his fellow Republicans managed to ram through the most pro-corporate tax legislation in modern history, dismantle the Environmental Protection Agency's initiatives on climate change, attack multilateral trade and security agreements with other countries, and embark on a comprehensive move to shut down government regulation of industry wherever possible. The anti-government agenda was clear as this administration continued to deregulate one industry after another while stripping the federal government of the revenue and means to enforce existing regulatory statutes. Although it was markedly more aggressive in the Trump years, the policy agenda of ripping down economic regulation by government and slashing taxes have been ongoing since the beginning of the Greenspan Era.

Over forty years ago, the Jimmy Carter administration carried out initiatives to repeal airlines, trucking, and rail regulations on behalf of companies in the transportation industry. The Ronald Reagan and administration followed by rolling back environmental protections, more industry deregulation, and massive tax cuts for corporations and wealthy members of the corporate class. The George H.W. Bush administration reversed some of the tax cuts, but to a small degree and

J. Magnuson, *Financing the Apocalypse*,
Palgrave Insights into Apocalypse Economics,
https://doi.org/10.1007/978-3-030-04720-7_5

continued on with free trade agreements, privatization, and industry deregulation. The most salient aspects of the Bill Clinton years were Wall Street deregulation, international free trade agreements, and scaling back public assistance. The momentum continued with George W. Bush's repeat of Reagan's tax cuts for the rich and this was followed by Barak Obama's spearheading more free trade agreements and a health care bill that overwhelmingly boosted health industry corporate profits while making basic care insurance unaffordable for most working people and small businesses.

A central provision of the Obama administration's *The Patient Protection and Affordable Care Act* (2010) was to develop state-level insurance exchanges on the assumption that by doing so, free market capitalism will would "increase competition and improve coverage."[1] The opposite happened as insurance premiums continued to rise steadily each year after the bill was passed. Proponents of the legislation claim that since 2010 premium growth was only 27% in the five years after the law was passed compared to the most dramatic rise of 69% between 2000 and 2005.[2] Though slowing the cost increases of something that was already beyond affordability is not the same thing as making it more affordable.

As we saw in the last chapter, the institutional matrix of corporate hegemony has produced a single-party political structure—the corporate party—such that the policy initiatives are consistently some variation on a pro-corporate theme that is pursued by Republicans and Democrats alike. In each round, the initiatives were sold to the public with bromides such as, "it is time to provide tax relief for American families," and to "get the government off the backs of businesses," and "government is the problem, not the solution." Pro-business, anti-government sentiments have been forthcoming throughout the Greenspan Era with religiosity among think tanks, cable television networks, university business and economics departments, and professional journals.

As we have been emphasizing here, institutional economists have been emphasizing the troubles associated with excessive corporate power since the Greenspan Era began. Over thirty years ago, Allan Gruchy warned that the U.S. political economy is shaping itself into a self-sustaining structure hegemony, but unlike the militaristic hegemonic structures of the past such as fascist states, "Little coercion is necessary to make use of this corporate power in the United States because the public has been culturally conditioned to accept the reality of this power without being aware of it."[3] A substantive aspect of such cultural conditioning is the constant drumbeat of the core beliefs of *neoliberalism*.

Neoliberalism took root in the US and the UK after the election victories Margaret Thatcher in 1979 and Ronald Reagan in 1980, then penetrated deeper into the collective mindset during the three decades of the Greenspan Era. As a belief system it is centered around these radical anti-government and pro-corporate government initiatives and stand as ideological justification for corporate hegemony. The canon of ideas along with the authorities who advocate them constitute what institutional economist Philip Mirowski calls, "The Neoliberal Thought Collective."[4]

This chapter and the next are devoted to exploring this neoliberal canon as part of the superstructure that provides normative justification for the corporate hegemony, and to see how it is bound up in the collective nerve cells of the American mentality. So deeply entrenched this ideology that it is nearly invisible, as Mirowski echoes Gruchy, "neoliberalism as a worldview has sunk its roots deep into everyday life, almost to the point of passing as the 'ideology as no ideology.'"[5] Whether invisible or not, a central point to be made is that neoliberal ideology is inseparable from the institutions that it supports. They are a package deal.

To keep themselves intact, all powerful institutions throughout history have developed their own version systems of ideological justification. As we explore the relationship between institutions and their supporting ideologies, there arises a chicken-and-egg question on which has primacy, the institution or the ideology? This question is overshadowed by the debate in the sociology of knowledge between idealism and materialism and weighing in on this debate is beyond the scope of our project here. If pressed, however, the materialist view seems to carry more weight.

In the institutionalist view, the emphasis is not on trying to solve this debate, but rather to see that institutions and ideologies are two aspects of a broader cultural whole that evolves with time. There is a dynamic interplay between the structure of institutions that determine how we do things and the structure of beliefs that determine how we think about things. How we think about the world affects how we act in the world, which affects how we think about the world and so on. The men and women who advocate neoliberal doctrines have the privilege of orthodoxy because they are supported by the vast financial resources of the corporation and by the social classes that reside in its citadels. At the same time, corporate institutions evolved into a hegemony in part because they are supported by the coevolution of neoliberal economic doctrine. It is not a coincidence that as corporate institutions orchestrated their capture of other institutions in media, government, and academia, these institutions became the home base for neoliberal intellectuals. In other words, corporate hegemony and neoliberalism are coevolving in such a way that they mutually strengthen each other. We cannot fully understand one without the other. To that end, we will flesh out some of the cornerstone elements of neoliberalism:

- The sanctity of economic individualism
- Greed is necessary for well-being
- The sanctity of the market system
- The "Janus Face" of government
- What is good for corporations is good for everyone
- Capitalism equals democracy
- Economic and Financial Innovation are Unassailable.

In the corporate hegemony that is packaged in these beliefs, the tenets of neoliberalism are not just economic viewpoints, they stand as pieties deeply embedded in American culture.

As such, when the federal government decides to pass legislation that is designed specifically to benefit the corporation and its affluent social class, it only needs a few neoliberal soundbites to receive acceptance.

The Sanctity of Economic Individualism

Margaret Thatcher and Ronald Regan popularized the arguments that people should not count on government for economic support nor should government be meddling in the affairs of business. These arguments stress that everyone has the opportunity to succeed in a functioning, market-driven capitalist system. Individuals are responsible for their own poverty as well as for their own success by the choices they make. The poor have opportunities to pull themselves out of poverty and could even become rich, and businesses are there to help them as long as the government stays out of the way. Individual workers, consumers, and entrepreneurs make their own choices in an open marketplace, and the extent to which they rise or fall depends on those choices. People are individually responsible for their own fate, and society, organized labor, or government should not bear any responsibility or take any credit.

Economic individualism runs deep in American culture. It can be traced back to the late nineteenth century and the social philosophy of Herbert Spencer in Britain and his American acolyte, William Graham Sumner. This was the same intellectual environment that led to the genesis of institutional economics. Spencer was writing about biological, intellectual, and social evolution before Charles Darwin and produce a comprehensive philosophical system he called Synthetic Philosophy.[6] The main goal of his of his work was to demonstrate that society evolves toward an ideal of maximum individual welfare as a result of competition in the open markets where the result is certain to be survival of the fittest.[7] Spencer emphasized how the stronger elements of any system, whether biological or social "organisms," will prevail as a result of the fierce discipline of competitive struggle to survive. The biological or social organisms, "which are best fitted to their environment, or which change to fit themselves to their environment, will survive. The least fit will die out, leaving the strongest and 'best.'"[8]

William Graham Sumner was inspired by Spencer's social philosophy and taught his work in the classes at Yale University, where Veblen was one of his students.[9] For Sumner, society evolves if it can change and adapt according to Spencerian rules of survival through competition.

Social institutions that interfere with eliminating the "weaker" individuals of the population such as social welfare programs or labor unions act as a hindrance to progress. Sumner writes emphatically that poverty is proof of indolence and a lack of morals and affluence is proof of industriousness and virtue.[10] A heavy dose of open competition will allow the elite to rise to prominence and the lazy, ignorant, and weak will taper off into extinction.

Spencer and Sumner's ideas were less well-received in Britain as they were in the United States where steel magnate Andrew Carnegie became an avid fan. It is helpful to look closely at Carnegie's worldview as he was arguably the wealthiest business tycoon of his age and was influential in the evolutionary process of corporate hegemony. In an article he published in the *North American Review* simply titled "Wealth" Andrew Carnegie gave reassurances that the free market and individualism were not only responsible for his own success but were best for the society as a whole. His article appeared the same year as the Sherman antitrust law was passed, corporate empire-building was on the ascent, his company was savagely attacking organized labor.[11]

Carnegie opens by assuaging skeptics who have witnessed his company's monopoly power and violent suppression of labor strikes at his steel plants and that vast polarization of wealth is a good thing, "The problem of our age is the proper administration of wealth, so that the ties of brotherhood may still bind together the rich and poor in harmonious relationship."[12] He went on to argue that the egalitarian lifestyles of Native Americans is primitive and underdeveloped. That tribal leaders' standard of living is not much different from the rest of their tribes, at least in appearance, for Carnegie is evidence of a stunted state of social development and less "civilized." He argues in corporate monopoly capitalism, however, "The contrast between the palace of the millionaire and the cottage of the laborer with us to-day measures the change which has come with civilization."[13] For Carnegie widely polarize economic inequality is a sign of social evolution in a civilized society where survival of the fittest has allowed the individual millionaire to assume a natural position at the top of the food chain.

Carnegie pressed on about technology, "One illustration will serve for almost every phase of the cause. In the manufacture of products we have the whole story. It applies to all combinations of human industry, as stimulated and enlarged by the inventions of this scientific age" (ibid).[14] In his view, inventions, industry, technology, and general human development all arise from competitive markets and individual enterprise,

> Under the law of competition, the employer of thousands is forced into the strictest economies, among which the rates paid to labor figure prominently, and often there is friction between the employer and the employed. The price which society pays for the law of competition, like the price it pays for cheap comforts and luxuries, is also great; but the advantage of this law are also greater still, for it is to this law that we owe our wonderful material development, which brings improved conditions in its train… and while the law may be sometimes hard for the individual, it is best for the race, because it insures the survival of the fittest in every department… We accept and welcome therefore, as conditions to which we must accommodate ourselves, great inequality of environment, the concentration of business, industrial and commercial, in the hands of a few, and the law of competition between these, as being not only beneficial, but essential for the future progress of the race.[15]

As he mentions concentration of business, Carnegie is referring to the corporate monopolies of his day. Although a corporate monopoly is an institution and not an actual person, he justifies it with philosophical individualism in the same tenor of religious fervor as Sumner and claims that individualism that "the angels derive their happiness."[16] From there Carnegie launches a polemic against progressive taxation, organized labor, socialism, and government regulation of business and any attempt to create a more equitable economy as a violation of the laws of competition and wealth creation, "Individualism, Private Property, the Law of Accumulation of Wealth, and the Law of Competition; for these are the highest results of human experience, the soil in which society so far has produced the best fruit. Unequally or unjustly, perhaps, as these laws sometimes operate, and imperfect as they appear to the Idealist, they are, nevertheless, like the highest type of man, the best and most valuable of all that humanity has yet accomplished."[17]

Carnegie concludes by going back to his original question about how to properly administer wealth. He attempts to make a case for the millionaire who has survived as a result of their fitness to be the steward of societal wellbeing, "Thus is the problem of Rich and Poor to be solved. The laws of accumulation will be left free; the laws of distribution free. Individualism will continue, but the millionaire will be but a trustee for the poor; entrusted for a season with a great part of the increased wealth of the community, but administering it for the community far better than it could or would have done for itself."[18]

Carnegie may not have truly believed that the laws of competitive markets and individualism should be left free to achieve social progress, for he could not have gained his monopoly privilege in the steel industry were not for the government tariffs on that blocked imported steel from entering US markets. Carnegie's steel empire and personal wealth were protected with the Morrill Tariff (1861) and other government legislation. With a twist of irony, Carnegie asserts that his steel business represents "inventions of the scientific age," though the tariffs specifically targeted British steel imports, which at the time were manufactured under the most technologically advanced production systems. As we will see, government intervention in economic affairs is implicitly endorsed in neoliberal ideology. The acid test for whether it should be supported is whether it leads to corporate profits and shareholder interests.

Carnegie established a legacy as an entrepreneurial success story. He personified the legend that with individual hard work and tenacity, anyone can climb to the top of the wealth pyramid as long as they are up to the challenge or fit enough to survive the struggles of competition in the open market. With the philanthropic foundations established in his name, his legacy endures as an iconic figure in the world of business. He is a poster symbol of rugged individualism that is affixed in the American cultural milieu. But washed out of the Carnegie success story are the institutional forces at work including the financial trust arrangement that was engineered by the investment banking house J.P. Morgan, which gave his company monopoly control in the steel industry. The Carnegie story usually edits out the part about his using government militia and private mercenaries to wage wars of violence against steelworker unions trying to organize workers at his plants, nor does it typically include the protections federal government provided with tariffs on steel imports.

The deeper truth of the Carnegie story is that it symbolized the triumph of the corporate institution over the countervailing institutions of labor and government. Economic individualism shifts the focus of attention away from these institutional forces. It mystifies the impression that economic success derives from an individual's hard work and good choices and that economic failure derives from a lack of effort and bad choices. When there are times of systemic crises characterized by widespread business and bank failures and unemployment that extend beyond anything that can be traced to individual action, such crises are seen as aberrant conditions like bizarre weather. The storms pass and all can return to their individual work in a mystical economy where, as suggested by Margaret Thatcher, that social institutions do not exist.

Greed Is Necessary for Wellbeing

In standard neoliberal economics, individuals are held to be driven purely by self-interest, which usually means a quest for financial gain and shopping for more things to buy with money. This notion fits squarely with the vision of economic individualism where each person is a competitor in a marketplace teeming with others who are also pursuing goals for themselves. In this open competitive struggle in the marketplace all become more active and more productive. As they do, there is more wealth to be enjoyed overall, particularly for those who survive and rise to the top.

The notion that the individual self-interest leads to prosperity underscores the sentiments of economic individualism presented by Spencer, Graham, and Carnegie. But the argument dates back another century to the beginnings of capitalism. Economist and philosopher Adam Smith writing in the latter half of the eighteenth century, argued that although there are multiple ways that humans can muster the motivation to work hard and be industrious, nothing compares to self-interest and greed. His writings on self-love resonated a century later with the corporate class as it rose to power and was surrounding itself with neoliberal ideology. Smith writes, "It is not from the benevolence of the butcher, the brewer, or the baker, that we expect our dinner, but from their regard to their own interest. We address ourselves, not to their humanity but of their self-love, and never to them of our own necessities but of their advantages."[19]

This was further developed with nineteenth-century utilitarian economics. Here consumer choice-making behavior is based on utility theory—a pleasure/pain principle in which people are rationally calculating what things to buy so as to maximize pleasure of consumption and to minimize pain of sacrifice. Similarly, businesses strive for more profit because ever more profits, which translates into ever more pleasure.[20] Greed is a good thing as long as it keeps everyone running, like rodents on a hamster wheel, in a continuous chase after consumer goods and financial gain. It is as if everyone has an internal voice in their head that keeps repeating, more, not enough, faster, newer, better, more. In a society where the corporation is the dominant institution, having the entire population running nonstop on a hamster wheel is godsend. It is necessary to keep the corporation expanding and forever generating returns for investors. Thus in the corporate world, greed has to be seen as a good thing.

Depression era economist John Maynard Keynes was captured by the alluring notion that greed is a good thing. Keynes writes, "The love of money as a possession … will be recognised for what it is, a somewhat disgusting morbidity, one of those semi-criminal, semi-pathological propensities which one hands over with a shudder to the specialists in mental disease." Though Keynes sounds moralizing, he nonetheless holds on to the idea that societies need to embrace greed for another century in order to be set free from economic depressions and insecurity. "For at least another hundred years," Keynes writes, "we must pretend to ourselves and to everyone that fair is foul and foul is fair; for foul is useful and fair is not. Avarice and usury and precaution must be our gods for a little longer still. For only they can lead us out of the tunnel of economic necessity into daylight."[21] Thus elevated to god-like status, greed and egoism in neoliberalism are seen as natural and unequivocal. In an economic field dominate by corporations in which bottom-line gains is the guiding rule, individual and consumers and producers are expected to behave accordingly.

The Sanctity of the Market System

Neoliberalism uses standard economic theory to build a normative framework that defines an economy as a system of markets where structures of institutional power are considered exogenous. By delimiting the purview of economic activity to market activity, it also normalizes a belief in mainstream textbooks that, "everything has a price—each commodity and each service. Even the different kinds of human labor have prices."[22] As it is presented as *fact* in this way, the market system is also held to be natural and unequivocal. This normalizes what Marx refers to a "commodity fetishism" and opens the way to financialization. If every possible thing has a price and is commodified as such, then everything can be turned into a security that can be traded on speculation. Wheat and corn are not food, houses are not homes, labor is not our livelihoods or crafts, they are instruments to be bought and sold for financial gain.

For Marx, commodification of all things is a social construct that has little or no bearing in the physical existence of things. A physical object is perceptible in the mind in part because of the physical existence of light that connects the object to the eye to the brain. Marx argues that commodities are not objectively situated in the physical world as they,

> …have absolutely no connexion with their physical properties and with the material relations arising therefrom… to find an analogy, we must have recourse to the mist-enveloped regions of the religious world. In that world the productions of the human brain appear as independent beings endowed with life, and entering into relation both with one another and the human race. So it is in the world of commodities with the products of men's hand. This I call the Fetishism which attaches itself to the products of labor.[23]

The same can be said to be true of securitization and financialization. One day a bushel of wheat is seen in the human imagination as food, then once the human brain is saturated with market ideology, it is refashioned as a commodity. One day a home is a shelter, then is refashioned into real estate, then at a higher level of abstraction into a security traded on Wall Street like a stock or bond.

Another normative assumption in neoliberalism is that the market system is supremely efficient. When everything is commodified and securitized, markets need to be created for their exchange. To normalize the creation of a ubiquity of markets, neoliberalism sublimates their existence as an optimally efficient way to distribute products, resources, and money. This ideological assumption is grounded in the idea that market prices are continually adjusting to market conditions. It also predicated on the assumption that consumers are considered to be sovereign and everything in the system adjusts to what consumers demand.

If the consumer prefers large SUVs for their mode of transportation, then they send their demand signals to the auto market accordingly. As signals hit the market, prices start to rise, and the auto manufacturers have an incentive to produce more SUVs because they are more profitable to make. To do this, auto manufacturers have to send their demand signals to labor, resource, and capital markets. The prices of these start to rise and workers are drawn to the higher wage, steel producers have an incentive to produce more steel for the auto industry, and investors are drawn to higher rates of return in capital markets. If the opposite were the case and people lose interest in SUVs, then the process is reversed. Prices fall, the auto industry slows down, auto workers get laid off and their wages are cut such that they are forced to look for jobs elsewhere, steel producers lose interest as demand and prices fall, and investors pull out as returns evaporate. In this chain of command, the markets move goods and resources toward where they are in demand and away from where they are not. Everything is placed under the discipline of the market that keeps prices within a range of affordability and acceptable quality to satisfy consumers. The economy is therefore optimized by achieving consumer satisfaction, while providing employment opportunities where labor is needed most, and provides investment income for entrepreneurs. At least that is the theory. But in standard economics it is not presented as theory, it is presented as the ontology of an economy: an Eden of cost/benefit choice behavior in an open market that is as natural as freshwater and sunlight. Anything that might interfere with this such as regulation or organized labor, is a pathology because it leads to diminished efficiency. In the early 1970s, the religion of market efficiency was elevated to mathematical sophistication with the Efficient Market Hypothesis.

The Efficient Market Hypothesis

The central idea in the Efficient Market Hypothesis (EMH) is that commodities, securities, and financial instruments in general, when traded in an open unregulated market, the price is always gravitating toward that which is correct and undistorted, and therefore capital is allocated toward optimal efficiency. It was first articulated by Eugene Fama in the Journal of Finance in 1970 where he observed that as buy and sell signals bombard financial markets, prices of financial instruments will respond and continually adjust.[24] Occasionally inefficiencies arise in the maelstrom of speculative trading that goes on in markets daily, but Fama argued that these inefficiencies can only last for a short time as speculators take advantage of opportunities for speculation that arise with the inefficiencies. For example, if there is an inefficiency, say a shortage of supply relative to demand the price should naturally rise and the higher price draws in suppliers who will eliminate the efficiency. Similarly, if a publicly traded stock is underpriced, speculators will move in and start buying on the anticipation that the market will correct itself and the stock price will rise. The buying frenzy drives the price upward and the market price is returned to its optimal point and the inefficiency is eliminated—the stock can never stay overpriced or underpriced. By extension, capital can never be overallocated or underallocated.

The EMH became the ideological centerpiece for financial market deregulation during the Greenspan Era. It stands to reason that if a free market will always produce fundamentally correct asset prices, then the entire financial should be able to function properly on its own without government interference. In this hypothesis, asset price bubbles cannot exist and if there are spikes in one direction or another it is because there are changes in the asset's underlying fundamental value, which will be reflected in the markets. If a stock price rises, it is due to stock traders seeing the market value increasing as a result of the company becoming more profitable or in better financial standing with its creditors.

This argument was used to dismiss concerns about the rapidly growing and poorly understood mortgage derivatives market in the runup to the banking crisis that started in 2007. At the time, mortgage-backed securities (MBSs) began to rise in price as investors saw the income streams that flowed from mortgage payments to be considered stable investments and secured with collateral. Speculators jumped into the MBS market, and eventually, bubbles began forming all around the mortgage universe. According to the EMH, however, distortions such as bubbles cannot be sustained and therefore the prices of the securities reflect optimal efficiency—there cannot be systemic failures preventing market correctness. The EMH provided justification for the argument that banks should be allowed to do as they pleased, and that financial innovation in a free market environment would always lead to socially optimal outcomes.[25]

The hypothesis, though elaborated with sophisticated mathematical models such as the famous Black-Scholes Model, is predicated on a remarkably unrealistic assumption that socially optimal outcomes arise out of a general condition of perfect information. That is, there is full open access to all relevant information about the value, earnings potential, debts, technology, and every other possible thing that could influence the underlying fundamental value of an asset. The EMH also assumes that all have access to this information at all times. Given that everyone presumably knows everything there is to know, the EMH concludes that market participants will always make rational market decisions. The contention that everyone involved in markets trades have the ability to collect all relevant information to use in making rational decisions is highly improbable. Nonetheless, the EMH became the premier justification for financial market deregulation, though it did not go unchallenged. Many well-known economists such as Joseph Stiglitz, Larry Summers, and Robert Shiller energetically assailed the EMH.

When herds of speculators are drawn to a securities market, most of their buy or sell decisions are based on what is known as "noise trading." This means that buyers and sellers are not acting on the basis of solid information about an asset's true fundamental value, but rather on general buzz, media hype, and gossip. The critics of EMH argue that "noise trading can lead to a large divergence between market prices and fundamental values."[26] Financial market analyst George Cooper studied the statistical probably of markets having a condition of perfect information and determined that the likelihood is so microscopically small that it is invisible. He concludes that the EMH is "an example of bad statistics and bad science."[27] Be that as it may, the EMH served the interests of Wall Street, and the Greenspan Federal Reserve held steadfast to the belief in perfect market efficiency and maintained that there are no bubbles in stocks, derivatives, or real estate right up to the moment when they burst and crashed.

The subtext of the EMH is that market forces and adjusting prices are, like individualism and greed, part of the natural order of things. More important, though, is that these are considered orthodox assumptions because this is what corporate capitalism needs.

The EMH is a more contemporary and sophisticated version of Adam Smith's slogan of the "invisible hand" in which everyone is driven by self-indulgent impulses as if these were built into our DNA. In the neoliberal scheme of things, the market system is treated as an inexorable state of mankind. The market system and the corporation are therefore arranged as the ideal institutional habitat for human beings. In these institutions' sphere of influence, which is now total and complete, not only are resources allocated optimally, they are also more consistent with our natural tendencies to pursue financial gain, and to be competitive and aggressive in the Spencerian struggle for survival of the fittest. Within this ideological and institutional structure of corporate hegemony, all our institutions become isomorphic; that is, the distinctions among the corporation, the market system, the state, and the central bank are erased in a political project directed at subordinating everything under the sun to corporate rule.

The Janus Face of Government

In neoliberalism the role of government is treated in a way that seems inconsistent or even contradictory. Like Janus, the Roman god of duality, government is seen as having two faces: one for the world to see and the other to serve corporate hegemony. One face shows the government as something that needs to be kept to a minimum with an understanding that the economy functions best if government is not there to gum up the works of the capitalist machine. The other face shows an implicit recognition that government has been an active and vigilant part of economic affairs since the beginning of capitalism as it was instrumental in creating and maintaining the market system. One face is for the public, the other is for the corporate hegemony.

This duality of government creates some confusion. Part of the confusion comes from associating neoliberalism with classical liberalism or laissez-faire. The French phrase laissez-faire literally means "let people do as they please" and it was born out of the revolutionary movements in Europe and North America in the eighteenth century. The aim these movements was to dismantle the rule of the monarchical forms of government and replace with modern democratic nation-states. Classical liberalism was a radical notion of individual liberty in which people were untethered to the arbitrary powers of the aristocracy and the crown. This notion of individual freedom extended into the economic sphere in which businesses, too, were set free to conduct their affairs in an open market environment.

The most notable economist to contribute to the ideology economic liberalism was Adam Smith. Smith's famous tome, *The Wealth of Nations*, was published in 1776 coinciding with the American revolution and struggle for independence from British colonialism. Smith challenged the British monarch's total control over commerce as unnatural and gave too much power to government. Instead, Smith proposed that the role of government in the economy would more naturally be limited to "Defence, Justice, and Public Works and Public Institutions."[28] And with the public works and institutions, these are chiefly institutions for facilitating commerce.[29] As Smith's work on restricted government and individual economic self-interest unfolded simultaneously with Thomas Jefferson's Declaration of Independence they became economic doctrines that are firmly embedded in the collective imagination of Americans. Classical liberalism in economics is associated with political freedom and democracy.

But in the real, non-imaginary economic world of corporate hegemony, government shows a different face. Government institutions are not to be restricted so much as to be put into the service of the corporate market system. The active role of government is upheld behind a veil of rhetoric in which its authority is outwardly criticized yet quietly empowered to be the producer and custodian of the market system. On this, scholar Jaime Peck writes, "Neoliberalism was always concerned… with the challenge of first seizing and then retasking the state."[30] All the public outcries from neoliberal circles about the heavy hand of government regulation, excessive tax burdens, and government waste (the antithesis to market efficiency) are surreptitiously directed at building a case for corporate rule using government as an agent. Neoliberalism "is the remaking and redeployment of the state as the core agency that actively fabricates the subjectivities, social relations, and collective representations suited to making the fiction of markets real and consequential."[31] By seizing and retasking the state, it brought to heel as a servant to the interests of the corporation and the corporate class. The neoliberal agenda was never intended to anarchize or move to a restricted laissez-faire model as Smith envisioned; it is a case of bait and switch to publicly vilify government as an enemy of free enterprise while privately making it the best of friends.

Jaime Peck's point about market fiction resonates with the work of economic historian, Karl Polanyi. For Polanyi, markets for goods and services have existed for thousands of years, but what led to the development of capitalism was the modern creation of a total system of integrated markets that had to be forcibly and unnaturally imposed on society as a kind of "commodity fiction."[32]

Capitalism came into being as something historically unique with the creation of labor markets, markets for land and natural resources, and capital markets. In the capitalist market system human labor is hired in labor markets for money, natural resources and capital equipment are acquired in markets for money, land is rented or purchased with money and the final goods and services are sold for money in markets. In this way a capitalist makes money purely through buying on the input side and selling on the output side—buying low and selling high in the market system. Prior to the ascent of capitalism in the sixteenth century, such a system was not possible. Land and its resources were then considered the domain of God and were not ordinarily thought of as commodities to be bought and sold for money in markets. Nor was labor hired for wages in labor markets. Human labor was embedded in a system of hierarchy of servile relationships that revolved around the control of land, not money. There were few or no institutions created for raising finance capital, and human-made resources such as the equipment and tools used in production were not so much privately owned as they were used collectively in peasant communities or controlled by guild masters. Polanyi described the process of transforming land, labor, and capital into marketable commodities as a historical sea change leading to modern capitalist development in the eighteenth and nineteenth centuries.

Polanyi refers to this sea change as "The Great Transformation" and was imposed on society by the state.[33] The institution of the nation-state forced working people into wage labor, turned land into real estate, and created the original corporate prototypes for capital formation. All the principal resources—labor, land, and capital—were forcibly transformed into marketable commodities. Historically, this was by far the most important step toward the corporatization and financialization of economic systems, and that was just the beginning. Beyond that state institutions developed patent protections, erected tariffs on trade, subsidized railroad monopolies with land grants, subsidized tech companies with research and development, helped corporations keep down labor costs with union bashing, gave tax abatements to the highest bidder, ratified trade agreement, orchestrated taxpayer-funded bailouts, and the list goes on. Yet while all this is going on, neoliberals proclaim the sanctity of individualism, free markets, and limited government. As Mirowski puts it, "A primary ambition of the neoliberal project is to redefine the shape and functions of the state, *not to destroy it*. Neoliberals thus maintain an uneasy and troubled alliance with their sometimes fellow-travelers the anarchists."[34]

One of the greatest ironies of neoliberalism is that a free and unregulated market is probably the last thing that most well-established corporations actually want. For most businesses, a free market is an undesirable environment in which new competitors are free to challenge existing businesses, where prices are uncertain, and there is a constant threat of losing market share and profits. No businesses actually want to see their product markets openly flooded by competitors who threaten to drive prices and profits into the ground. In the several hundred years of capitalism, businesses have always embraced the interventions of government so long as those interventions protect their profitability from the wild uncertainties of unregulated competition in markets.

Neoliberal ideology sustains a belief that government regulatory agencies are unwanted encumbrances that prevent the realization of perfect efficiency in the marketplace resulting in imbalances and inefficiencies. It perpetuates the myth that the market system is self-regulating, and by doing so is able to weaken public support for any other institution that may not be aligned with their interests. It has served to mold public opinion in ways that will always favor corporate interests over organized labor, and markets over government regulation. It has also served to create a climate of opinion that is slavishly accepting of large corporations' ascent to commanding heights of wealth and power. I neoliberalism, government institutions are pet instruments, but crucial instruments in corporate hegemony. Yet they are seldom acknowledged as such. Government is bad when it takes away profit-making, but good when it does what corporations want from it, particularly when it is saving the market system from itself.

Despite the magical powers of market self-regulation, neoliberalism concedes that occasionally "weird" things happen in the economy such as recessions or financial market instabilities. Since the publication of John M. Keynes *General Theory of Employment, Interest and Money* in 1936, central banks and government treasuries have been brought to the front stage to save the capitalist system from recurring recessionary spirals.

Keynes and other Depression-era economists refocused economic thinking to highlight the efficacy of using government powers to lessen the downward pull of recessions and to restore stability. Keynes's model was comfortably nestled into the neoliberal paradigm, but kept government on the margins unless needed as a last resort in the corporate sphere.

What Is Good for Corporations Is Good for Everyone

As he crossed through the revolving door between corporation and state, Charles Erwin Wilson stepped down from his post as CEO of General Motors to become Secretary of Defense in the Dwight D. Eisenhower Administration in the 1950s. In his confirmation hearing, he was pressured to sell his substantial holdings of General Motors stock to avoid possible conflict of interest. That struck Wilson as odd as he commented, "because for years I thought what was good for our country was good for General Motors, and vice versa."[35] Wilson's statement was frequently paraphrased as "What's good for General Motors is good for the country" and the paraphrased version was handed down as a piece of American folklore.

A similar sentiment in another famous quote by President Calvin Coolidge a few decades earlier in an address to the Society of American Newspaper Editors in 1925 where he told the press, "the chief business of the American people is business."[36] Coolidge was attempting to mollify concerns that were being raised about a conflict of interest for corporate media to both maximize profits for shareholders and fulfill its obligation to inform the public. Coolidge said, "There does not seem to be cause for alarm in the dual relationship of the press to the public, whereby it is on one side a purveyor of information and opinion and on the other side a purely business enterprise. Rather, it is probable that a press which maintains an intimate touch with the business currents of the nation, is likely to be more reliable than it would be if it were a stranger to these influences."[37] His claim was that since America's business is business, a corporation is in the best position to protect the interests of the population at large.

Echoing the sentiments of Carnegie, Coolidge went on to say that the successful business tycoon specifically is in a unique position to serve the public, "Just a little time ago we read in your newspapers that two leaders of American business, whose efforts at accumulation had been most astonishingly successful, had given fifty or sixty million dollars as endowments to educational works. That was real news. It was characteristic of our American experience with men of large resources. They use their power to serve, not themselves and their own families, but the public."[38] Of course, his speech resonated with the corporate class as it reinforced the notion that what is good for corporate CEOs, the corporations themselves, and their principal shareholders, is good for everyone.

It should be noted also this view of the corporation as social benefactor was a break from traditional the laissez-faire ideology of classical liberalism. Adam Smith and others in the classical liberal tradition were as distrustful of corporate power as they were of state power. But as Mills and Galbraith observed, the corporation broke away from the state to become a force in its own right. As it did neoliberalism and the coronation of the corporation became the new ideology. The corporation was being conceptually transformed from a ruthless monopoly power working against the public interest like Standard Oil, to a socially beneficial vehicle for wealth creation and livelihoods for the general population. By the Greenspan Era, it became vogue to look to the corporation as a model institution for not only social benefit but also for the environmental movement. With a public relations tweak here and profit incentive there, the corporation is seen as of having positive impacts on people's lives while simultaneously making shareholders wealth. As corporate hegemony came into full form, the corporation was refashioned as a force for public wellbeing and the market system was refashioned as a new form of democracy.

Capitalism Equals Democracy

Many Americans have been raised on the belief that capitalism and democracy are two dimensions of the same system. Free markets, stars and stripes, the Declaration of Independence, and the invisible hand are all symbols imbued in the popular American imagination. As they continue to mystify corporate hegemony, business and political leaders regularly incorporate these symbols in their public statements on economic policy, particularly in an effort to deregulate and use the terms "free market capitalism" and "democracy" interchangeably. In neoliberal ideology, corporate enterprise and the market system are frequently heralded by economists as democratic institutions where entrepreneurs and consumers are always "free to choose" in the marketplace—voting with their pocketbooks as they say.

Real democracy, however, is a political system sovereignty of the population either directly or through representation. Under capitalism, the majority of the working population provides labor under the direction of a proportionally small number of members of the investor class and their agents. The class of shareholders and bondholders and executives is not democratically accountable to the people who work in their businesses or to the communities in which they conduct business, nor do working people have the power to decide how or what is to be produced or for whom. In the corporate universe there are no such things such as voter equality, universal suffrage, referendums, or any other of the key elements that would make up a democratic system. There is no mechanism in a privileged class structure of ownership centered on ownership that would render it popularly sovereign.

Nor is the market system a democratic institution. It is a strange twist of logic to see buying and selling in markets is seen as an exercise of popular democratic will. The market system rations products, resources, and capital to those who have money and away from those who do not. Such a system necessarily weighs heavily in favor of those with money, and a system financial wealth over people cannot claim to be democratic.

Equating private enterprise and markets with democracy makes powerful political rhetoric frosted with the mystification of "freedom." In a fundamental way capitalism and democracy stand in antagonistic opposition primarily because it strips those without the money to buy, or what John M. Keynes called "effective demand," of political franchise and lavishes it on those who do. Yet, as we will see in subsequent chapters, the cliché of equating capitalism with democracy has the status of a philosophical axiom in American culture.

Economic and Financial Innovation Are Unassailable

The word innovation enjoys unquestioned status as something positive. It generally implies introducing a new idea, concept, or device that will cause a beneficial shift in the established way of doing things. Innovation indicates moving forward, and to question something that is being presented as innovative will risk coming across as against progress, backward, curmudgeonly, or technophobic. In the project of mystification, therefore, one of the most effective ways for neoliberalists to push through deregulation initiatives was to present it as innovative.

During the Greenspan Era, the lines between innovation in so-called high tech and financial innovation have been blurred. What was once considered capital investment or capital formation has increasingly become financial engineering. From computerized trading programs in the 1980s to online trading platforms in the 1990s and to the millennial age of complex derivatives and blockchain, all is subsumed under the heading of innovation. To question usefulness or economic efficacy of these things is to risk being branded as a Luddite and lose credibility. General discourse is framed in such a way that those who raise concerns about the need for collateral debt obligations, credit default swaps, or structured investment vehicles are made to appear unsophisticated and clash with the lore of technology-driven economic progress.

Making financial innovation unassailable falls in line with same piety of what is good for corporations is good for everyone. The notion of a technologically sophisticated financial sector is heralded as good for the public overall. Given all the material gains and productivity increased given by technological innovation, it stands to reason that the same is true of financial innovation. In the 1990s, Robert Merton, MIT business professor and EMH guru, gushed about financial innovation as "the force driving the global financial system towards its goal of greater economic efficiency. In particular, innovations involving derivatives can improve efficiency by expanding opportunities for risk sharing."[39] A couple of years later, Greenspan expressed his adoration of financial innovation and the far-reaching innovation of the technology of securitization.[40] And as the process of financialization spread through the Greenspan era, former Treasury Secretary and President of the Federal Reserve Bank in New York, Timothy Geithner, waxed enthusiastically about how innovation in the financialization process is allowing for gaining a better grip on managing systemic risk. For Geithner, financial innovation has "contributed to a substantial improvement in the financial strength of the core financial intermediaries and in the overall flexibility and resilience of the financial system in the United States."[41]

In the runup to the crisis in '07–'09, there were many on Wall Street arguing that the engineering complex mortgage derivatives were improving credit availability, providing more options for businesses, and reducing transaction costs for the housing industry. By throwing complex financial engineering under the general heading of innovation, Wall Street gains the unassailable privilege of defying doubt or lack of merit. Looking at the crisis that unfolded in retrospect, we see that instead of reducing risk, mortgage derivatives massively increased systemic risk. But because these instruments were lauded as innovative, their usefulness was beyond reproach or question. Economist Hyman Minsky saw this problem decades earlier as he warned that unexamined innovation opens the door to speculation, reckless, which inevitably leads to conditions of instability. Minsky drew his warning from observing historical patterns in which financial innovation and instability being repeated again and again in history.

Among the few who are willing to question blind faith in financial innovation, authors Simon Johnson and James Kwak express their concern and shed light in the dark world of blind faith that gave rise to a flurry of financial innovation that led to the crisis, "turned out so badly because financial innovations *not* like technological innovation. There are financial innovations that do benefit society, such as the debit card… But there is no law of physics or economics that dictates that all financial innovations are beneficial."[42] But if the plan is to turn the world into a giant portfolio of financial investments, this is the sales pitch.

It was the drumbeat of innovation that created the mad dance of deregulation in the years before the crises, and the trend continues with blockchain, cryptocurrency, internet equity crowdfunding platforms, such that there is no distinguishing between electronic-based financial engineering and the technological infrastructure with which it is structured.

During the Greenspan Era, innovation bloomed into its own structure with a purpose that has little or nothing to do with economic well-being. Wall Street became increasingly preoccupied with creating and brokering instruments that have become nearly impossible to explain in terms of why we would need them: currency swaps, indexed sinking fund debentures, puttable convertible bonds, and the list could go on for pages. Looking at these innovations from the long view the question begs as to what is the point of all this?

The answer is multifaceted. In the Marxian view, it is inextricably linked to the process of financialization where innovation becomes a necessity of late capitalism as it is unable to generate profits for the investor class through traditional commodity production. The drive to make money for investors or shareholders forced the financial system to find new methods of generating returns. Financial instruments, rather than functioning as a means of supporting real economic production, became an intrinsic gimmick for money-making schemes for those savvy enough to pull it off, and as a proxy for the more challenging work of producing goods and services.

It is becoming increasingly evident to Wall Street companies that trying to make money by producing actual goods and services is cumbersome, long term, and sketchy in the context of increasingly intense global market competition. As Wall Street investment banks see this, they fabricate financial "products" as a strategy for investors that can see their returns staying ahead of the market saturation and decaying orbit of profit-making from commodity production. Instruments that were created to help facilitate real economic production have always been subject to market speculation, but now they have drifted way from that facility and are themselves replacing commodities as the principal means by which investors sustain returns. In other words, the necessity of capitalism to show bottom line return for investors has turned to what amounts to speculative gambling rather than production. With each round of innovation, the newly created instruments are the most lucrative for those who get into the markets early enough, The windfall from buying low and selling high dissipates quickly as more speculators are drawn to the table. All the players in the markets learn that with innovation they can create another game and with each game comes volatility, and with volatility the potential for great gains as well as great losses intensifies. Booms and busts create opportunities for those who know how to take positions on both sides of the trades. With exotic instruments, money can be made on market upswings, downswings, and both. Wall Street has become addicted to innovation for this reason. Innovation is like a new drug.

Another factor is that the financial innovation that was spawned during the Greenspan Era was partially in response to the central bank's "zero bound" rate policy. Interest rates were pushed to near zero levels, which meant that fund managers of 401s, foundations, pensions, had to look far beyond bond funds to find ways to generate returns for their clients. Speculation in new innovative instruments provided fat returns for a time for those who were able to take advantage of the opportunities early as they arose. This in turn would provide stable portfolio returns for their clients, which represent a fairly broad cross section of pensioners, trust fund beneficiaries, and endowment stakeholders. Everyone was getting involved.

Economist Joseph Schumpeter writing decades before financial innovation became all the rage, took note that "it is one of the most characteristic features of the financial side of capitalist evolution so to 'mobilize' all, even the longest, maturities as to make any commitment to a promise of future balances amenable to being in turn financed to being in turn financed by any sort of funds and especially by funds available for short time, even overnight, only. This is not mere technique. This is part of the core of the capitalist process."[43]

Schumpeter was writing in the late 1930s, so extending to the Greenspan Era, and the speed-of-light quickness with which funds are mobilized on the web, and again by the sheer numbers of those involved, the system condition for mass instability is unprecedented. This is a certainty because throughout the history of capitalism, speculation on innovative financial instruments has always resulted in boom-bust patterns of instability. We allow this to keep happening because we have become dependent on those processes and we accordingly, under the spell of neoliberal ideology, hesitate to question innovation. To keep this going it requires that a certain buy-in from the population that the solution to any problem is renewed financial market innovation.

Marxist intellectual Antonio Gramsci wrote most of his important work while sitting behind prison bars in Mussolini's Italy in the 1930s. Like so many others throughout human history, Gramsci was severely punished for his ideas. The most important of which is his theory of cultural hegemony. He observed that as capitalist institutions became entrenched into, it was unnecessary for the political establishment to use force to gain acceptance and compliance from the population of working people. Instead, the corporate class exercised its control over cultural production to massage the values, beliefs, and norms into the accepted belief of all. Gramsci describes cultural hegemony as "the spontaneous consent given by the great masses of the population to the general direction imposed on social life by the dominant fundamental group."[44] The dominant group of our time is the corporate hegemony—a powerful network of corporate institutions, and its attending social class, and its subordinate institutions in government. Its control over the American economy and society stands largely unchallenged and extends its influence everywhere. As we will see in the next chapter, the American population hold onto a popular consensus around the core elements of neoliberalism, which prevails as both corporate ideology and as popular folklore. American believe wholeheartedly that their economic society is exemplified as a system of free markets, individualism, and innovation. Neoliberalism is so deeply entrenched in the popular imagination that most Americans are unable to see that economic institutions even exist.

There is a popular myth that runs through certain new age circles that tells a peculiar story about when the large ships of European explorers first arrived in coasts of North America, they were considered invisible to the indigenous people. They were invisible to these people, so the story goes, because such ships and foreign ways were so alien to their collective mindset and shared experience that they were unable to actually see the ships. In all likelihood, the story is not true, but like all myths there is an element of truth value in the fiction. When people believe in something so wholeheartedly, they become blind to facts that contradict the belief and hold onto to it every more steadfastly, even though it eventually leads them toward their own destruction.

Notes

1. Zachary Tracer and Alex Nussbaum, "Heath Insurance Exchanges," *Bloomberg*, January 5, 2017.
2. See Kaiser's data on health statistics at https://www.kff.org/report-section/ehbs-2015-section-one-cost-of-health-insurance/.
3. Allan Gruchy, *The Reconstruction of Economics: An Analysis of the Fundamentals of Institutional Economics* (New York, NY: Greenwood Press, 1987), p. 133.
4. Philip Mirowski, *Never Let a Serious Crisis Go to Waste: How Neoliberalism Survived the Financial Meltdown* (New York, NY: Verso, 2013), pp. 42–43.
5. Ibid., p. 28.
6. Joseph Dorfman, *Thorstein Veblen and His America* (New York, NY: Augustus Kelley, 1966), p. 74.
7. The phrase "survival of the fittest" was coined by Spencer, though often incorrectly used as synonymously with Darwin's "natural selection."
8. Herbert Spencer, *The Principles of Sociology* (New York, NY: D. Appleton and Co., 1876–1896), Vol. III, p. 594.
9. Dorfman, 1966, p. 43
10. William Graham Sumner, *What Social Classes Owe to Each Other* [1883] (New York, NY: Harper and Brothers, 1911), pp. 43–48.
11. The Sherman Act was passed in 1890 during a time when the federal government was becoming more concerned about labor strikes turning into revolutions. The strikes at Carnegie's steel mills were in the middle of violent conflicts at this time.
12. Andrew Carnegie, "Wealth," *North American Review*, June 1889, No. CCCXCI, p. 1.
13. Ibid.
14. Ibid.
15. Ibid., pp. 1–2.
16. Ibid., p. 2.
17. Ibid., p. 3.

18. Ibid.
19. Adam Smith, *An Inquiry into the Nature and Causes of the Wealth of Nations* [1776] (The University of Chicago Press, 1976), Book I, Chapter II, p. 18.
20. See the "marginal analysis" sections on consumer and business theory in any standard neoclassical economics textbook.
21. John M. Keynes, *Collected Writings*, Donald E. Moggridge, ed. (London: Macmillan, 1971),Vol. IX, pp. 329, 331.
22. George Cooper, *The Origin of Financial Crises: Central Banks, Credit Bubbles and the Efficient Market Fallacy* (New York, NY: Vintage, 2008), pp. 4–5.
23. Karl Marx, "The Fetishism of Commodities and the Secret Thereof," *Capital*, Vol. 1, p. 77.
24. Eugene F. Fama, "Efficient Capital Markets: A Review of Theory and Empirical Work," *The Journal of Finance*, Vol. 25, 1970, pp. 383–417.
25. Johnson and Kwak, 2010, p. 70.
26. Bradford DeLong, Andrei Shleifer, Lawrence H Summers, and Robert J. Waldmann, "Noise Trader Risk in Financial Markets," *The Journal of Political Economy*, Vol. 98, 1990.
27. Cooper, *The Origin of Financial Crises*, p. 11.
28. Adam Smith, *An Inquiry into the Nature and Causes of the Wealth of Nations* [1776] (Chicago: University of Chicago Press, 1976), Book V, pp. 213–244.
29. Ibid., p. 244.
30. Mirowski, 2013, p. 54.
31. Ibid.
32. Karl Polanyi, *The Great Transformation: The Political and Economic Origins of Our Time* (Boston, MA: Beacon Press, 1944), p. 73.
33. Ibid, p. 141..
34. Mirowski, 2013, p. 56.
35. Penelope Simons and Audrey Macklin, *The Governance Gap: Extractive Industries, Human Rights, and the Home State Advantage* (New York, NY: Routledge, 2014), p. 53.
36. See the full text of Coolidge's speech at http://www.presidency.ucsb.edu/ws/?pid=24180.
37. Ibid.
38. Ibid.

39. Robert Merton, "Financial Innovation and the Management and Regulation of Financial Institutions," *Journal of Banking and Finance*, Vol. 19, 1995, pp. 461–481.
40. Alan Greenspan, "Technological Change and the Design of Bank Supervisory Policies," May 1997. See https://fraser.stlouisfed.org/title/452/item/8597.
41. Timothy F. Geithner, "Risk Management Challenges in the U.S. Financial System," February 26, 2006. See https://www.newyorkfed.org/newsevents/speeches/2006/gei060228.
42. Johnson and Kwak, 2010, p. 108.
43. Joseph Schumpeter, *Business Cycles: A Theoretical, Historical, and Statistical Analysis of the Capitalist Process* (New York, NY: McGraw-Hill, 1939), Vol. 2, p. 613.
44. T.J. Jackson Lears, "The Concept of Cultural Hegemony: Problems and Possibilities," *The American Historical Review*, Vol. 90, No. 3, June 1985, p. 568.

References

Carnegie, Andrew. "Wealth," *North American Review*, June 1889, No. CCCXCI.

Cooper, George. *The Origin of Financial Crises: Central Banks, Credit Bubbles and the Efficient Market Fallacy* (New York, NY: Vintage, 2008).

Coolidge, Calvin. "Address to the American Society of Newspaper Editors," 1925. http://www.presidency.ucsb.edu/ws/?pid=24180.

DeLong, Bradford, Andrei Shleifer, Lawrence H. Summers and Robert J. Waldmann. "Noise Trader Risk in Financial Markets," *The Journal of Political Economy*, Vol. 98, 1990, pp. 703–738.

Fama, Eugene F. "Efficient Capital Markets: A Review of Theory and Empirical Work," *The Journal of Finance*, Vol. 25, 1970, pp. 383–417.

Geithner, Timothy F. "Risk Management Challenges in the U.S. Financial System," *Federal Reserve Bank of New York*, 2006. https://www.newyorkfed.org/newsevents/speeches/2006/gei060228.

Greenspan, Alan. "Technological Change and the Design of Bank Supervisory Policies," *Federal Reserve Bank of Chicago*, 1997. https://fraser.stlouisfed.org/title/452/item/8597.

Gruchy, Allan. *The Reconstruction of Economics: An Analysis of the Fundamentals of Institutional Economics* (New York, NY: Greenwood Press, 1987).

Johnson, Simon and James Kwak. *Thirteen Bankers: The Wall Street Takeover and the Next Financial Meltdown* (New York, NY: Pantheon, 2010).

Kaiser Foundation. "2015 Employer Health Benefits Survey," 2015. https://www.kff.org/report-section/ehbs-2015-section-one-cost-of-health-insurance/.

Keynes, John M. *Collected Writings*, Donald E. Moggridge, ed. (London: Macmillan, 1971), Vol. IX.

Lears, T.J. Jackson. "The Concept of Cultural Hegemony: Problems and Possibilities," *The American Historical Review*, Vol. 90, No. 3, June 1985, p. 591.

Marx, Karl. "The Fetishism of Commodities and the Secret Thereof," *Capital*, Vol. 1. (Moscow: Progress Publishers, 1970), p. 76.

Merton, Robert. "Financial Innovation and the Management and Regulation of Financial Institutions," *Journal of Banking and Finance*, Vol. 19, 1995, pp. 461–481.

Mirowski, Philip. *Never Let a Serious Crisis Go to Waste: How Neoliberalism Survived the Financial Meltdown* (New York, NY: Verso, 2013).

Polanyi, Karl. *The Great Transformation: The Political and Economic Origins of Our Time* (Boston, MA: Beacon Press, 1944).

Schumpeter, Joseph. *Business Cycles: A Theoretical, Historical, and Statistical Analysis of the Capitalist Process* (New York, NY: McGraw-Hill, 1939), Vol. 2.

Smith, Adam. *An Inquiry into the Nature and Causes of the Wealth of Nations* [1776] (Chicago, IL: The University of Chicago Press, 1976), Book I, Chapter II.

Simons, Penelope and Audrey Macklin. *The Governance Gap: Extractive Industries, Human Rights, and the Home State Advantage* (New York, NY: Routledge, 2014).

Spencer, Herbert. *The Principles of Sociology* (New York, NY: D. Appleton and Co., 1876–1896), Vol. III.

Sumner, William Graham. *What Social Classes Owe to Each Other* [1883] (New York, NY: Harper and Brothers, 1911).

Tracer, Zachary and Alex Nussbaum. "Heath Insurance Exchanges," *Bloomberg*, January 5, 2017.

6
Everyday Neoliberalism

After three decades into the Greenspan Era, the project of consolidating corporate power entered into its final stage. All the major economic institutions had become either directly under corporate control or were rendered irrelevant to corporate interests and pushed to the margins. Organized labor had all but disappeared from the private sector and government watchdog agencies were either defunded or ignored. Media became wholly absorbed into the sphere of corporate interests as a sales tool and propaganda machine. Neoliberalism became the unquestioned ideology for policymakers regardless of their political party affiliations. Democrat and Republican parties have absorbed themselves into what is now a single institution that transcends political affiliations—the corporate hegemony. In this final stage, corporate neoliberalism has captured the imagination and intellect of the general population and has forged itself into a popular consensus. Neoliberalism stands largely as the accepted ideology of the American population, though when put into practice it largely runs against the economic interests of most people. Genuine advocacy for models that truly stand outside business as usual is barely audible in public discourse. Most economic models in the United States that are included in public discourse as standing

J. Magnuson, *Financing the Apocalypse*,
Palgrave Insights into Apocalypse Economics,
https://doi.org/10.1007/978-3-030-04720-7_6

outside the mainstream have been co-opted into a neoliberal framework. As we will explore in later chapters, so-called alternatives such as peer-to-peer finance, microfinance, and green capitalism are mainly ersatz alternatives—alternatives in form but not substance.

In his theory of cultural hegemony, Gramsci articulated that popular consent is often ambiguous as a result of a conflict between people's own conception of things and that which they adopt. Even with a consensus, there remains opposition and public demonstration in defiance of corporate rule. Though rare, we can even encounter attempts to create counter-hegemonic institutions. But in the main, most find it too difficult to maintain an outlook that runs counter to dominant culture, no matter how bootless that outlook may be. Consent, for Gramsci, entails a complex mindset in which there is an ideological mixture ranging from staunch adherence to orthodox ideology to approval held with apathy to resistance held with resignation. The dominant ideology is not merely a set of beliefs reflecting interests and structures of power but is a more complex "spontaneous philosophy" that is nestled within "the entire system of beliefs, superstitions, opinions, ways of seeing things and of acting, which are collective bundled together under the name of folklore."[1] In this sense, the often repeated American shibboleths such as "rugged individualism" or "the marketplace of ideas" where everyone is "free to choose" are part of this folklore that is extrapolated from both tradition and neoliberal ideology. The elements of neoliberalism that problematize government or the blind worship of innovation have worked their way up to the status of conventional lore. These are symbols of piety that represent "the American way" and carry much weight. Perhaps the most compelling of all is the popular and ephemeral notion of equating the capitalist market system with democracy.

Gramsci's theory of cultural hegemony is consistent with the holistic view in institutional economics in which powerful institutions and ideological consensus among the population are bound together in the whole of culture. Gruchy and Dugger echoes Gramsci as they both assert that American corporate hegemony uses popular belief systems rather than military force to sustain itself. As C. Wright Mills also argued, Americans are fond of saying that they are free individuals living in a free country, though actual political and economic actions are delimited by what is conditioned for them by corporate institutions that control media, education, finance, and political choices.

In popular neoliberalism, the Janus-face of government is evident. Throughout the Greenspan Era, deregulation movements were dressed in anti-government rhetoric which resonated with the public. There exists a near total consensus that maligns as an unwanted encumbrance to American prosperity. Yet even with the popular view of government as being "the problem" most Americans expect to benefit from public institutions. The result is a general state of confused ambivalence.

A recurring theme found in popular surveys of Americans is that they are both for government involvement in economic affairs and against. One survey conducted in 2011 found that 95% of the respondents support cutting government spending, yet the vast majority oppose cutting the largest pieces of the budget pie: Social Security, Medicare, Medicaid, and the defense budget.[2] In another survey in 2008 showed that nearly half of the recipients of Social Security, Medicaid, and unemployment insurance benefits, claim to have never been a beneficiary of government social programs. At a Republican town hall meeting, South Carolina citizens met with their representative from Congress and a person stood up and demanded from the representative to "keep your government hands off my Medicare."[3] The constant push of neoliberal ideology and programs during the Greenspan Era has deepened this state of confusion. A highlight moment of this came around the turn of the new millennium as corporate and government officials were making promises of economic miracles and fortunes for everyone in what they called "the New Economy."

Hype, Irony, and the New Economy

The Berlin Wall tumbled on November 9, 1989. Cable network pundits, motivational speakers, columnists, and market analysts were shouting with jubilation that the Cold War had come to an end. It was a historical milestone that coincided with the beginning of the Greenspan Era, and the Wall Street-Washington establishment began celebrating the notion that American capitalism had emerged triumphantly in the world as the premier economic system with neoliberalism guiding belief system. A new global division of labor was to establish itself as a "New World Economic Order" in which Americans were promised to become the more affluent information workers, while the workers in the emerging markets of Asia and elsewhere would become the labor force for a globalized manufacturing sector. Robert Reich, Secretary of Labor in the Clinton Administration, told American workers they were to become better-paid, highly skilled "information" workers and manipulators of symbols (words, computer codes, and numbers) rather than assembly line workers in factories.[4] They were going to deal with ideas rather than things. Newly minted millionaires and well-paid information workers alike were all promised to be on the path to riches on America's "information superhighway."[5] And so it went with all the hyperbole and fanfare, the new order was called the New Economy and it promised miracles.

Part of the miraculousness of it all stemmed from tremendous increases in computing power and internet technology brought the world of finance much closer together and dramatically facilitated the movement of finance capital around the world. Millionaires and billionaires were popping up almost every day as entire new industries were erupting like volcanoes in the dot.com sector. New technology companies were breeding, and with each new company there were initial public offerings of stocks that offered fresh opportunities for financial market innovation and speculation.

Incidentally, 1990s were remarkably similar to conditions in 1920 leading up to the great stock market crash of 1929. The mood of euphoric optimism of the 1920s was given the dramatic name of the New Era, reflected again in the New Economy. Both eras were at the end of global conflict as the New Era came at the end of World War I in 1918, and the New Economy emerged after the end of the Cold War in 1989. Both were boom periods characterized by get-rich-quick schemes, flurries of technological innovation and growth industries, media hype, and a general feeling of capitalist triumph. The roaring twenties and the booming nineties were periods during which financial speculation became all the rage, both had massive market bubble inflation, ended in profound financial market crashes and meltdowns.

In the Greenspan Era, historical patterns and parallels were ignored and the New Economy was hyped as a veritable cornucopia of wealth creating opportunities for everyone.

It was also a political opportunity for Washington to direct countries into a global neoliberal system. American foreign policy leaders traveled the globe pressuring countries, particularly the "emerging markets" in Eastern Europe, East Asia and elsewhere to begin restructuring their economies along guidelines that conformed with neoliberalism. These policy prescriptions came through the traditional Washington D.C.-based institutions such as the International Monetary Fund, the World Bank, and the U.S. Treasury Department, and subsequently came to be known as the "Washington Consensus."

The Washington Consensus preached to the world a vision of a global system of capitalism in which financial investments could travel seamlessly from one country to another. It was important, therefore, for countries to liberalize their financial markets so that they could be part of the new system where finance capital could be allocated around the world most efficiently by following neoliberal principles. In a global free market environment, capital will automatically flow around the world to wherever it is needed the most, that is, where it is scarcest and where it pays higher returns.

Wall Street investment companies were eager to jump on high returns in the so-called emerging markets and pushed the global neoliberal agenda. Wall Street became a kind of surrogate foreign policy institution. Investment firms pressured the largely compliant government to deregulate financial markets as quickly as possible thereby making it easier for these companies to move their money in and out of these countries as they pleased. Accordingly, everyone was promised to be a potential stakeholder in the New Economy, regardless of where they were located, and they could share in the benefits of economic growth stimulated by capital investments.

Everyone in the world was promised to have the opportunity to become rich, though such promises were most popular among Americans. Neoliberalism had already been established as gospel in the United States by that time. On this, historian and author Thomas Frank provides important insights, "Aside from the technological advances of recent years… very little of the 'New Economy' is new. What the term describes is not some novel state of human affairs but the final accomplishment of the long-standing agenda of the nation's richest class."[6] Justification of extreme affluence during the Greenspan Era resonates with Carnegie's sublimation of the rich and became part of popular culture. The affluent members of the corporate class extended neoliberal ideology to the general public to influence how people view wealth. The ideology of economic individualism provided justification as it spread the belief that billionaires were self-made and those who were left of the fortune-making business simply lacked ambition. The opportunities are there, so the argument goes, all is required is a bit of initiative to take advantage of them.

Thomas Frank describes development during the Greenspan Era as the rise of "market populism." Market populism was partially a byproduct of a shift in politics in which traditionally progressive political parties were embracing corporate influence and neoliberal ideology. "From Deadheads to Nobel-laureate economists," writes Frank, "leaders in the nineties came to believe that markets were a popular system, a far more democratic form of organization than (democratically elected) governments." Frank notes that markets were being refashioned not as just mediums of exchange, but as models for democratic consent in which members from all socio-economic classes are seen equal market players. "Markets were serving all tastes, markets were humiliating the pretentious, markets were permitting good art to triumph over bad, markets were overthrowing the man, markets were extinguishing discrimination, markets were making everyone rich."[7] Market populism in America conveyed the myth that it was becoming a classless society even though it was becoming more class divided.

Multimillionaires and billionaires have been reconstructing their public images in ways that give the appearance of blurring socio-economic distinctions. Rather than staying aloof in exclusive estates far from the rabble in the world of Mills's power elite, they could be seen hanging out at popular nightclubs, doing poetry slams at Starbucks, or commuting to work on bicycles (ibid.).[8] They can be seen doing TED talks in casual attire, eating fast food, donating money for progressive or environmental causes, and working long hours at the office. The rich portray themselves as one of us and thus they earned their position with a newly energized sense of righteous indignation. The wealthy investor class morphs into the working class; the working class given the opportunity and the right portfolio, morphs into the leisure class and everyone becomes equal.

The process of fashioning capitalism into something hip and egalitarian is nothing new in the American experience. In *The Making of a Counter Culture* (1969), Theodore Roszak observed it as a kind of commercial verminization that captured youth culture in the sixties,

> [I]t is the cultural experimentation of the young that often runs the worst risk of commercial verminization—and so of having the force of its dissent dissipated. It is the cultural experiments that draw the giddy interest of just those middle-class swingers who are the bastion of the technocratic order… Visiting bohemia to peer at the 'flower children,' dropping by the rock clubs, laying out the $5.00 minimum it costs to play voyeur at Le Cimetiere des Voitures, has become the contemporary version of 'slumming for our big spenders: a breezy flirtation with the off-beat inevitably destroys the genuineness of the phenomenon.[9]

The Greenspan Era, however, stands apart as the coopting of dissenting styles and images took on a new fervor and presented itself as democratizing: that consumer trends in the marketplace are a force for popular sovereignty.

The political administrations of Bill Clinton in the US and Tony Blair in the UK exploited the culture of market populism. They worked to forge a consensus around a belief that economies of the world are best served by free markets shaken loose from government regulation. Trade and banking deregulation policies followed in a flurry, along with the global presence of institutional investors and hot money. Market speculation became all the rage. People flocked to speculation schemes on the internet. The media buzzed so profoundly about the promises of new markets and technologies at the turn of the millennium, it was sublimated as nothing short of a miracle.

At the end of the Cold War and the beginning of the Greenspan Era, the American foreign policy establishment took the ideas of economic individualism, disdain for organized labor, efficiency of free markets, and contempt for government regulation to the rest of the world as gospel. Frank observes, "the determination of American leaders to extend it to all the world the general belief among opinion-makers that there is something natural, something divine something inherently democratic about markets."[10] The widespread acceptance of the neoliberal movement in America at the turn of the twenty-first century is a salient example of Gramsci's conception of cultural hegemony. In the Marxist view, contemporary neoliberalism is the part of the superstructure extending from the economic base of corporate capitalism. Also, from the view of institutional economics, culture is never neutral. It is the same forces that cause the evolutionary drift of our economic institutions that cause changes in cultural symbols and our mindset. Both views point in the same direction to the ideology of corporate imperialism that magically aligns itself with the treasures of democracy that now can span the globe in the post-Cold War era.

Once the notion of equating markets with democracy was drilled into the American population and into the ears of anyone else who would listen, it was not difficult to forge a neoliberal consensus worldwide. Neoliberalism gained widespread and spontaneous acceptance while the corporate sphere extended is imperial dominance and cultural influence everywhere. Frank asserts that "…making the world safe for billionaires has been as much as cultural and political operation as an economic one."[11]

The free market version of liberty, equality, fraternity was popularized by bestselling books such as *The World is Flat* (2015), by journalist Thomas Friedman. Friedman was best-selling book celebrated global neoliberalism as a profound equalizing force by providing access to the structure of opportunity to raise living standards for everyone through free commerce, individual initiative, and competition. Great masses were drawn to the promises of easy money through speculation in emerging markets. It was as if an epidemic of gambling addiction spread everywhere and was sustained on a delusion that markets were not only democratic, they would remain bullish for all time—the delusion that everyone would become rich by playing the markets because financial markets will always continue to rise in value. As we see from the historical record, wherever and whenever the general population is caught up in financial market get-rich schemes, mass instability follows. This reality was brought into full view through a series of global financial crises over a few decades culminating in the epic turbulence that began in 2008.

It did not take long for a more sobering vision of reality to set in. Global neoliberalism and the imperial dominance of the corporation caused the distribution of wealth to move in the opposite direction away from flattening equality to widening polarization. The new global division of labor did create millionaires and billionaires all over the world, but it also caused much ruin and was never really a promise that extended to anyone who wasn't already wealthy anyway. Wealth and income distribution have become profoundly more unequal since then. Perhaps the most outstanding characteristics of the New Economy were dramatically widening wealth inequality and financial instability—the two most foreboding signs of apocalyptic economic ruin to come. We will explore the financial instability part of these stories in the next few chapters.

The World Is Far from Flat

Perhaps the most noticeable economic indicator of the New Economy is that it became rapidly characterized by widening inequality. The great prosperity generated from the new technology and globalization did not trickle down to the majority of American working people as promised. As would be expected under corporate hegemony, the corporate sphere was doing well as stock prices soared with massive corporate profits, and superstar CEO compensation ballooned while the wages of the average worker either fell or stayed constant with inflation. For decades the top 10% wealthiest members of society have been collecting the largest percentages of income generated in the US economy. The chart below shows that the share of the wealthy remained relatively constant for nearly four decades, then with the onset of the Greenspan Era it took a significant jump and has been on a steady climb upward since.

Concurrent with rising incomes of the top 10% is more polarized income distribution. One of the most commonly used measurements for income distribution in a country is the Gini Index or Gini Coefficient. It is a numerical index scaled between zero and one where an index of zero would signify an extreme case of "perfect equality" meaning that the incomes received by all households in the country are exactly equal. An index of one, or perfect inequality, would be the other extreme, one household receives all the income earned in the economy and everyone else receives nothing. Obviously neither extreme is possible, so the Gini stands as a fraction somewhere between zero and one.

The next chart below shows Gini numbers for the United States on a time series between 1967 and 2015. The trend line shows a steady upward march of inequality. This data set was developed by the Federal Reserve District Bank of St. Louis goes up to 2016. But it is probably safe to assume that after the changes in tax law that occurred in 2017 that overwhelmingly favors the wealthy and the corporate class, the Gini is heading upward. The United States has achieved the most unequal distribution of after-tax income compared to any other developed country.[12] This is not by accident, it is by economic policy design—neoliberalism (Fig. 6.1).

Notice that the long-term trend is basically the same upward slope of about a 2.5% increase each year, but the whole structure jumped upward at the onset of the Greenspan Era and the full implementation of neoliberal policies; that is when the income shares of the wealthy pull away from the rest of the population.

The neoliberal agenda was globalized and where it spread, it dismantled the structure of opportunity for working people to gain from economic growth. Mass layoffs accompanied the sizeable corporate mergers of that decade and downsizing and outsourcing were made more possible with a global race to the bottom in labor markets, all of which was celebrated as sound business practices that improved the corporate bottom line. Working people everywhere suddenly found that their jobs were far less secure as they were thrown into a fierce competition for a decent job with a globalized labor force. For Greenspan Era neoliberal economists, this is necessary for keeping down price inflation. Corporate industries became more concentrated and creating fantastic

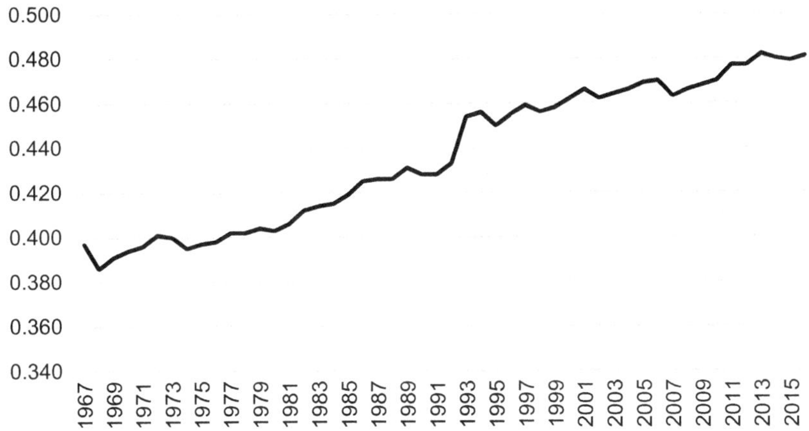

Fig. 6.1 Gini Index for the United States, 1967–2015 (*Source* Federal Reserve District Bank of St. Louis, https://fred.stlouisfed.org/graph/?graph_id=212325&updated=2000 and Luxembourg income study, https://www.lisdatacenter.org/our-data/lis-database/)

wealth for those at the top of the food chain, while the labor markets became a global game of survival of the fittest. Despite the economic models present in most textbooks, higher productivity rates measured by output/labor ratios did not lead to higher incomes for workers. Productivity soared while wages stagnated.

Wealth inequality of the nineties was becoming much more visible as the corporate class pulled away from the rest. Rising levels of wealth and income for the upper-income families provide them with access to a structure of opportunity for further gain that is inaccessible to middle and low-income classes. Wealthier families have the resources to send their children to prestigious schools and universities, assuring access to the highest paying jobs and income security. The affluent typically use their top-tier incomes to gain even more wealth as they buy income-earning property and make financial investments. The income derived from these assets can be used to acquire more assets, and so on. Wealth begets wealth in the virtuous ascent to prosperity.

Low-income families, on the other hand, have been largely shut out of the structure of opportunity, and the vast majority experience little upward class mobility. Most tend to borrow and rent, and thus are paying the rent and interest income that flows to the wealthier property owners. Low-income families find it more difficult to accumulate wealth in the form of income-earning assets as ownership remains and accumulates in the hands of the wealthiest segment of American society. Low-income families stand as the most likely to be drained of resources as they spend all their income mainly to pay their bills, have higher debt burdens, and thus are far more likely to descend into a vicious circle of poverty, foreclosures, and lack of decent health care.

In the era of Donald Trump, class distinctions are becoming more rigid, and social mobility for those at the bottom is becoming increasingly difficult, if not impossible. Under the boot of corporate hegemony, the economic system will not result in class equity because this is not a priority of such a system. The livelihoods of working people are held down as much as possible to keep the corporate class in its upward spiral of affluence. As inequality climbs higher and faster, it is just a matter of time that the Gini will top over the .50 mark. This will signify that the income distribution pattern will resemble something closer to slavery than a democratic commonwealth. The common features of all nations of the world where the Gini is .50 and over is splendid affluence standing alongside poverty in a society that fundamentally lacks democratic institutions. Nonetheless, the American population views this as the untampered natural order of things as it should be. The question begs as to why would such a lopsided, unequal be supported by a group of people who stand little or nothing to gain from it.

Living with Our Moral Discord

Over half a century ago the Nobel laureate institutional economist, Gunnar Myrdal, noted this contradiction in his *Rich Lands and Poor* (1958). Myrdal saw that in countries like the United States there exists a "moral discord" between the common adherence to egalitarian principles of governance such as the basic political rights and enfranchisement of all persons and the starkly inegalitarian conditions of real life where corporate power rules. The mythology of neoliberalism provides an easy way out of this contradiction because for many it is easier to live with moral discord than to face the deeper problem of institutional changes needed for resolution. And it is even easier still if it can be dismissed with economic theory. On this Myrdal writes, "Economic theory is only a segment of total culture. It becomes modulated to serve opportunistic rationalization needs. In order to live as comfortably as possible with the moral discord in their hearts, people [in America] need an economic theory that diverts attention from this moral discord."[13]

Cultural historian Morris Berman addresses this question in the third installment in his trilogy on America: *Why America Failed: The Roots of Imperial Decline* (2012). For Berman, the country from the beginning has never been committed to creating a democratic commonwealth and is incapable of reconciling the moral discord Myrdal observed. Evidence of this lies in the historical tendency for Americans to be more interested in building institutions aimed at financial accumulation than social provisioning. For Berman, a commonwealth is "a truly human way of life, that Americans had largely rejected from early on."[14] From the start, the vision for America was torn between that of a land destined for unrepentant acquisitiveness on the one hand, or that of a nobler commonwealth for the collective good on the other. Under the evolving corporate hegemony, acquisitiveness won out. Americans accept this discordant way of life because they envision that in the neoliberal scheme of things, even if it's mostly fictional, all can rise to be members of that very affluent class. To question this vision is to question the "American Dream" no matter how ephemeral that dream may be. On this, Berman writes,

> ...if the American Dream is really about unlimited abundance, and if we are addicted to that as a goal, then alternatives to that way of life are simple too scary to contemplate. Try telling a full-blown alcoholic to put down that glass of Scotch... addiction has a certain 'systemic' pattern to it that is typically not self-corrective. Both capitalism and alcoholism are characterized by cycles of increasing dysfunction, 'runaway,' and breakdown, and the system can do this for a fairly long time.[15]

Berman is looking in retrospect at what Veblen was seeing for the future a century ago. The image is essentially the same—the interests of the *Interests* are dominant, including what constitutes the most cherished American values. The US post-colonial history began simultaneously with the rise of the corporation. The history of the corporation is inextricably tied to the history of the corporation. Corporate-dominated cultural hegemony has woven itself into folklore or popular beliefs such that markets are seen as freedom, corporations are entrepreneurs, and all forms of innovation, including financial innovation, should not be questioned. These beliefs are deeply attached to the collective brain stem, which leads to strict acceptance of anything that resonates with the American Dream, even if they are destructive, nondemocratic, or blatantly false. The institutions of corporate capitalism in America are seen as a natural, normative aspect of life. Suggestions that this system is fostering inequality, instability, environmental damage, or anything but growing prosperity are met with suspicion even when the evidence is overwhelming. In other words, an important dimension to this particular brand of cultural hegemony is the phenomenon of cognitive dissonance.

Cognitive Dissonance, Delusion, and Apocalypse

Along with rising inequality, financial market instability, and environmental damage, cognitive dissonance is another pathological system condition associated with corporate cultural hegemony. When it affects a wide segment of the population, it becomes a general condition of mentally whitewashing Myrdal's state of moral discord. It is a general state of anxiety in which people are unable to reconcile deep schisms in their beliefs about the social and physical reality around them. To alleviate anxiety, the population distances itself from reality and retreats into a state of denial.

Leon Festinger, one of the most influential figures in modern social psychology is renowned for his trailblazing work on cognitive dissonance theory. He was inspired after reading a story about a series of rumors that began to spread in India after a mild earthquake.

Among the people who experienced the earthquake rumors began to circulate that this was just the beginning of more apocalyptic earthquakes and other disasters on the way. The rumors turned into beliefs, and when the disaster did not arrive, a schism opened between the beliefs and actual experiences. This inconsistency, or dissonance, between belief and experience caused widespread anxiety. In order to reduce their anxiety, people hold more firmly to their beliefs and reject experience or information that would present a contradiction no matter how fanciful or bizarre the belief.[16]

A common example of cognitive dissonance is a smoker who decides to hold on to a belief that there are certain health benefits from smoking and rejects information that would suggest otherwise, including conclusive health research data. Festinger points out that if an individual believes something wholeheartedly then it is presented with "unequivocal and undeniable evidence that his belief is wrong: what will happen? The individual will frequently emerge, not only unshaken, but even more convinced of the truth of his beliefs than ever before."[17]

As we have argued, standard economic theory assumes consumers to be rational choice-makers in the open market, but such a concept of rationality gets fuzzy in social and economic life. This assumption, too, is an example of cognitive dissonance. Mainstream economists believe with their whole hearts that we are all rational and respond to objective reality, yet the evidence of greed-inspired irrationality in financial market speculation is obvious evidence of widespread irrationality. Economists cling to the Efficient Market Hypothesis even though such a condition of efficiency is statistically impossible. Nonetheless, economists cling to these assumptions and hypothesis even more tightly when presented with contrary evidence.

Understanding cognitive dissonance as a widespread phenomenon helps our understanding of how so many of us choose to hold on such beliefs as financial markets are riding an elevator of prosperity that always goes up even though there is a mass of evidence that indicates otherwise. That physical limits to economic growth do not exist even though the basic realities of the finiteness of our planet and anthropogenic climate change are unequivocal. We hold onto to these beliefs because our corporate system needs us to. It is perfectly natural for us to expect continuously compounding financial returns without giving it a second thought. Even if the markets crash, which they do on occasion, the general assumption is that they will bounce back and continue appreciating. The mantra on Wall Street is that markets always bounce back. If we look at the last two hundred years of stock market history, that certainly seems to be the case—a long-term trend showing a 7% rate of return after factoring out price inflation. It is no surprise, then, that people see this as a normal aspect of our economy.

Cultural norms, however, are not always grounded in reality. Is it truly valid to expect that just because the market value of Wall Street securities has always grown in the past, they will continue to do so in the future? The growth of our bodies is something that happens in our adolescent phase of life and stops at maturity. We have natural limits to growth and it would be madness to argue that since a person has grown zero to six-feet-tall in their first twenty years, they can be expected to twelve feet in the next twenty years, and to eighteen in the next twenty, and so on. In fact, continuing growth after maturity is pathological: obesity or cancerous tumors. All forms of growth are bounded by limitations, yet in our culture we tend to believe otherwise when it comes to economics.

We believe in this because the endless accumulation of money is a very alluring idea and also we have become dependent on it. People pour trillions into pension funds, hedge funds, mutual funds, etc., because of the promise that these investments are going to continuously appreciate in value and will provide for us in our retirement or pay for our children's education. Because the Fed's zero-bound rate policy rendered savings on bond funds are essentially useless, institutional investors had to explore riskier funds in equity and derivative speculation. When these funds began racking up double-digit returns, dreams of becoming millionaires spread, everyone wanted more. Institutional investors including pension funds with defined benefits sought higher and higher returns wherever they could find them. Bond returns were too low, and the allure of risky ventures became irresistible. A kind of institutionalized gambling addiction was created. Parents used to say to their children that money doesn't grow on trees implying that you have to work for it. That has changed and money now is always expected to grow at an extraordinarily fast rate in investment funds stretching out into an infinite horizon of financial wealth.

By the same logic and cultural norms, businesses expect their earnings to grow and working people expect their paychecks to grow. For all this growth in money and financial wealth to be appreciable or meaningful to people, the amount of stuff you can buy with the money must also grow—real economic growth. After all, what good is it to become a millionaire if you can't buy a million dollars' worth of stuff with the money?

This expectation is a major force for economic expansion. If the money side of the economy is expected to keep ballooning out, it follows that businesses are pushed to generate new sales and create new markets. If they succeed, then the businesses are rewarded with higher stock prices and management with hefty bonuses. The profits businesses make from their new sales provide financing for new capital, which will drive production and sales even higher. For that, though, they need to find more consumers with voracious appetites. In time, this forms into a perfect circle or positive feedback loop. We expect and demand that our financial wealth continue to accumulate, this financial growth is derived from expanding business profits, business profits are derived from expanding sales, and expanding sales are predicated on the creation of a consumer culture that idolizes the accumulation of financial wealth.

Most of us will find it nearly impossible to let go of these deeply held beliefs. Even when the physical world is reeling from climate change, the defensive response is to deny the evidence. When the evidence becomes irrefutable, we are compelled to find logical loopholes or that the science is biased. Widespread cognitive dissonance obliges us to cling even harder to the belief that unencumbered financial markets will always accrue and our wealth will always compound are the true one and only destiny. To suggest otherwise is tantamount to inviting an angry mob with torches outside your window.

In the aftermath of the banking crisis of 2007–2009 crisis, the most widely accepted argument for its occurrence was the "opaqueness" of the derivative markets. The mortgage-backed securities particularly were seen as that were created such that market trades and investors could not see clearly their inherent risk factors, nor could they assess their market values. Trouble bloomed out like the spread of an unseen pathogen, but this eventually became comforting because it suggested that the problems were caused by a glitch. There were a few villains who could be propped up in the media as the ones who caused the mess. A few heads had to roll to appease the population. The general public found relief in the promise that the glitch was fixed, there is nothing wrong with the system, securities have been exposed to the healing power of sunlight, and the markets will resume their eternal upward climb. In this process, the crisis actually reinforced the neoliberal tenets of market efficiency. After a brief respite, popular neoliberalism was restored and has become more entrenched than before. By the 2016 election cycle, voters overwhelming put into office politicians who had campaigned on a neoliberal platform promising less government regulation, less taxes for the wealthy, huge tax cuts for corporations, and less government-sponsored health care programs. In this almost surreal environment, Donald J. Trump became president.

The nearly two-century evolution of corporate hegemony is now complete. From its infancy in the nineteenth century to a powerful alliance twenty-first century, it is now a complete hegemonic structure surrounded by a protective bubble wrap of neoliberal ideology, market populism, and cognitive dissonance. The pathological system conditions that are embedded in this hegemony are accordingly fixed. There is no turning back from this and there is no fix. All the basic elements that gave rise to the crises of the Greenspan Era are intact and are destined to be replayed with the same dose of rationalizations and the same solemn pronouncements about the need for bailouts. It is to these elements and the apocalyptic conditions they create that we now turn our focus.

Notes

1. T.J. Jackson Lears, "The Concept of Cultural Hegemony: Problems and Possibilities," *The American Historical Review*, Vol. 90, No. 3, June 1985, p. 570.
2. Joint Committee on Taxation, Estimates of Federal Tax Expenditures for Fiscal Years 2010–2014, JCS-3-10, Table 1, pp. 39, 49. https://www.jct.gov/publications.html?func=startdown&id=3718.

3. Quoted in Philip Rucker, "Sen. DeMint of South Carolina Is Voice of Opposition to Health-Care Reform," *The Washington Post*, July 28, 2009.
4. Richard Barnet and John Cavanagh, *Global Dreams: Imperial Corporations and the New World Order* (New York, NY: Touchstone, 1994), pp. 280–281.
5. The phrase "information superhighway" was first used by then Vice President Al Gore in speech sponsored by the Benton Foundation on March 29, 1994.
6. Thomas Frank, *One Market Under God: Extreme Capitalism, Market Populism, and the End of Economic Democracy* (New York, NY: Doubleday, 2000), p. 15.
7. Thomas Frank, "The Rise of Market Populism," *The Nation*, October 30, 2000.
8. Thomas Frank, *One Market Under God*, p. 10.
9. Theodore Roszak, *The Making of a Counter Culture* (New York, NY: Anchor Books, 1969), p. 70.
10. Frank, *One Market Under God*, p. 15.
11. Ibid.
12. By net income we mean after taxes and transfer redistribution. See http://www.pewresearch.org/fact-tank/2013/12/19/global-inequality-how-the-u-s-compares/.
13. Gunnar Myrdal, *Rich Lands and Poor: The Road to World Prosperity* (New York, NY: Harper, 1958), p. 172.
14. Morris Berman, *Why America Failed: The Roots of Imperial Decline* (New York, NY: Wiley, 2012), p. 24.
15. Ibid., p. 66.
16. Leon Festinger, *A Theory of Cognitive Dissonance* (Palo Alto, CA: Stanford University Press, 1957), pp. 236–239.
17. Leon Festinger, Henry Riecken, and Stanley Schachter, *When Prophecy Fails* [1956] (London: Pinter Martin, 2008), p. 3.

References

Barnet, Richard, and John Cavanagh. *Global Dreams: Imperial Corporations and the New World Order* (New York, NY: Touchstone, 1994).

Berman, Morris. *Why America Failed: The Roots of Imperial Decline* (New York, NY: Wiley, 2012).

Festinger, Leon. *A Theory of Cognitive Dissonance* (Palo Alto, CA: Stanford University Press, 1957).
Frank, Thomas. *One Market Under God: Extreme Capitalism, Market Populism, and the End of Economic Democracy* (New York, NY: Doubleday, 2000), p. 15.
Frank, Thomas. "The Rise of Market Populism," *The Nation*, October 30, 2000.
Joint Committee on Taxation. "Estimates of Federal Tax Expenditures for Fiscal Years 2010–2014," 2010. https://www.jct.gov/publications.html?func=startdown&id=3718.
Lears, T.J. Jackson. "The Concept of Cultural Hegemony: Problems and Possibilities," *The American Historical Review*, Vol. 90, No. 3, June 1985, p. 591.
Mettler, Suzanne. "Reconstituting the Submerged State: The Challenge of Social Policy Reform in the Obama Era," *Perspectives on Politics*, Vol. 8, September 2010, pp. 803–824.
Myrdal, Gunnar. *Rich Lands and Poor: The Road to World Prosperity* (New York, NY: Harper, 1958).
Pew Research Center. "Global Inequality: How the U.S. Compares," 2013. http://www.pewresearch.org/fact-tank/2013/12/19/global-inequality-how-the-u-s-compares/.
Roszak, Theodore. *The Making of a Counter Culture* (New York, NY: Anchor Books, 1969).
Rucker, Philip. "Sen. DeMint of South Carolina Is Voice of Opposition to Health-Care Reform," *The Washington Post*, July 28, 2009.

7

The Crises of the Eighties and the Ascent of the Greenspan Era

Morris Berman tells us that creating a stable commonwealth that prioritizes social provisioning was never a priority in the plan for America. As we continue to drift through the Greenspan Era into the Trump Era and beyond, the hope for making that a priority or achieving some measure of sustainability have all but faded to oblivion. The policies of the Trump administration—a seemingly random mixture of neoliberalism, nationalism, and cronyism—mostly served the interests of the corporate class with tax cuts and rollbacks on environmental regulations. What Dugger refers to as the social irresponsibility of corporate hegemony intensifies with widening wealth inequality, more fuel adding to climate change, and worsening conditions for instability. As our economic systems continue along the evolutionary drift toward more concentrated power and wealth, corporate hegemony has evolved into a raging behemoth bringing social, financial, and environmental damage everywhere. The damage is permanent, irreparable, and growing in severity.

What will eventually follow will likely be an era of reckoning in which we will be forced to look in retrospect how we squandered every opportunity to change course. Our reckoning will also include an assessment of how as a society we took our institutions of money and

J. Magnuson, *Financing the Apocalypse*,
Palgrave Insights into Apocalypse Economics,
https://doi.org/10.1007/978-3-030-04720-7_7

finance for granted. Blinded by the false promises of neoliberalism, we have all but completely lost sight of just how important our financial institutions really are for provisioning and wellbeing. Instead we have allowed them to drift away from their original mission to support economic development and become supercharged gambling casinos.

Author and one of the founders of the Occupy Money movement, Magrit Kennedy, emphasizes the importance of money and finance as "humanity's most important invention."[1] In the corporate hegemony, money is merely an object for greed-inspired accumulation where its importance is only found on financial statement bottom lines. As an invention instruments of finance can be used as forms of social technology with the potential for serving human wellbeing by facilitating trade, aggregating capital for development, securing resources for retirement and education, and so on. As with all technology, the extent to which any instruments of finance will be in this way depends on institutional context.

Metalsmithing, for example, is technology that can be used produce cooking utensils or weapons and the degree to which it is used for one other the other depends on the prevailing institutions. Digital technology can be used for education, state surveillance systems, or pornography depending on institutional context. The same is true with instruments of finance. It can be used to fund development projects that help people better their lives or used for speculation depending on the mission of our financial institutions. Thus from this institutional perspective, we see money and what it does or does not do in society not as a piece of paper or artifact, but as an institutional construct.

The physical form of money is continually evolving. It's importance, however, is not derived from what it looks or feels like—paper, galvanized metal, electronic transfers, or blockchain ledgers—money matters as a social convention. The most important function of financial institutions everywhere is to set the rules and practices that allow money, whatever physical form it takes, to be accepted among the economic population as a medium of exchange. That is its power. Without a medium of exchange, there would be no markets, without markets, there would be no basis for transactions. There would be no commerce or trade and there would be no division of labor. People would not be able to buy anything of the things they need for living and businesses would not be able to buy resources they need for production of those things. The cycles of production and consumption would be broken.

Without money, exchange would be limited to direct good-for-good or good-for-service barter, and this could only be done at a very rudimentary level. A half dozen eggs exchanging for a loaf of bread, or maybe a coffee table for a car repair. Even if this were possible at the scale of current activity, which is unlikely, barter is still problematic. If someone wanted to exchange eggs for something else, how would they get the chicken feed needed to produce eggs? How could someone bake bread without buying flour, pans, ovens, and electricity? How would someone get the parts needed to repair a car? The point here is that without money economies could not function, economic activity would grind down, and eventually the majority of the population would fall into poverty. In time, most of us would starve. We know this because this is the result from the many instances in the historical record of what happens to societies when their monetary institutions break down.

In our age of reckoning we will also look back and see how important banking and credit was for social provisioning. In a well-developed financial system, money necessarily flows from one place to the next as people use it. Financial and depository institutions collect, store and amass money so that it may be available in concentrated amounts for investment. While money facilitates exchange, banks facilitate capital formation to be used for advancing production, to build housing and infrastructure, keep farms alive, or finance schools. Without financial instruments and institutions our ability to provide for the wellbeing of our population would be knocked back to the stone age.

When we look at this from an institutional perspective, these social provisioning aspects of our financial system are taken for granted and deprioritized under corporate hegemony. Rather than being treated as a means to support these ends, the process of aggregating wealth into concentrated pockets for the affluent members of the corporate class has become an end in itself. In Veblenian terms, money and what people can buy with it are nothing more than pecuniary trophies that signify the economic conquests. As such, they are trophies that signify a social status that is coveted by the mass population. It is with this understanding of our financial system as dichotomized between a system necessary for wellbeing and a system used for conspicuous self-aggrandizement that we will have our reckoning; for the wellbeing functions are being drowned out.

If there is a post-apocalyptic era following our era of reckoning, populations everywhere would have to return to the question of how to craft instruments and institutions of finance. They would have to return to the questions of how we use these things and with what priorities. To provide capital for healthy economic development, or to provide leverage for corporate mergers, wars of aggression, obsessive-compulsive consumerism, and market speculation? Capital markets were created to capitalize business and support economic development. The original idea was to open exchange so that shares could be sold to a wide segment of the investor population. This was a very expedient way to aggregate large amounts of finance capital so that the company could do something big like build railroads, auto manufacturing plants, or steel mills. The success or failure of the enterprise would be measured in terms of the returns the shareholders would receive on their investments. The financial standing of the company would be audited by weighing these returns against debts, and this would determine the fundamental value of the shares. But even though we can see this as the original purpose of capital markets, what takes place in them there has very little to do with capitalization and development and much more about serving corporate interests and creating casino-like speculation.

It is in the context of this question that we focus on corporate hegemony as it is made of institutions that are financial at their core—comprised of securities and commodities trading—and are largely indifferent to social provisioning. It is in the context of the institutionalist perspective on corporate hegemony that we also take a fresh look at the troubling phenomenon of *financialization* and the role it plays in recurring cycles of financial system instability.

Financialization Revisited

Since the Banking Crisis of '07–'09, there has been much discussion in heterodox circles about the economic phenomenon of financialization, though ignored in the mainstream like so many other important issues.

Financialization is a process in which financial institutions and markets systematically gain influence and control over increasingly large segments of the economy. The process has roots that go back to the beginning of capitalism, but has risen to a very high profile in the last few decades with the ascent of corporate hegemony, implementation of neoliberal policies, and the development of a global digital technological-financial infrastructure.

As has been a central theme running through this book, the corporation is a specific institution that is as much a financial entity as it is a legal one. Its very existence is predicated on its ability to raise financing through securities trades and its ability to sustain the value of these securities as they are traded in markets. As the corporate sector evolved into a dominant global economic force, the financial sector that underwrites, innovates, and trades its securities also raises in profile. With the push of neoliberalism, web technology, and the cult of innovation, an endless array of different types of securities and markets for trading these securities have stretched around the globe. Looming large at the center of this global system is Wall Street. In this process, finance has shifted from being a support network within the capitalist commodity producing system, to a new version of capitalism that is controlled by Wall Street companies and eventually rise to bypassing production.

Recall that a tenet of neoliberalism is that society must never question innovation. This tenet particularly applies to Wall Street's obsession with financial innovation and technology. Electronic securities trading systems have been around for decades. Among the largest is Nasdaq, which has been trading stocks in various types of electronic exchanges since 1971. Such systems, however, were limited until the 1990s with the full expansion of web-based technology, desktop computing power, and the rise of neoliberalism. Once internet infrastructure was globally set into place and computer terminals everywhere were armed with state-of-the-art software, securities price quotations and deal-making were revolutionized. Wall Street melded with Silicon Valley to create a global geography of lightning-fast systems of buying and selling.

Traditional methods of brokering and trading using telephones and handshakes were rendered obsolete within a historical blink of an eye. But what stands the test of historical time is a certain immutable truth:

wherever there are securities trades, there is speculation; and where there is speculation, there is financial instability.

Part of why this is happening stems from a deeper crisis that can be traced directly to the heart of capitalism and the problem of systemic stagnation. Underneath all the glitter and technological razzmatazz of contemporary finance is a looming problem of fundamentals. There are basically two ways one can assess the value of stocks and other publicly traded instruments: by looking at "technical" or "fundamentals." The technicals approach to valuation has to do with looking at a security in a broader trend where it value might be connected to a bunch of other things going on around it. These things could be changes in market conditions, government policies, or broader trends that affect a whole class of instruments. The fundamentals approach has to do with looking at the underlying profits, sales projections, debts that are reflected the corporations' balance sheets. The problem with stagnation in modern corporate capitalism lies in the fundamentals. It is a problem in which companies in significant numbers are finding that they just cannot generate profits through actual producing things for sale in markets.

The Great Depression of the 1930s unveiled this problem in a major way. It showed the world that capitalism, left tow its own devices, would inevitably grind down into a condition of saturation and stagnation, which is a death sentence for capitalist enterprise. Built into the core logic of capitalism is the need to generate returns for investors and to plow back a portion of those returns to fuel expansion. The imperative to generate returns every quarter of every year into perpetuity means that companies must continuously find or fabricate new markets and new places to channel plowed-back profits. Eventually this expansion hits a wall. Business sales slows down in one industry after another, and everything stops moving like a river that has gone dry. Authors John Bellamy Foster and Robert McChesney describe this process as capitalism's long-run tendency toward an "endless crisis." The only way out of which is to receive injections of "external stimuli" to keep it going.[2] Part of this stimuli comes from governments stepping in with its powers of borrowing and spending to inject transfusions into production and consumption cycles. Other stimuli can come from new technological innovation that can be worked into new products or from countries that open themselves to world trade—the so-called emerging markets—or mounting consumer debt. Whatever the case, these stimuli create new markets and new vehicles that constitute a new field within which capitalism can grow. As corporations expand into these fields of external stimuli, stagnation was put off for another day.

The financial system provides crucial services in this process. Stagnation is the default downward trend and external stimuli gives the system a bounce up from the trend. The economy is continuously churning through cycles of stagnation-induced recessions and stimulus-induced growth and this requires corporations to have certain flexibility or malleability. But eventually those sources of stimuli start to become exhausted. The hunt for profitable opportunities becomes more desperate. Companies have to jump into profitable opportunities as quickly as possible and jump out just as quickly when profits disappear. This requires a facile investment system in which capital is liquid (in the form of cash) in one moment where money can easily and swiftly move anywhere, solidify into real capital where is settles, then in another moment turn back into to cash. The more rapidly this take place, the more pressure there is on the financial system to mobilize liquidity and to underwrite the instruments—stock, bonds, commodities, derivatives—that get traded for liquidity. Financial services are indeed becoming an increasingly significant sector. In the mid-twentieth century, financial services constituted about 2.5% of national output, then it grew to about 4% in 1980, then soared to 8.3% by 2006 right before the banking crisis began.[3]

Under corporate hegemony and Wall Street's cult of innovation, everything suddenly becomes fair game for securitization—transformed into a security or derivative. And thanks to neoliberal market deregulation, new exchanges for these instruments sprout up everywhere. The world becomes a playground for speculative trades—buy low, sell high; get in get out—and instability inevitably follows.

Another key part of financialization is the expansion of credit and debt. Stagnation can be kept at arms length by constantly tossing out new things to be sold in new markets, but this can function as long as buyers have purchasing power. If they don't, it becomes a necessity to make cheap and abundant credit available for debt-driven purchasing.

Among the most outstanding characteristics of the Greenspan Era is cheap credit and soaring debt. Household debt was 56% of national output in 1987, then it steadily rose to reach 63% in 2000, and then soared to 98% by the first quarter of 2008 on the eve of the banking crisis.[4]

Public debt as a percentage of GDP has mostly increased during the Greenspan Era. It was 48% in 1987, hit a 65% peak in 1995 and gradually tapered off. When the George W. Bush tax cuts for the wealthy were put into effect in 2001, public debt resumed its upward climb and then soared during the Great Recession and continued to climb after the recession was over to hit 105% of GDP by 2016. As mentioned in an earlier chapter, the Trump tax cuts pushed deficits and debts to new highs (Fig. 7.1).

As the corporation seeks to create or conquer markets wherever it can, it has the effect of transforming everything in its path to a commodity or security. It is part of its institutional DNA. As Veblen witnessed a century ago, the corporation is an institution that is disconnected from actual creative or productive work. It is only concerned with buying and selling commodities and securities so as to generate returns for the *Interests*. If the corporation were a kind of institution that was of minor importance in the scheme of things, then its impact on the economy would also be minor. But it is huge and dominant.

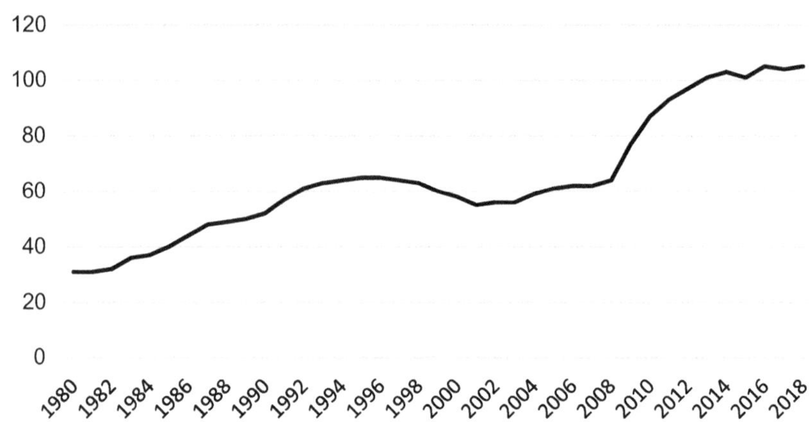

Fig. 7.1 Federal debt as a percentage of GDP, 1980–2018 (*Source* Federal Reserve Bank St. Louis, https://fred.stlouisfed.org/data/GFDEGDQ188S.txt)

The institutional and technological developments during the Greenspan Era had a profound effect on the global economy. It ushered in a period characterized by not only financialization and soaring debt, but also the global expansion of corporate enterprise, an explosion of digital trading technology, implementation of neoliberal policies, the spread of market populism, and mountains of cheap credit made available by the Federal Reserve. The result was a heightened profile of financial market speculation as it was justified with "greed-is-good" ideology, made easier for everyone with technology, and facilitated with low-interest credit. If corporations could feel emotions like real human beings, they would be thrilled.

If thrill is what everyone is after, then our financial system has been on a veritable roller coaster ride for decades. Speculation in the stock market, measured in trading volume as a percentage of global economic output, has fluctuated dramatically during the Greenspan Era. The world is becoming financially unstable. Stock market trading volume in the early to mid-eighties was hovering around 20% of global output. It went through a period of turbulence in the late eighties, but then soared to astronomical heights in the nineties. Stock trading volume went from about 22% of global output in 1992 to 146% in 2000, fell to 76% by 2003, ascended to 162% in 2007, fell to 83% in 2012, soared again 163% in 2015, then dropped to 118% in 2018. As we will see in the pages and chapters that follow, these are market bubbles that inflate and pop in predictable, recurring patterns, and are becoming increasingly large in magnitude (Fig. 7.2).

Three major conclusions we can draw from this data are that (1) corporate-driven financialization and technology are spreading speculation, (2) households and governments are becoming buried in debt, and (3) the world is becoming more economically unstable.

Speculation and Instability

While leveling his attack on the neoliberal Efficient Market Hypothesis, analyst George Cooper provided consolation that there is a more plausible theory about the workings of financial markets. "Fortunately, there

Fig. 7.2 Stocks traded in total value as a percentage of global GDP (*Source* The World Bank: World Federation of Exchanges database. https://data.worldbank.org/indicator/CM.MKT.TRAD.GD.ZS?view=chart)

is an alternative theory of how financial markets operate… one that can explain the erratic behavior of financial markets."[5] Cooper is referring to the Financial Instability Hypothesis originally developed by economist Hyman Minsky[6] and further elaborated by economic historian Charles Kindleberger.[7] The model summarized here provides an important link between financialization and systemic instability.[8]

Looking at financial market booms and busts throughout the history of capitalism, Kindleberger and others identified a distinct pattern that is replicated with almost perfect statistical certainty. At the core of this pattern and all the cycles of market booms and busts is speculation. Though the term is often used synonymously with investment in the financial press, they are not the same. The distinction is important. In economics, investment is capitalizing production with the proper plant, equipment, resource, and technology needed to get the work done. Speculation is just buying and selling things, usually financial instruments or real estate, with the expectation of yielding financial gains. With speculation there is no real capital or production, in fact speculators do not even need to know, see, or care about what the instrument represents. The only important thing for a speculator is to buy in, cash out, and pocket an easy profit. Real investment can serve the broader project of social provisioning whereas speculation serves extracting money with an indifference toward social provisioning.

Speculation, capitalism, corporations, and instability are institutionally and historically locked together. As capitalism evolved over several centuries, the institutions of the corporation and market system evolved with it in lock step. Wherever there emerged corporations there emerged financial markets; and there were financial markets there were speculative manias that reappeared over time in a remarkable consistent pattern. Kindleberger breaks the pattern down in an observable sequence that always begins when a new opportunity for speculation presents itself.

The pattern begins with a financial instrument—a security, commodity, or derivative—which is relatively liquid and captures the interest of speculators who begin to buy on the anticipation they can easily resell a yield a profit. Speculative manias general occur in highly liquid markets in which players can convert cash to an instrument and back to cash quickly. The exception is real estate, which is subject to huge speculative trading, but is not particularly liquid. Whatever the case, if the object of speculation is sufficiently pervasive it will attract the attention of a larger population of speculators and will begin to magnet cash away from other instruments. Minsky called this "displacement" as cash begins to move from one instrument to another.[9] As more people or institutional investor buy the instrument, the price will start to rise.

This process can become supercharged with bank credit and leveraged trading. Once the displacement occurs and attracts interest, it is not unusual for speculators to leverage their purchases of these instruments with borrowed money. If money is cheap to borrow, it makes it easier for speculators to borrow in one place and make speculative bets in another, even if the bets are based on a modest percentage gain. The price of the instrument gets pushed even higher at it is being chased with borrowed money. Eventually a speculative boom be underway, and it will cause prices to inflate into bubbles, which means they rise far above any reasonable value.

Market bubbles always burst and rapidly deflate. As we can see from the chart on the previous page, stock market speculators jump in and out of the market with a certain regularity. Speculator interest turns to revulsion, buy commands turn to sell commands, and prices fall. The collective impulse that once drove the price sky high reverses and drives the price to rock bottom. In the digital universe, this can happen almost instantaneously. At that point, the cloud of speculator cash lifts off of the instrument and drifts elsewhere in search of another instrument; another displacement. The process starts over again in another location.

This basic pattern has a history of repetition stretching back about four hundred years. In the early-seventeenth century Amsterdam there was a commodity market boom and bust in which people went collectively insane over tulip bulbs. The pattern was repeated again in markets for government bonds, corporate stocks, gold and silver, dot.com companies, currencies, mortgage derivatives, and cryptocurrencies, just to name a few examples. Depending on the instrument, the size of the bubble, and the amount of leverage was used to inflate it, bursting bubbles always come with the potential to precipitate a financial crisis.

Under the current regime of corporate hegemony, this process is not only repeated, it is encouraged and normalized. Speculation has become big business and with market populism everyone is invited to play. Pension funds, foundations, money managers, and institutional investors of all kinds are pulled into the game of speculation in the hopes of securing high returns and fund growth for their clients. Stock, bond, commodities, and currency market conditions are quoted ceaselessly in news reports, though rarely if ever is the intention of speculation is ever mentioned. It is as if it has become accepted yet remains a taboo subject or secret. In the mass psychology of market populism and cognitive dissonance, continuously rising asset prices is upheld as the normal state of things, and when prices fall, it is a shocking abnormality like an unexpected storm. Frederich Nietzsche reflects on how such collective pathology can be appear to be normal if enough are drawn in, "Madness is something rare in individuals but in groups, parties, peoples, ages, it is the rule."[10]

With time and much neoliberal conditioning, the collective American mind has been nestled into a comforting hallucination that financial markets will always appreciate and that exist purely for us to pick easy money like fruit from a tree; that is, as long as enough people feel that they have a chance to get a share. But when the promise of gains turns to ruin, the population feels robbed of an entitlement. The strangeness of these expectations is buried from sight and kept quiet as if it is not supposed to be a function our financial system. The Federal Reserve during the Greenspan Era celebrated debt driven stock market inflation, housing market inflation, and assisted the process by pretending that systemic bubbles cannot exist, yet kept interest rates very low to make sure they did. And the Fed could always be relied upon to express shock when bursting bubbles led to financial turmoil.

Innovation, Crises, "Surprise," and Bailouts

As the neoliberal movement unfolded over the last few decades, a new discernable pattern emerged. Deregulation unleashed recklessness, which led to a crisis followed public expression of "shock" and "surprise," and then earnest pronouncements about how bailouts will be forthcoming to contain the problem. The pattern usually begins when major corporations pressure government to deregulate their industries with the claims that regulations were antiquated and at odds with the new realities of the global economy. Once the government conceded and ignored the reasons for regulation in the first place, it was expected that the companies could become more flexible, competitive, and able to self-regulate in the open market. But instead they became reckless and ran roughshod over their industries. The period of recklessness invariably concluded with troubled conditions and threats of mass bankruptcies. Although part of process was the implicit (ultimately proven correct) understanding that if things go wrong for corporations, government and central bank institutions are there to assist them out of their troubles. Government officials would express an appropriate amount of "shock" while appealing to taxpayers for bailouts. Such is the "moral hazard" of allowing businesses to run amok, not be held accountable for their recklessness and given bailout money, which encourages more recklessness.

Among the first examples of this was late seventies and eighties. The Carter administration began deregulating specific industries on a case by case basis such as trucking and airlines. But it was with the Reagan administration that neoliberalism became a wholesale crusade. The president famously announced that "government is not the solution to our problem; government is the problem."[11] For corporations, Reagan's proclamation was a godsend and put in motion the movement to dismantle a bundle of rules that constrained the activities of banks and other financial institutions. His first treasury secretary was Donald Regan, formerly Merrill Lynch CEO, was eager to get the movement to deregulate the financial system underway, "as quickly as possible in the field of interest rates, mandatory ceilings, things of that nature."[12] And their first target was the Savings and Loans mortgage lending business.

The Savings and Loans Debacle

American Savings and Loans banks (S & Ls) were originally chartered to exclusively provide mortgages and promote home ownership, particularly in the post-war decades of the fifties and sixties. The S & Ls deposits were insured by the federal government and the government imposed restrictions that these banks could only lend for home mortgages and imposed rate ceilings on what the S & Ls could pay depositors. The decade of the seventies was plagued by rapid price inflation. As always during periods of inflation interest rates on the whole spectrum of credit were in an effort to slow it down. Because their savings rates were capped, S & L depositors began to pull their money out and putting their money higher-yielding bonds in the newly created short-term money markets. Money market funds are mutual funds that pool money from investors and put it short-term government and corporate bonds. S & Ls started running out of deposit money and turned to their powerful lobbying organization—the United States League of Savings Institutions—to pressure the federal government into changing the rules. S & Ls were typically small and numerous, so their presence was felt everywhere. This gave their lobby a great deal of clout with the government as commented by of their bankers, "When it came to [S &

Ls] matters in Congress, the US League and many of its affiliates were the de facto government."[13] The plan was to deregulate the interest rate cap, which would allow them to raise rates in tandem with price inflation as did the rest of the banking industry.[14]

It all made sense and in 1980 the federal government passed the Depository Institutions Deregulation and Monetary Control Act, which was followed two years later with the Garn-St. Germain Depository Institutions Act. Unrestrained by deregulation, S & L banks embarked on wild program of lending for high-risk ventures. Journalist and author Frederick Sheehan writes, "S & Ls were an attractive platform for a businessman with a certain turn of mind. Deregulation of the industry permitted a panorama of investment classes that had previously been forbidden."[15] Another provision in Garn-St. Germain was that it allowed S & Ls to merge across state lines. This set off the first of a series of merger waves that permanently transformed the landscape of banking in the United States.

The newly deregulated and larger banks proceeded to entice people to bring their deposits into the bank and open checkable money market accounts that paid competitive interest rates. Depositors' money poured into the banks and the banks poured it back out again into a greed-inspired festival of lending for land speculation, shopping mall development, and questionable real estate schemes. The S & Ls were borrowing from depositors at high rates, but also charging even higher rates on the loans, some of which were collateralized by rising land prices. According to author, Martin Mayer, the S & L bankers "could raise endless money and take it to whatever gambling table was most convenient. If they won, the kept it… if they lost, the government would pay." The reason being is that the deposits, like any other bank's deposits, were federally insured.[16]

The global recession of 1981–1982 started unraveling the whole arrangement as it caused, among other things, land prices to fall. The borrowers who were speculating in land deals and using S & L loans as leverage began defaulting on their loans. To make matters worse, the bankers were investing heavily in junk bonds sold largely by the infamous Drexel Burnam Lambert's bond brokers under the guidance of convicted felons Ivan Boesky and Michael Milken. Milken mischievously manipulated bond markets by trading back and forth within his own company to make it look like the bonds were hotly traded instruments.[17] Milken and his gang finally were caught, and by 1987, their fake bond market fell apart about the same time as the stock market. The industry, of course, fell into ruin. The speculative deals made by the S & Ls were based on the delusion that phony bond markets and dubious land speculation ventures were somehow an appropriate use of federally insured deposits.

By 1988, about one-third of all S & Ls that were operating in the United States failed.[18] Political leaders in Washington were, once again, expressing shock and made grave resolutions to bailout the banks. The bailout plan came the following year when the federal government passed The Financial Institutions Reform, Recovery, and Enforcement Act of 1989.[19] The bill created the Resolution Trust Corporation, which in the industry is referred to as a "bad bank." A bad bank is a government institution that uses taxpayers' dollars to buy the junk or nonperforming assets from private sector banks. By doing so, the government cleans the bad assets off the balance sheets of the banks with the idea that it will sell off the assets after the crisis has abated. It took a number of years and several hundred billion in losses of taxpayer dollars before the government to finally rid itself of the junk it absorbed in its service to the S & L industry.[20] The large banking community was taking notice. Further moral hazard and more trouble were inevitable.

Unconcerned about the spectacular failure of the S & L deregulation plan, the government soldiered on with its neoliberal agenda. In 1983, they took a stab at the Glass Steagall Act that has been on the books since the Depression years. The Financial Institutions Deregulations Act was designed to repeal Glass Steagall, which covered a broad scope of banking and securities trades business, but crucial among them was the provision that maintained an institutional separation between commercial banking, investment banking, and insurance. The act failed in Congress, but was resurrected again fifteen years later under a different name and succeeded.

The passage of the Secondary Mortgage Enhancement Act (1984) allowed the securitization of mortgages by Wall Street. With this bill it became clear that the government the was to take great strides to show its deferential treatment of Wall Street. Since 1968 the federal government had been assisting the banking sector with its own corporate entities Fannie Mae, Ginnie Mae, and Freddie Mac. The entities were originally chartered to help expand home ownership for a broad segment of the population. To this end, they began the process of securitizing mortgages by buying mortgages from lenders, assembling them into large pools, then issuing mortgage-backed securities to the investor public, and they guaranteed the principal in case of default. By acting as an intermediary in this way, the government helped banks access a much larger source of funds than just deposits and interbank lending. These government entities Mortgage securitization was not meant to be for speculation or money-making schemes, but that changed.

By the 1970s, the legendary bond trading company Salomon Brothers saw an opportunity. They wanted to elbow in on the mortgage securitization business because they saw money to be made, but ran into tax and regulation obstacles. The Secondary Mortgage Enhancement Act along with the Tax Reform Act (1986) cleared out these obstacles. The tax reform legislation also provided tax changes that incentivized private-sector mortgage securitization. Together these pieces of legislation opened the path that led toward building a giant and extremely volatile mortgage derivative pyramid that collapsed two decades later and left a devastating trail of ruin and prompted that largest government bailout in world history.

Meanwhile, Alan Greenspan, who had just assumed his role as chair of the Federal Reserve Board, and seemingly oblivious to this emerging pattern, noted that "…deregulation was working according to plan."[21] It is unclear whether he meant that part of the "plan" was to turn to taxpayers for a bailout, but by then that pattern was being established. In the case of the S & L crisis, leveraged speculation and large-scale crises left the government in a position to have no choice but to orchestrate a bailout of depositors with a total cost of approximately $160 billion, which included $132 billion from taxpayers.[22] Emboldened, the banking industry lobbyists pressed on for more deregulation even as the world watched stock markets crash spectacularly in October, 1987, for similar reasons.

Speculation and Instability Go Global and the Crash of 1987

The crash of '87 revealed some instabilities that were building in the financial system. One factor was the growing market for derivatives. These instruments were poorly understood and were sold to the investor public as a way to protect their investment portfolios against risk, though in actuality it was the opposite.

Wall Street's corporate culture was being fashioned around the neoliberal tenet that financial innovation, like technological innovation, was unequivocally a good thing. As the financial sector grew to be the glistening centerpiece of the economy, Wall Street was the most seductive place to pursue a career in ways that traditional banking could never be.

People with real talent, particularly those gifted with skills in creating mathematical algorithms, gravitated toward the steel and glass towers in the financial district of New York. Math models and computer models for trading became more complex and sophisticated and the cult of technological wizardry gave the illusion that the more complex the instruments created by investment banks, the more investors could speculate without risk. Innovation became the justification for the creation and new derivatives and new markets. This combined with a growing digital infrastructure heightened the process of financialization and accelerated the expansion of corporate hegemony. Financial engineers were continuously contriving new ways to aggregate massive amounts of cash for multinational corporations and to make speculative trades in staggering amounts on computer screens. Wall Street corporations were at the center of financial world and the people there knew it. Their jobs were to score profits for themselves and their clients even if this meant running the risk of destabilizing economies everywhere—which is precisely what they did.

By the Greenspan Era, the institutional amalgamation of Wall Street, the Treasury, and the Federal Reserve was complete. These became among the most powerful within an elite club of institutional giants that included tech companies and oligopolies in retail, auto, pharmaceuticals, media cartels, and a stunning array of joint ventures among all of them. With this amalgamation, sugar-coated neoliberalism lulled policymakers to dismiss the economic dangers that were building in the system. These institutions no longer represented a good old boy network of corruption, together they constituted a fortress of corporate, financial, and political power. Corporate hegemony uses wealth, power, and connections to make money by sweeping away regulatory interference and take on more risk. And Wall Street with its wealth, talent, and sophistication exercised their will over the political sphere to stifle any initiatives to place new regulations. Commercial banks, investment banks, insurance companies, brokerage firms all started to merge, and everyone was getting into the game of securitization, financialization, and the expansion of derivatives.

As with most early generation derivatives, these were contracts created to hedge against risk or unwanted price movements. Say a company wants to finance expansion and investment by $100 million. The company could put together a deal with an investment bank to borrow the principal, pay say a 2% finance charge, plus the difference on oil prices based on specific time and quantity. Say oil is $100 per barrel in today's prices, then the contract would specify that the debtor has to deliver 1 million barrels of oil at a specified date. If the price of oil rises to $105 per barrel, then the debtor has to pay an extra $5 per barrel as a cost of financing, or 5% plus the 2% finance charge, for a total of 7%. In this case the debtor loses and the creditor wins. If, on the other hand, the price of oil falls to $95 per barrel, then debtor can borrow $100 million, turn around and buy 1 million barrels of oil at $95, deliver the oil at the specified date, pay a finance charge of $2 million, and pocket $3 million. The debtor wins and the creditor loses.

The deals can be made more complex by throwing in other instruments besides oil such as its own company stock, or other commodities, or bonds. Corporate finance, in other words, has become a highly leveraged, high stakes, and very risky poker game in which companies and their counter-parties are both gambling on price movements in the open market.

As the markets for derivatives were deregulated, they were also subject to speculation and leveraged trading. Those who believed that price movements were going to be in their favor—based on their mathematical models—they up their risks by borrowing money to place large bets by buying these derivatives in huge numbers. Brokerage firms, private equity companies, shadow banks, and investment banks, placed such bets on both their own accounts and on behalf of their clients. The largest of which are institutional investors. Commercial banks that were lending the money were willing to lend the money because they were operating on the same belief. If the models turned out to be accurate, then big money was made. If not big money was lost. As the Fed made borrowing money for these deals as cheap as possible, while maintaining the position that the markets would never become unstable for long, they allowed for massive bubbles to form. Derivative bubbles as well as stock market bubbles began to form along side the expansion of bank credit. Everything balloons. Meanwhile the Fed's position was to allow these bubbles to inflate without taking any initiatives to prevent the inflation. And if the bubbles pop, it would stand as lender of last resort to allow those who were losing money to shore up their cash reserves.

This Fed policy was established by Greenspan, but it has remained intact through the Bernanke, Yellen, and Powell tenures. Their assumption is that they have to do things this way, because if they don't it would lead to something like the Depression of thirties. It never seems to occur to them that they should never have allowed such a risky, bubbly unstable system to form in the first place. But as soon as their role of lender of last resort is played, those who are culpable hide their tracks, the general public loses interest, and the whole process gets a reboot.

With the advent of wonky finance, our system loses touch with the reason for finance in the first place—economic development, public finance, homeownership, etc. The Fed's charter is to create stability, but ironically it does the opposite. Traditionally, central banks downplayed their lender of last resort role for this very reason. But from Greenspan on, the Fed advertised itself as officially being in the risk management business which emphasized that Wall Street should not be concerned about risk because the Fed will come to their aid with a low-budget carte blanche of credit to use freely.

The particular derivatives that played a role in the crash of 1987 were called "portfolio insurance."[23] Portfolio insurance was fixed to a questionable assumption that investors would be *insured* against losses in the stock market.[24] The basic idea was that if there were unwanted moves in prices in one direction, the derivative allowed a trade in the opposite direction. With these derivatives, at least in theory, speculators would have a built-in mechanism to adjusting to movements of any wanted shifts in the markets. They were led to believe that they could automatically preempt a market panic. Investment bankers and fund managers created and brokered these instruments as magic elixirs. But like all magic tricks, it was an illusion. The risks and potential instabilities were not eliminated only hidden. In the imagination of portfolio managers for institutional investors—mutual funds, pensions, endowments, and trust funds—derivatives nullified the risk side of speculation, leaving only the sky as the limit to the gain side.

By allowing risk to be hidden in this way, prices expressed in markets were becoming divorced from any real meaning of underlying fundamental value. In other words, it was becoming very difficult to see whether stocks represented anything real in terms of the value of assets of a company, its debts, or its earnings.

As financialization evolved, markets were becoming opaque and abstract. The cloud of hot money was becoming larger and dense, like a fog. The strange thing about these derivatives is that when stock prices started to fall in a big way, those who owned the derivatives could simultaneously exercise their option to buy at those lower prices *and* sell the stocks to make a profit. In other words, portfolio insurance derivatives made sure that speculators would profit enormously from downward pressure on stock market prices if they exercised their options the moment the moment the market appeared vulnerable. The only thing that could possibly have happened after that was a crash, and it did dramatically.

Part of the reason that derivatives were a fast-growing segment of the financial industry was mission drift. With spreading financialization, the industry itself was becoming less directed at raising capital for real investment purposes and more at how to deal with the risk associated speculative ventures. The traditional notion of speculation had always been that the speculator gambles on two fundamental principles: potential gains and the risk of potential losses. The two principles are inversely related, which means that higher gains usually implies higher risk. This began to change as Wall Street tried to foster a mass delusion that risk no longer existed with the invention of derivatives.

Another factor was that computers were being programmed to make trades in such a way that they could respond to bits and pieces of information at lightning speed, which served to intensify selloffs when they occurred. A third factor was the Federal Reserve itself under the leadership of freshly appointed Alan Greenspan.

The advent of computerized trading hastened the process. Institutional investors and brokers were increasingly employing people with backgrounds in math and computer programs to write algorithms to automatically execute these trade based on bits of information. The programs, not people, dictated what stocks and futures were to be sold. As stock prices began to fall, this automatically triggered sell orders from computers.

Various bits of bad economic news started streaming in throughout the year. In the weeks leading up to the crash, the stock market took a series of tumbles. These tumbles were the triggers to the computers needed to make a programmed trade. Since the use of computers was widespread, the programmed trades were synchronized and responded massively in like fashion—to sell. Institutionalized greed turned into institutionalized fear and computerized panic in a second. The system was overwhelmed in a trading frenzy on October 19th, and at the end of the day, the Dow Jones Industrial Average lost 22.6% of its stock value. In the span of a few days the S&P 500 Index tanked by 28.5% and investors lost about a trillion in paper wealth.[25]

The leaders at the Federal Reserve expressed surprise, but their feathers remain unruffled. Market crashes, "…always come as a surprise, otherwise they wouldn't be crashes" says former Fed governor, Robert Heller.[26] For those who have ascended professionally to one of the most powerful positions in finance to express "surprise" is either remarkably naïve or remarkably disingenuous. According to Stockman, "… the Greenspan Fed misunderstood the most thunderous wake-up call in financial history."[27] These criticisms may be accurate unless the official central bank position was to be deceptive and publicly deny that such bubbles even exist; which was the temperament of the Fed from the Greenspan years forward. The central bank of the United States, a major force in financial system regulation, showed indifference in public testimony to the instabilities caused by an overpriced stock market or leveraged computerized trading, nor did it show interest in regulating the increasingly volatile derivative industry.

By the late eighties, the derivative industry was booming. It was driven by a single mission: to make the world of finance safe from risk. It was around this same time that first Basel Accord was ratified by the main economic superpowers including the United States. The accord was put in place to ensure that banks around the world would meet certain minimum capital requirements, or cash, to be held on reserve against risky assets and debts. The idea was to create a cushion against insolvency in of rash of foreclosures or failing bonds so that the banks could continue to meet their own debt obligations during such a crisis. In response, Wall Street began looking for ways to hide their debt liabilities in the shadows and thereby sneak around the Basel restrictions. With deregulation, the financial engineers began fabricating an astonishing array of things they would call collateral to hold against debt. What made them particularly hidden is that they were traded in particular markets that were not regulated. There was no data being compiled, no oversight, and no reporting requirements and there was nothing to keep them from being entirely fictional. It was here that the wickedly unstable mortgage-backed securities were born. We will return to these mortgage derivatives later, but it is important to note here that this was a business that required a lot of cheap liquidity—cash—like a factory that requires a lot of cheap electricity. For this Wall Street turned to the newly minted chair at the Federal Reserve, Alan Greenspan.

The Greenspan Put

Since the 1980s, Alan Greenspan has been devoted to implementing a neoliberal agenda in banking and finance. In his many public presentations, he consistently attempted to make the case that financial innovation and deregulation were the best medicine for maintaining efficient and "self-regulating" markets. At every opportunity, Greenspan makes the association of deregulated markets with modernization as he does here, "As we move into a new century the market-stabilizing private regulatory forces should gradually displace many cumbersome, increasingly ineffective government structures."[28]

Greenspan also played the technological innovation card to gloss over overinflated asset prices or market bubbles. He established a trend for central bank policy called the "Greenspan Put." The basic strategy of the policy is to deny the existence of speculative bubbles, but when they inevitably burst, express a politically correct amount of surprise then calm the markets by tossing unlimited amounts of cheap cash into the banking system. Greenspan set the plan in motion by asserting on the day after the crash that, "The Federal Reserve, consistent with its responsibilities as the Nation's central bank, affirmed today its readiness to serve as a source of liquidity to support the economic and financial system."[29] Everyone on Wall Street understood the subtext of Greenspan's message that the Fed would build into the system a market floor to stop the downward spiral that results from bursting price bubbles of risky assets. The process of financialization was sent in hyperdrive because investment banks could build mountains of speculative assets that are inherently unstable without the fear of collapse. The policy was called the Greenspan Put as a metaphor for "put" options which is a contract that allows a speculator to profit from a price decrease of their securities. With Greenspan firmly established as their dutiful servant, Wall Street could not be more pleased. For two decades, Greenspan led the Federal Reserve with a conviction that financial innovation and maintaining the bubbles when they become overinflated was more important stability.

The Greenspan Put is a classic expression of neoliberalism and has been emulated by central banks everywhere. Outwardly the central bankers their belief in confidence in the efficiency of markets and innovation. If bubbles occur, markets will automatically correct themselves. But inwardly always being ready to have the public sector push through policies directed at keeping the bubbles from collapsing at all costs. One of the reasons for they do this is to perpetuate bubbly illusions of paper prosperity to create a "wealth effect." The assumption is that as people in general feel wealthier after looking at the returns in their portfolios, they will spend more on consumer goods, which stimulates growth for the rest of the economy. In other words, with the spread of financialization, the Greenspan Put became the primary device in monetary policy.

It all made sense. The wealth effect would stimulate a spending binge, factory inventories would start disappearing, which would signal to businesses that they need to produce more stuff for people to buy. More production means more jobs and more income and away the process goes. The only problem was that it did not work. Evidence of the wealth effect trickling down to households and working people is nonexistent.[30] Instead, the Fed instigated an endless cycle of leveraged speculation in everything that could be traded, causing bubble markets, leading to bursting bubbles and crises and panic, followed by another round of leveraged speculation.

The Greenspan Fed represents the essence of contemporary neoliberalism—minimum genuine accountability to the population it is supposed to serve while providing the institutional connective tissue between leviathan banks and the federal government structures of power. His stated mission was to "engage in efforts to advance free-market capitalism as an insider."[31]

After 1987, the predictable patterns of neoliberal deregulation and financial market instability escalated. Speculative cash began moving more rapidly around the world as worldwide electronic trading infrastructure developed and institutional investors desperately searched the globe new opportunities for returns. The electronic herd of speculators and institutional investors once again nestled into a "this-time-is-different" belief that somehow large-scale financial market crises would not happen again. That belief, of course, changed with the onset of the financial crises in East Asia and the stock market crash 2000–2001.

Notes

1. Margrit Kennedy, *Occupy Money: Creating an Economy Where Everybody Wins* (Vancouver, Canada: New Society Publishers, 2012), p. 9.
2. John Bellamy Foster and Robert McChesney, *The Endless Crisis*, p. 12.

3. Thomas Phillippon, "The Future of the Financial Industry," New York University, Leonard N. Stern School of Business, http://w4.stern.nyu.edu/blogs/sternonfinance/2008/11/the-future-of-the-financial-in.html.
4. Household Debt to GDP for the United States, Federal Reserve Bank of St. Louis, https://fred.stlouisfed.org/series/HDTGPDUSQ163N.
5. George Cooper, *The Origin of Financial Crises*, p. 11.
6. Hyman P. Minsky, *Can 'It' Happen Again? Essays on Instability and Finance* (Armonk, NY: M.E. Sharpe, 1982); Hyman P. Minsky, "The Financial Instability Hypothesis," in M. Feldstein (ed.), *The Risk of Economic Crisis* (University of Chicago Press, Chicago, IL, 1991).
7. Charles Kindelberger, *Mania, Panics and Crashes: A History of Financial Crises* (New York, NY: Wiley, 1978), pp. 11–19.
8. See John Bellamy Foster, "The Financialization of Capital and the Crisis," *Monthly Review*, Vol. 59, No. 11, April 2008.
9. Kindleberger, *Mania, Panics and Crashes*, p. 12.
10. Frederich Nietzsche, *Beyond Good and Evil: Prelude to a Philosophy of the Future* [1886] (Cambridge University Press, 2002 [1886]), p. 156.
11. Johnson and Kwak, *Thirteen Bankers*, p. 71.
12. Edward Cowan, "How Reagan Sees the Budget," *The New York Times*, October 18, 1981.
13. Gretchen Morgenson and Andrew Martin, "Citigroup Hires Mr. Inside," *The New York Times*, October 10, 2009.
14. Nomi Prins, *All the President's Bankers: The Hidden Alliances That Drive American Power* (New York, NY: Nation Book, 2014), p. 340.
15. Frederick Sheehan, *Panderer to Power: The Untold Story of How Alan Greenspan Enriched Wall Street and Left a Legacy of Recession* (New York, NY: McGraw-Hill, 2010), p. 88.
16. Martin Mayer, *The Greatest-Ever Bank Robbery: The Collapse of the Savings and Loan Industry* (New York, NY: Scribner's and Sons, 1990).
17. Sheehan, *Panderer to Power*, p. 89.
18. T. Curry and L. Shibut, "The Cost of the Saving and Loan Crisis," *FDIC Banking Review*, 2000, pp. 26–35.
19. Ibid.
20. Ibid., p. 341.
21. Sheehan, *Panderer to Power*, p. 92.
22. Ibid.
23. Stockman, *The Great Deformation*, p. 317.
24. Portfolio insurance was a derivative that was structured around stock index futures and options. If stock prices started to seem unreasonably

high, the instrument would allow an option to cash out with without directly impacting the market. If prices fall, the instrument would allow the option of short selling that would offset losses from the fall in price. In this way, large numbers of owners of derivatives could put downward pressure on stock prices even though the stocks themselves had not been traded. This is what happened in 1987.

25. "Stocks Plunge 508 Points, A Drop of 22.6%; 604 Million Volume Nearly Doubles Record," *The New York Times*, October 20, 1987. See also Danielle Booth, *Fed Up: An Insider's Take on Why the Federal Reserve Is Bad for America* (New York, NY: Penguin, 2017).
26. Justin Martin, *Greenspan: The Man Behind the Money* (Cambridge, MA: Perseus, 2000), pp. 173–174.
27. David Stockman, *The Great Deformation: The Corruption of Capitalism in America* (New York, NY: Public Affairs, 2013) p. 318.
28. Alan Greenspan lecture at the Annual Conference of the Association of Private Enterprise Education, April 12, 1997. See https://www.federalreserve.gov/boarddocs/speeches/1997/19970412.htm.
29. Danielle Booth, *Fed Up*, p. 65.
30. Ibid., p. 217.
31. Alan Greenspan, *The Age of Turbulence: Adventures in a New World* (New York, NY: Penguin, 2007), p. 52.

References

Cowan, Edward. "How Reagan Sees the Budget," *The New York Times*, October 18, 1981.

Foster, John Bellamy. "The Financialization of Capital and the Crisis," *Monthly Review*, Vol. 59, No. 11, April, 2008.

Johnson, Simon, and James Kwak. *Thirteen Bankers: The Wall Street Takeover and the Next Financial Meltdown* (New York, NY: Pantheon, 2010).

Kindelberger, Charles. *Mania, Panics and Crashes: A History of Financial Crises* (New York, NY: Wiley, 1978).

Martin, Justin. *Greenspan: The Man Behind the Money* (Cambridge, MA: Perseus, 2000).

Mayer, Martin. *The Greatest-Ever Bank Robbery: The Collapse of the Savings and Loan Industry* (New York, NY: Scribner's and Sons, 1990).

Minsky, Hyman P. *Can 'It' Happen Again? Essays on Instability and Finance* (Armonk, NY: M.E. Sharpe, 1982).

Minsky, Hyman P. "The Financial Instability Hypothesis," in M. Feldstein (ed.), *The Risk of Economic Crisis* (University of Chicago Press: Chicago, IL, 1991).

Morgenson, Gretchen, and Andrew Martin. "Citigroup Hires Mr. Inside," *The New York Times*, October 10, 2009.

Nietzsche, Frederich. *Beyond Good and Evil: Prelude to a Philosophy of the Future* (Cambridge University Press, 2002 [1886]).

Prins, Nomi. *All the President's Bankers: The Hidden Alliances That Drive American Power* (New York, NY: Nation Book, 2014).

Sheehan, Frederick. *Panderer to Power: The Untold Story of How Alan Greenspan Enriched Wall Street and Left a Legacy of Recession* (New York, NY: McGraw-Hill, 2010).

Stockman, David. *The Great Deformation: The Corruption of Capitalism in America* (New York, NY: Public Affairs, 2013).

8

The Epic Crises of the Nineties

By the nineties, large corporations and the Washington political establishment melded into a single firmament of power. The revolving door between corporate boardrooms, the halls of Congress, the White House, and the Federal Reserve disappeared, leaving a wide open corridor teeming with expensive suits and briefcases. Dugger's vision of corporate hegemony has become distinctly real. The people who climbed to the top executive rungs of the corporate ladder are indistinguishable from the lobbyists who do their bidding, from the lawmakers who cut deals for them, from the members of the Fed's open market committee, or from those serving in the president's cabinet. But to characterize this establishment as corruption does not quite fit. Corruption implies a situation in which one institution is unduly influenced by the money and power of another. Instead, the corporate-Washington establishment is a single, composite entity—an amalgamation of wealth and license into an institutional joint venture.

That the Fed and Treasury would pursue a political agenda that was crafted to extend corporate interests worldwide seems to no longer require explanation. It is a forgone conclusion that this is how things are done now. By 1999, the global economy was experiencing its own kind

J. Magnuson, *Financing the Apocalypse*,
Palgrave Insights into Apocalypse Economics,
https://doi.org/10.1007/978-3-030-04720-7_8

post-traumatic stress disorder after a decade of financial market turbulence. In February that year, Alan Greenspan from the Federal Reserve, and Robert Rubin and Larry Summers from the Clinton administration's Treasury Department posed together for a photo to be pasted on the cover of Time magazine. Time referred to them as "The Committee to Save the World"[1] as it canonized them as saviors for the global economy, which made little sense because the world was pressured by these people and institutions to restructure their economies to conform to a neoliberal set of policies that embroiled the economies into financial chaos.

Neoliberalism as policy was pushed into the political scene around the world by United States and international institutions based in Washington DC as we identified earlier the Washington Consensus. Under this consensus, free-market capitalism was to be developed such that finance capital and speculative cash could from one country to another without interference. Governments everywhere, including our own, were told they needed to slash public spending on social programs, reduce government regulations on banking and finance, open their financial markets to the global investing community. Massive instability followed.

The cyclone of instability in second half of the decade of the nineties was building from as a result of institutional developments. Wall Street banks and their international partners, the Federal Reserve, the U.S. Treasury and other powerful economic institutions that by then formed into the corporate hegemony that stands astride the global economy. This behemoth of economic and political power pushed neoliberalism on the rest of the world at the same time orchestrating global financialization. Ample supplies of cheap credit from the Federal Reserve, the largest central banking institution in the world, were washing saturating into financial institutions around the world while those institutions were being pushed into deregulation. This opened the flood gates for financial market speculation on an unprecedented scale. Speed-of-light capital flows combined to create a massive cloud of speculative cash, or "hot money" as it came to be known, that orbited the planet at dazzling speeds. Hot money began moving more rapidly around the world as worldwide electronic trading infrastructure developed and speculators feverishly scoured the globe looking for new opportunities and new markets. Financial markets everywhere were becoming increasingly unstable and subject to high-speed reckless endangerment. The electronic herd of speculators and institutional investors once again nestled into a "this-time-is-different" belief that somehow large-scale financial market crises would not happen again. Corporate hegemony is like the hardware and neoliberalism is the software and together—institution and ideology—created a dangerously unstable system.

Pulled into this vortex of this massive structure of electronic financial market speculation were the so-called "emerging markets" in Asia, Eastern Europe, Mexico and other countries that were struggling to develop. In their effort to become members of the privileged club of developed nations, they sought to be integrated into the financial system that was dominated by the world's largest financial institutions, though their own financial systems were fragile due failing currencies or weak securities markets. They turned to the United States and international institutions like the International Monetary Fund (IMF) for help and in return, as will see, they got pummeled.

Yet in this context Time referred to the top officials of these institutions as the *committee to save the world*. Looking at this from the institutional view, this is not surprising. A recurring theme within the structure of corporate hegemony is that what is drummed out as a solution is the same neoliberal game plan that created the problems in the first place. Cognitive dissonance has become institutionalized.

The principal neoliberal argument behind policies for emerging market liberalization was that finance capital could be allocated around the world most efficiently by following free market principles. Finance capital is scarce in many parts of the world. The forces of supply and demand drive up returns to capital in places where it is most scarce and lower returns where there are not scarcities. Finance capital is typically scarce in developing countries and therefore the markets could command higher returns for investors. Hedge funds, shadow banks, institutional investors, etc., could borrow at very low rates in the US or Europe, rush money into emerging markets, and take advantage of those higher returns. Presumably a win-win scenario in which developing countries acquire capital they can use for development and investors get premium returns if they are willing to take the risks. But the risk factor was largely nullified by the Fed, Treasury and to some extent the IMF, because everyone knew these institutions would bail out the biggest players. These institutions created the phenomenon of "moral hazard," meaning incentivizing financial recklessness. With the institutionalized moral hazard in place, the stage was set for epic speculation followed by epic instability.

This was heightened by the fact that the cloud of hot money was electronically transferred. In an open market environment that meant it could rush from one market to another on a whim. With each rush, prices would jump up and down and eventually turn into a crisis which created serious problems for the developing economies and the people in them. Among the first to experience such a crisis was Mexico between 1994 and 1995.

Mexico's December Mistake

After being pressured to deregulate its currency and bond markets in 1994, Mexico's financial system was flooded with speculative cash mostly coming from the United States. The North American Free Trade Agreement (NAFTA) created a severely imbalanced multilateral trade environment. Mexico's trade deficits soared and along with that came soaring debt using short-term bonds. The bonds were supported by the government and backed by dollars to give reassurances to foreign investors. In December 1994, a grassroots movement coalesced to rebel against the neoliberal programs adopted by the Mexican government and negative effect they were having in some of the poorest regions of the country. Despite the reassurances, American investors became skittish because of the political situation and began demanding higher returns as a risk premium.

The investor public began to dump the Mexican peso as they considered it to have an artificially high exchange rate with the US dollar. Mexico's central bank began borrowing more and dollars to keep the currency from collapsing, but eventually ran out of credit. Investors rapidly pulled their money out Mexico by dumping bonds and dumping the peso. A crisis of instability followed along with government officials in Washington claiming their surprise over these unfortunate circumstances as if they were caused by an earthquake. The U.S. Treasury quickly orchestrated a $30 billion bailout package that was mainly to the benefit of Wall Street.[2] Approximately $20 billion of the bailout funds came from the U.S. Treasury's Exchange Stabilization Fund (ESF) supervised by newly appointed Secretary of Treasury, Robert Rubin and his sidekick Larry Summers. American politician, Newt Gingrich, soon to be Speaker of the House, also expressed "shock" and informed the public that the bailout was necessary to stop the crisis before it caused millions illegal immigrants to surge across the US/Mexico border.[3] The bailout did very little to improve the living conditions of the Mexican people who were protesting neoliberalism and damage it was doing to their livelihoods.

The cloud of speculative hot money lifted up and away from Mexico and began trolling the planet for other emerging markets. It found them in Asia, quickly moved to the other side of the world to settle there and started another round of instability. In the meantime, there were warning signs of homegrown trouble brewing in California.

Orange County's Derivative Debacle

In 1994, Orange County, California suffered major losses in investments in derivatives and plunged into bankruptcy. The experience of Orange County tells a slightly different story of the financial troubles created by neoliberalism. The county, located in the suburbs south of Los Angeles, is arguably one of the most prosperous counties in the country. But, like public service institutions everywhere, it has been starved of funds because of a deteriorating tax base. Increasingly, public agencies and pension funds are pushed toward speculation in financial markets as a method of paying for government services.

The county scraped together about $8 billion of its reserves and borrowed about $12 billion and placed the bets on particular derivatives called "inverse floaters." Inverse floaters are a kind of bond in which the yield floats in an inverse relationship to benchmark rates such as the rate paid on Treasury bonds. When the benchmark rates rise, the floater rate goes down and vice versa. Placing bets is based on the assumption that the benchmark rate is high and should be going down in the future. If the assumption is true and the benchmark rate falls, the floater rate will rise. Typically, the rates on bonds and bond prices move in opposite directions. But with inverse floaters falling benchmark rates will cause both the rates on the bonds *and* the bond price to rise. In such a case, they can be sold for a profit.

Orange county tried this, and their turned sour. Local agencies that invested in Orange County's investment pool suddenly saw their taxpayers money vanish as it lost over $1.5 billion.[4] The news sent major shock waves through bond markets, particularly in municipal bonds. As investors began dumping bonds, bond prices fell and the yield on those bonds jumped by 2% in a single day of trading. The decline represented contagious fears that what happened in Orange County would happen elsewhere. It also represented panic from the creditors that lent the county funds to make such risky investments.

A financial advisor for local governments in California commented that, "You can pin this almost 100 percent on Proposition 13." The anti-tax neoliberals in California had pushed through a referendum that reduced property taxes—the main source of funding for local governments—by a staggering 57%.[5] The advisor continues, "The only reason people are out there trying to turn two dimes into a quarter is they can't finance basic needs anyway else. The Music Man comes in and says, 'I can get you 10 percent when everyone else gets 5 percent and he is a hero.'"

Foundations, pension funds, scholarships, face the same problems as local governments. By mid-2016, returns to pension funds have dropped to their lowest levels on record, which has created a $1.25 trillion funding gap.[6] Unable to raise funds or generate decent returns on bonds, they are forced into riskier territory just to pay their bills. Meanwhile, Merrill Lynch, being the music man in this case, made $100 million in fees for the deals it arranged with Orange County.[7] The zero-bound rate policy of the Fed has created a situation in which Wall Street companies can borrow billions at dirt cheap rates from the Fed, while these funds that serve legitimate social functions are stripped bare.

At the time, former investment banker and diplomat for the Clinton administration Felix Rohatyn commented, "The more complicated and the fancier these so-called investments are, the more the question of appropriateness comes to the fore." Rohatyn was an outspoken critic of derivatives and characterized them as "financial hydrogen bombs, built on personal computers by 26-year-olds with MBAs."[8] He and others were advocating at Congressional hearings that public funds should not be gambled with in this manner and pressed for legislation that would restrict local investment policies. Their voices were drowned out by stalwart neoliberals, including Greenspan who complained in a meandering testimony that "The trouble with legislation is that it is very likely in this type of market to become obsolete, and could very readily become counterproductive to the required flexibility that we need to address the types of problems that we are addressing."[9] In typical Greenspan fashion, he argues that financial innovation, no matter what problems it causes should always take precedent over regulation.

Thailand and the Crises in East Asia

Shortly after the crisis in Mexico and a heavy dose of neoliberal medicine, similar instabilities were building in the financial markets in East Asia. The governments in Thailand, Malaysia, Singapore, Hong Kong, and South Korea were convinced by Washington to deregulate their controls on international capital flows in financial markets. Wall Street firms once again were given the green light to move speculative cash in and out of these countries as they saw fit. The cloud of money drifted to Thailand for speculation on its currency, the Thai baht.

In April of 1995, the United States began negotiating a process whereby the dollar would rise in value against the Japanese yen in order to assist Japan out of its recession. By weakening the yen relative to the dollar, Japanese exports would become more competitive in US markets. With a boost in its export sector, it was believed that Japan would pull out of its recession. As the US dollar became stronger relative to the yen and other currencies, including the Thai baht (THB), also strengthened as they were fixed to the dollar. Just as weakening the yen boosted Japan's ability to export to foreign markets, strengthening the baht compromised Thailand's ability to export. This was a significant problem for a country like Thailand, whose economic growth was almost entirely driven by its export sector. In their earlier years of development, Thailand and other Asian countries patterned their export-led growth after the Japanese model which was based on a pluralist system of careful government planning and management and private enterprise—a model which is antithetical to America's push for a global system of pure capitalism.

After adopting a more free-market approach, and after tying its currency to the dollar, Thailand's export sales plummeted and trade deficits began to soar. To make matters worse, China burst into the world trading system as the premier producer of low-cost exports and Thailand lost much of its share of the world export market.

Losing its export earnings, Thailand began borrowing large sums of money by selling bonds to Wall Street banks and investment firms at relatively high-interest rates. With the borrowed money, Thai banks, in turn, made loans to local businesses for economic development projects (a policy that was also recommended by the Washington Consensus) including commercial real estate development in hotels and resorts to augment tourism, and in export-oriented manufacturing infrastructure. Much of this development was directed toward restoring Thailand's earnings of foreign currency needed to pay their high-interest debt obligations to Wall Street.

As Thailand agreed to follow open-market policies set by the Washington Consensus, its financial sector became vulnerable to instabilities that come with currency speculation. As with the Dutch tulip bulbs centuries before, the Thai baht became an object of speculator interest and was quickly destabilized. Speculators observed Thailand's mounting deficit and debt problems and began to place bets that Thailand would not be able to sustain its fixed exchange rate with the dollar. But the speculators were not anticipating that the baht would rise in value, rather that it would fall. In other words, they were "short-selling" Thailand's currency, and they were doing so in huge volume.

The process of short-selling the Thai currency goes something as follows. Thailand had for some time been maintaining a fixed exchange rate of about 25 THB to the dollar. Speculators who believed that the currency would fall in value began borrowing baht and then used the baht to buy dollars. They would then wait for the currency to devalue, buy the baht at a cheaper price, pay back the loan and walk away with a profit. Say for example, a speculator borrows 25 million bahts and with that money immediately buys $1 million US dollars at the $1 = 25 THB exchange rate. The speculator sits on the million dollars and waits for the baht to devalue, to say $1 = 30 THB. At that point, the speculator can buy the 25 million bahts it needs to pay back the loan, and at a $1 = 30 THB, the speculator only needs about $833,000 to buy the 25 million bahts and pocket the remaining $167,000.

Like other forms of speculation, short-selling has a way of becoming a self-fulfilling prophecy. Large hedge funds and other US investors were positioning to short-sell the Thai baht. By doing so, they were siphoning dollars out of Thailand's banks. As more speculators decided to short-sell, more were demanding US dollars and therefore placed more stress on Thailand's reserve of foreign currency. Eventually Thailand ran out of dollars. Those who were not short-selling began a panicked sell-off of the baht, and the currency went into a free fall. In a vain attempt to stabilize its currency at its agreed fixed rate, Thailand's government borrowed huge amounts of dollars in order to buy enough baht to raise its value. But those dollars immediately fled back out of its banks as speculators sold off their holdings of baht. The self-fulfilling prophecy for the speculators was realized, and Thailand's currency collapsed. Within a matter of months, Thailand's currency lost half of its value, and at its lowest point it was trading at 56 THB to the dollar.

As the currency collapsed, the panic spread to other sectors of Thailand's financial markets. US banks and investment firms that purchased Thai stocks and bonds stood to lose as these securities, priced in baht, collapsed in value along with the currency. The collapsing currency dragged the stock and bond markets down with it. Free and open markets in Thailand came to mean that Wall Street firms were free to openly move their money into Thailand's markets for speculation, and were freely to openly pull it back out, en masse, leaving a tsunami of financial wreckage behind. In a wave of panic selling, these Wall Street firms sold out their holdings of Thai securities, which contributed heavily to the destabilization of Thailand's stock and bond markets. In 1997, Thailand's stock market dropped by a staggering 75%.[10]

Observing what was happening in Thailand, speculators became skittish in other markets and the speculative panic began to spread to other countries, specifically among those that followed the Washington Consensus's prescription of liberalized capital markets.

A brand of gambling casinos opened and speculators rushed into place their bets. As in Mexico, most of these bets were on an anticipation that the currency would lose its value relative to the US dollar. Speculative bets like this can be a self-fulfilling prophecy if enough money is drawn to it. The Thai baht tumbled into the target of speculators from the US and Europe who, in a self-fulfilling prophecy, anticipated that the baht would collapse from the weight of this speculation. They started pulling their money out of Thailand and in 1997 a massive panic selloff occurred in which investors began selling their holdings of Thai securities along with the currency. The Thai currency collapsed and Thailand's stock market dropped by a staggering 75%. Following a similar pattern, the panic spread to Malaysia, Indonesia, Hong Kong, and South Korea, leaving a wide swath of economic ruin everywhere.[11]

In October 1997, Hong Kong's Hang Seng stock market index showed a fall of 23% and its central bank had spent over $1 billion in US dollars—an amount equal to about half of Hong Kong's broadest measure of its money supply—to prevent a collapse in its currency. Unemployment soared in South Korea along with poverty rates. Interest rates everywhere in East Asia spun wildly out of control, and at one point had risen overnight to as high as 500%. Malaysia's and Indonesia's currencies collapsed and both countries plunged into deep recessions. In Malaysia, the national currency, the ringgit, also collapsed, the stock market crashed and the country plunged into a deep recession that was felt in every sector of the economy. Malaysia's real gross domestic product declined by 6.2% in one year. In Indonesia, the experience was similar: collapsing currency, crashing stock markets followed by a deep recession. Accompanying Indonesia's currency crash was skyrocketing price inflation. Steep increases in food prices precipitated riots and political instability.[12]

For all the Asian countries involved, this was among the worst economic crises in their histories and people suffered in large numbers.[13] Meanwhile the cloud of hot money lifted away from the Asian markets to seek fortunes elsewhere. Commenting on this series of crises, Nobel laureate and former World Bank economist, Joseph Stiglitz notes,

> I believe that the capital account liberalization was the single most important factor leading to the crisis...Indeed, in retrospect, it became clear that the IMF policies not only exacerbated the downturns but were partially responsible for the onset: excessively rapid financial and capital market liberalization was probably the single most important cause of the crisis, though mistaken policies on the part of the countries themselves played a role as well.[14]

The East Asian countries had no choice but to turn to the very same IMF for bailouts. The bailout deals were brokered by the former Chancellor of the Exchequer, Gordon Brown, who had nonetheless stood by his Prime Minister, Tony Blair, as they pursued the neoliberal game plan. In the US, Robert Rubin, a former Wall Street investment banker, was Treasury Department Secretary at the time and brought representation for the banking and finance industry directly to the White House cabinet. Rubin led the charge to crack open the financial markets in East Asia. Returning to the question of moral hazard, the element of risk in speculation was largely nullified as companies knew that the IMF, the US Treasury, and Her Majesty's Treasury would have their back if things went badly. The IMF distributed tens of billions of dollars in loans to the governments of the East Asian so that they could pay back their obligations to New York and London firms. In retrospect, Robert Rubin commented that he was "shocked" and had never seen anything like this before, which is remarkable considering that he had just finished administering the bailout deal in Mexico for precisely the same reasons.[15]

Then Prime Minister of Malaysia, Mahathir Mohamad, as a new form of capitalist imperialism, "In the old days you needed to conquer a country with military force, and then you could control that country. Today it's not necessary at all. You can destabilize a country, make it poor, and then make it request help." The help, in this case, would come from the IMF, which subsequently takes control over the policies of the country. "[And] when you gain control over the policies of a country," Mahathir asserted, "effectively you have colonized that country..." He called specifically on the international community to take note that the international financial institutions are acting in accordance with their own greed, not the wellbeing of people. The institutions, he argued, "are not in the business of attending to the social needs of people. They are only thinking about their profit, and if you allow the market to go free, unregulated, then the world will face monopolies of giants who will not care at all about what happens to people..."[16]

The warning signs that neoliberalism was making financial systems unstable and crisis prone was largely ignored in Washington and Wall Street, and most Americans could not feel what was happening as they were still caught up in market populism. Nonetheless, the United States was not entirely unscathed by the emerging market crises and financial market troubles swung back and came to roost at hedge fund Long-Term Capital Management (LTCM) and another homegrown crisis.

Long-Term Capital Management

Recall the merger waves in the banking sector in the 1990s. One of the waves occurred when investment banks were allowed to merge with commercial banks. This meant that firms that that engaged in making risking deals, underwriting derivatives, and doing massive proprietary trades on their own account now had access to commercial banks' deposit money. The waves also cemented the Too Big to Fail status of Wall Street leviathans.

Evidence of the TBTF status became clear when the Federal Reserve Bank of New York brokered a major rescue deal for one of the most prestigious hedge funds on Wall Street—LTCM. Part of its prestige came from having employed the two Nobel laureate economists Robert Merton and Myron Scholes who were mainly responsible for crafting the Efficient Market Hypothesis, headed by John Meriwether former head of legendary Salomon Brothers, and from having a former Federal Reserve vice chair David Mullins on board. With this superstar team, LTCM was flagship company that set the standards for the mathematic wizardry that came to characterize finance.

Deregulation allowed LTCM to craft massive arbitrage trades using $4 billion of its own capital and over $130 billion in money borrowed from a consortium of commercial banks. The arbitrage trades were based on bets that the prices of certain stocks or yields on certain bonds could be different in different markets, but only temporarily.[17] The basic idea was that securities are traded in markets scattered around the world and occasionally there will be differences in prices from one market to the next for the same security. The same assumption held for the yields on specific bonds. LTCM was trading "fixed income arbitrage" deals that were linked various government bonds, including bonds issued by the Russian Government. The Efficient Market Hypothesis was built around an assumption that these differences could not last for long and LTCM made bets accordingly. Huge bets. The math models that drove the bets did not take into consideration the crises unfolding in emerging markets and the capital flight that ensued. The crisis in East Asia triggered another crisis in Russian bonds and currency. When the Russian government was reeling from its financial and currency crises, it began to default on its bond obligations and the arbitrage deals began to unravel. LTCM was operating in near complete secrecy as hedge funds were not regulated. Investors from around the world panicked and a large cloud of hot money drifted to the safety of U.S. Treasury bonds. As a result, the yields on those bonds actually widened as they were traded in multiple markets. This was the opposite of what LTCM genius-inspired models predicted. and had quietly borrowed huge sums of money to underwrite these derivatives.

In 1998, LTCM lost massive amounts of money and its capital dropped total capital dropped to $1 billion.[18] What was even more alarming was that the company was on the verge of defaulting on the debt is piled up to make the deals. Because of its size, LTCM's troubles sent markets around the world roiling. Banks were panicking. The

Fed was shocked and began to worry that such a default could precipitate a wider crisis, including instigating depositors to make a run on the banks.

The Fed's New York bank brought together representatives from every major bank in New York that had a stake in the hedge fund's future, including J.P. Morgan Chase, Merrill Lynch, and Goldman Sachs. The Fed pushed the banks to collectively pony up $3.6 billion in a bailout deal. The Fed and Wall Street banks patted themselves on the back for containing a crisis that could have easily triggered a much wider meltdown. Greenspan, Rubin, and Summers were canonized on the cover of *Time* magazine's February 1999 issue as "The Committee to Save the World." But the implications of the rescue deal were much more far-reaching. It proved to the world that the electronic trading infrastructure was lightning fast and so interconnected that a crisis in one part of the world could easily trigger a crisis on the other side of the planet. It also demonstrated that the Fed was in bailout mode for hedge funds that took massive risks based on abstract mathematical models that turned out to be worthless. It was a green light to Wall Street to indulge in more debt-driven risky business and to do so dramatically.

For over a hundred years, the Federal Reserve's responsibility has been to maintain price and employment stability and to supervise banks. It was never intended to allow high flying hedge funds to achieve TBTF status, then orchestrate bailout after bailout. Not only does all of that amount to encouraging practices that lead to more instability, it represents a mission drift that swayed so far off center that it constitutes a violation of its charter.

These experiences should have made policymakers and people in general stand up and pay attention as they were clear warnings of dangers ahead. Instead, the bailouts made it easier to fall into apathy and amnesia. Other signs of cracks in the system were beginning to show in the nineties.

In the aftermath of the LTCM meltdown in the late 1990s, Brooksley Born, then head of the Commodities Futures Trading Commission, began to stitch together a proposal to regulate the derivatives industry. Born, unlike so many others around this time in the Clinton and Bush administrations, took her job as regulator seriously.

Her commission began investigating fraud in derivatives trades, including mortgage-backed securities. She was concerned mortgage-backed securities represent tens of trillions of dollars worth of risk, which could be dangerously unstable. She proposed to submit to Congress a plan for regulation and immediately came under attack by Wall Street companies and their partners in the Treasury, the Federal Reserve and the Securities Exchange Commission (SEC). Robert Rubin and Larry Summers at the Treasury, Alan Greenspan at the Federal Reserve, Arthur Leavitt at the SEC, and, of course, Phil Gramm in the Senate attacked Born openly in Senate hearings in a raw display of power and shut her down. Born's plan to regulate derivative trades never got off the ground in Congress.

The Dot.Com Crash of 2000–2001

Not long after the bailout and mop up of LTCM was complete, another major crisis was already on the horizon. This time it was in the very fashionable and volatile tech stocks. the cloud of hot money drifted back to the stock markets where a major stock market crash began to boil out of the tech sector. From the peak of the stock market boom to the trough of the bust, the dot.com crash between 2000–2001 was among the most startling stock market crashes in the history of the world.

By the mid-1990s, desktop computing power had become more affordable and user friendly. No longer were they merely a hobby for techies, personal computers became a regular tool for businesses as well as a common household appliance. Consumers began spending huge amounts of their disposable income on newer and faster machines, and on multiple generations of new software packages. Technology was a red-hot growth sector and this found expression in the stock market.

When the stock market bubbles started to take off, the baby boomer generation was making its way through the American population. The boomers are those born between the years 1945 and 1965, which meant that by 1995 they were between thirty and fifty years old. This is a time when most are in of their prime income earning years and had collectively amassed a substantial sum in their retirement and mutual fund nest eggs. They were also more inclined to be involved in financial market speculation than previous generations. Analyst Deborah Gregory notes that, "since 1987, individuals have become responsible for their retirement savings through defined contribution plans, the funds of which are tied up in the markets."[19] William Fleckenstein, journalist and author of *Greenspan's Bubbles: The Age of Ignorance at the Federal Reserve* (2008), elaborates, "The year 1995 marks the start of the biggest stock market bubble this country has ever experienced. Baby boomers, captivated by the Internet and the new financial networks like CNBC, believe they possess the know-how to invest for themselves and had earned the right to be rich."[20]

Alan Greenspan, testifying in a routine report to Congress in May 1994, also noted that, "[Lured] by consistently high returns in capital markets, people exhibited increasing willingness to take on market risk by extending the maturity of their investments." Interpreting his typical opaque language, Greenspan is saying that people were inclined to take long-term positions in the stock market and were shifting substantial amounts of money away from short-term money market accounts and savings deposits. He continued, "it is evident that all sorts of investors made their change in strategy—from the very sophisticated to the much less experienced."[21] According to Fed estimates, Americans moved approximately $282 billion from their piggy banks to the stock market in 1993 to get in on the bullish money-making phenomenon.[22] As Frederic J. Sheehan notes, "Money chases an inflating asset."[23]

If people at this time felt that they were entitled to become rich, it was not through wage growth. Former Federal Reserve Governor, Lawrence Lindsey, repeatedly reported to the Fed's policy making wing, the Federal Open Market Committee (FOMC), that wages and salaries of the working population in the 1990s were stagnating, while the wealthiest one percent were taking the majority of income growth from their investments. People on the rat wheel were falling into debt because, as Lindsey notes, "the non-rich, non-old live paycheck to paycheck, quite literally. That's where all their income comes from. Remember, virtually none of the capital income or business income goes to them. They have to live on their wages and that wage share is also declining… The middle-class, middle-ages people who are borrowing are really getting their income squeezed."[24]

Nonetheless undaunted, people in significant numbers were drawn into market speculation as a way to get what they considered their fair share. Equity growth, not wage growth, was fueling personal consumption expenditures. Increasingly, Americans were seeing their net worth, at least on paper, rise proportionally with expanding retirement portfolios and home equity. These were used as collateral to support consumer debt, and consumer debt was driving real economic growth measured in terms of GDP. The US economy was resting on a squishy foundation of equity bubbles. Lindsay warned again in 1996, that, "there is a long-term social cost we are going to pay from all this…. Consumption has expanded more quickly than the income of the great majority of American households." Lindsey was referring to the dangers awaiting as a majority were using bubbles to keep the economy alive and reiterated, "the long-term costs of a bubble to the economy and society are potentially great. They include a reduction in the long-term saving rate, a seemingly random redistribution of wealth, and the diversion of scarce financial human capital into the acquisition of wealth. As in the United States in the late 1920s and Japan in the late 1980s, the case for a central bank ultimately to burst that bubble becomes overwhelming." In other words, Lindsey was suggesting that the Fed take the air out of the bubble before it gets any bigger and thereby lessen the magnitude of the crisis that would follow. Chairman Greenspan responded, "On that note, we all can go for coffee" and after the coffee break, moved on to another topic. Lindsey's warnings were ignored and the public thereafter was subject to a seemingly endless feat of financial log-rolling.[25]

Greenspan not only ignored Lindsey's warnings, but believed that equity extraction, particularly from real estate, was a viable economic model. Sheehan tells how "Greenspan was living for the moment: 'I believe that equity extraction from homes will continue to be a source for positive growth in personal consumption expenditure.' Greenspan then extolled some Fed model… that calculated 20 percent of personal consumption came from consumers cashing out their 'wealth.' Rising house prices were essential to America's continuous shopping spree."[26]

Technology was not only the vehicle that moved capital around the world, but the stocks of technology companies themselves became the objects of financial speculation. The technology industry was both an area of growth and a source of increased productivity rates for other industries and for the economy overall. As hardware and software technology developed and became more affordable, such as with the introduction of the Pentium processor and Microsoft's Windows operating system, businesses and households spent heavily on computers and software throughout mid-to-late 1990s. Computing power became much more affordable and user friendly. No longer merely a hobby for techies, personal computers became a regular tool for business use and a household appliance. Households began spending huge amounts of their disposable income on newer and faster machines, and on a succession of new versions of software packages. By the mid 1990s, technology was a red-hot growth sector and this found expression in the stock market.

For businesses, investments in computer technology paid off in higher productivity levels. Rising productivity levels allowed for significant economic expansion without concerns of price inflation. Technology enthusiasts began making bold claims that digital technology has changed the US economy in such a way that price inflation would never again be an impediment to growth. With little worry about inflation, the Federal Reserve began expanding the availability of credit, lowering interest rates, and this cheap money was eventually channeled into stock market speculation.

With the development of the internet, entirely new industries were created seemingly overnight. Entrepreneurs came out every corner of the economy to create an explosion of "dot.com" service-sector companies. Internet-based companies that sold travel and dating services, pornography, music and books, movie rentals, banking services and practically every other service that does not require a physical human presence. Most of these companies were not profitable, but their stocks were publicly traded and they skyrocketed with speculation.

Speculators, blinded by the usual cognitive dissonance seemed not to notice, nor did they seem to want to notice. Just as journalists were on the pool operator payroll in the 1920s, research analysts of investment banking firms were issuing favorable reports on client's stocks, particularly new issues by corporations for whom their own investment banks were assisting in capitalizing for lucrative fees.

Another factor contributing to the rise of stock prices during the decade of the 1990s was the heightened role played by institutional investors and the so-called "day traders." A demographic wave coincided with the opening of financial markets in Asia and with digital technology. Baby-boomers were entering their prime income earning years and by the 1990s had collectively amassed a substantial nest egg in retirement funds and mutual funds. Moreover, the institutional investors had considerable influence and were pressuring corporate managers to squeeze maximum returns out of their stocks. As they did so, the stock prices rose. With the Internet and the power contained in desktop computing, online amateur speculators, or "day traders," were drawn to the bull market. Just as in the 1920s, just about anyone with a modest amount of money could potentially become obsessed with playing the stock market.

As with every other bubble in financial market history, when masses are caught up in the euphoria of easy money to be made in speculation, trouble inevitably follows. John K. Galbraith observed, "For built into this situation is the eventual and inevitable fall. Built in also is the circumstance that it cannot come gently or gradually. When it comes, it bears the grim face of disaster."[27] The disaster would be felt not by the rich, but by the millions of average Americans who watched the rapid deflation of their 401(k) accounts. The wealthy inside players that spearheaded bullish momentum on the up side, got out quickly, and triggered a reversal to bearish momentum on the down side.

The Dow Jones Industrial Average was at 2588 in January 1991. By January 2000 it had risen to 11,302, an increase of 337% in 10 years. The NASDAQ, which is heavily weighted with stocks of businesses in the computer and Internet sectors, rose from 414 in January 1991 to a peak of 5250 in March of 2000—an overall increase of 1168% in the same ten-year period and an average annual increase of 32%.[28] Considering that many of the new, high-tech companies listed in the NASDAQ were not earning profits, the NASDAQ stock market boom could not have been on rising fundamental values; rather it was a speculative bubble. Measured by the DOW and NASDAQ, the 1990s showed the largest stock market increase over a single decade in the history of capitalism. Like the New Era of the 1920s, the stock market bubble was evidence of massively overtraded stocks, and like the market of the 1920s, the bubble was doomed to burst.

As the likelihood of a crash became more evident, the hype became increasingly shrill. New Economy exaggeration reached its most intense moments with the publications of books such as *DOW 36,000: The New Strategy for Profiting from the Coming Rise in the Stock Market*, by James Glassman and Kevin Hassett. In 1999, Glassman and Hassett asserted that, "The stock market is a money machine.... The Dow should rise to 36,000 immediately, but to be realistic, we believe the rise will take some time, perhaps three to five years."[29] Glassman and Hasset were, of course, dead wrong and beginning in 2000, the stock market crashed with a resonance that could be heard around the world.

Depending on when and how one takes the measurement, the total dollar value loss of the 2000–2001 stock market crash was somewhere between $6 and $8 trillion. It stands the largest crash of all time and overwhelmingly eclipsed the crash of 1929 which, measured in 1992 dollars, obliterated about $676.5 billion. Tech stocks listed in NASDAQ lost 60% of their value, other indexes showed a decline in value around 10–20%, and banks that lent on margin suffered huge losses.[30] As the NASDAQ crash thundered downward, dot.com companies were wiped out. Panic selling ensued throughout the year 2000 and drove the index to as low as 800 in 2002.

The pattern of the crash was not unlike those of previous crashes going back to the Tulip mania 400 years ago: speculative buying, expansion of credit to be used in speculation, irrational euphoria as the bubble soared, and the notion that no matter how high the price went, there would always be the "greater fool" to buy. Stocks of the 1990s were driven to sky-high levels with the same self-reinforcing feedback mechanism as were stocks of the 1920s. As the ubiquity of greed—always present in a capitalist economy—turned inevitably to an epidemic of panic, stocks were thrown overboard in a self-reinforcing downward spiral of collapsing prices, panic sell offs. Millions of workers lost their jobs in the aftermath, and as the economy plunged into a recession millions more saw the hemorrhaging of their pension funds and the obliteration of their retirement nest eggs. Those who did not lose all of their investment cash began looking for a new vehicle for investment growth and they found it in real estate.

Notes

1. "The Three Marketeers," *Time Magazine*, February 15, 1999.
2. Jorge G. Castaneda, *The Mexican Shock: Its Meaning for the US* (New York, NY: The New Press, 1995), pp. 177–187.
3. Newt Gingrich, "Vindication of the Mexican Bailout," *The New York Times*, editorial, January 18, 1997.
4. Floyd Norris, "Orange County's Bankruptcy: The Overview; Orange County Crisis Jolts Bond Markets," *The New York Times*, 1994.
5. See californiataxdata.com/prop13.
6. Danielle Booth, *Fed Up*, p. 4.
7. Johnson and Kwak, *Thirteen Bankers*, p. 81.
8. Michiko Kakutani, "Books of The Times: Greed Layered on Greed, Frosted with Recklessness," *The New York Times*, June 15, 2009.
9. Norris, *The New York Times*, 1994.
10. Benjamin Friedman, "Globalization: Stiglitz Case," *New York Review of Books*, Vol. 49, No. 13, August 15, 2002, pp. 89–90.
11. Ibid.
12. See http://en.wikipedia.org/wiki/Asian_financial_crisis#Thailand.
13. Joseph Stiglitz, *Globalization and Its Discontents* (New York, NY: W.W. Norton, 2002), p. 97.
14. Ibid., p. 99.
15. From an interview for PBS, Frontline: Season 17, Episode 11, "The Crash," June 29, 1999.
16. See transcripts from the PBS documentary, "Commanding Heights." http://www.pbs.org/wgbh/commandingheights/.
17. Roger Lowenstein, *When Genius Failed* (New York, NY: Random House, 2000), pp. 179–180.
18. Gretchen Morgenson and Jushua Rosner, *Reckless Endangerment: How Outsized Ambition, Greed, and Corruption Led to Economic Armageddon* (New York, NY: Henry Holt and Company, 2011), p. 109.
19. Deborah Gregory, *Unmasking Financial Psychopaths: Inside the Minds of Investors in the Twenty-first Century* (New York, NY: Palgrave Macmillan, 2014), p. 74.

20. William A. Fleckenstein, *Greenspan's Bubbles: The Age of Ignorance at the Federal Reserve* (New York, NY: McGraw-Hill, 2008), p. 27.
21. Ibid., p. 18.
22. Steven Greenhouse, "For Clinton, a Place on the Bottom Line," *The New York Times*, October 1993.
23. Sheehan, *Panderer to Power*, p. 215.
24. See FOMC meeting transcript, February 3–4, 1994, pp. 20–21. http://www.federalreserve.gov/monetarypolicy/files/FOMC19940204meeting.pdf.
25. See FOMC meeting transcript, September 24, 1996, pp. 33, 20–21. http://www.federalreserve.gov/monetarypolicy/files/FOMC19940204meeting.pdf.
26. Sheehan, *Panderer to Power*, p. 260.
27. John K. Galbraith, *A Short History of Financial Euphoria* (New York, NY: Penguin Books, 1990), p. 4.
28. Joel Magnuson, *From Greed to Well Being: A Buddhist Approach to Resolving Our Economic and Financial Crises* (Bristo, UK: Policy Press, 2016), p. 135.
29. James Glassman and Kevin Hassett, *DOW 36,000: The New Strategy for Profiting from the Coming Rise in the Stock Market* (New York, NY: Times Books, 1999), p. 22.
30. "The Dot Com Bubble Bursts," *The New York Times*, December 2000.

References

Booth, Danielle. *Fed Up: An Insider's Take on Why the Federal Reserve Is Bad for America* (New York, NY: Penguin, 2017).

Castaneda, Jorge G. *The Mexican Shock: Its Meaning for the US* (New York, NY: The New Press, 1995).

Federal Open Market Committee Transcripts, February 3–4, 1994 and September 24, 1996. http://www.federalreserve.gov/.

Fleckenstein, William A. *Greenspan's Bubbles: The Age of Ignorance at the Federal Reserve* (New York, NY: McGraw-Hill, 2008).

Friedman, Benjamin. "Globalization: Stiglitz Case," *The New York Review of Books*.

Galbraith, John K. *A Short History of Financial Euphoria* (New York, NY: Penguin Books, 1990).

Gingrich, Newt. "Vindication of the Mexican Bailout," *The New York Times*, editorial, January 18, 1997.

Glassman, James, and Kevin Hassett. *DOW 36,000: The New Strategy for Profiting from the Coming Rise in the Stock Market* (New York, NY: Times Books, 1999).

Greenhouse, Steven. "For Clinton, a Place on the Bottom Line," *The New York Times*, October 1993.

Gregory, Deborah. *Unmasking Financial Psychopaths: Inside the Minds of Investors in the Twenty-First Century* (New York, NY: Palgrave Macmillan, 2014), p. 74.

Johnson, Simon, and James Kwak. *Thirteen Bankers: The Wall Street Takeover and the Next Financial Meltdown* (New York, NY: Pantheon, 2010).

Lowenstein, Roger. *When Genius Failed* (New York, NY: Random House, 2000).

Magnuson, Joel. *From Greed to Well Being: A Buddhist Approach to Resolving Our Economic and Financial Crises* (Bristol, UK: Policy Press, 2016).

Michiko, Kakutani. "Books of the Times: Greed Layered on Greed, Frosted with Recklessness," *The New York Times*, June 15, 2009.

Morgenson, Gretchen, and Joshua Rosner. *Reckless Endangerment: How Outsized Ambition, Greed, and Corruption Led to Economic Armageddon* (New York, NY: Henry Holt and Company, 2011).

The New York Times. "The Dot Com Bubble Bursts," December 2000.

Norris, Floyd. "Orange County's Bankruptcy: The Overview; Orange County Crisis Jolts Bond Markets," *The New York Times*, 1994.

PBS documentary. "Commanding Heights" Transcripts. http://www.pbs.org/wgbh/commandingheights/.

PBS, *Frontline*: Season 17, Episode 11, "The Crash," June 29, 1999.

Sheehan, Frederick. *Panderer to Power: The Untold Story of How Alan Greenspan Enriched Wall Street and Left a Legacy of Recession* (New York, NY: McGraw-Hill, 2010).

Stiglitz, Joseph. *Globalization and Its Discontents* (New York, NY: W.W. Norton, 2002).

Time Magazine. "The Three Marketeers," February 15, 1999. https://en.wikipedia.org/wiki/1997_Asian_financial_crisis#Thailand.

9

The 2008 Meltdown

As the US economy was fire dancing its way into the third millennium, some discernable patterns became visible. One was that the cloud of speculative funds continued to drift around the planet looking for a place to land. Individual speculators, institutional investors, hedge funds, foundations, banks, government agencies were all putting whatever money they could scrape together into the funds. It became larger and able to travel at whatever speed electronic infrastructure would allow. Wherever it settled, that is, on whatever became the new object of speculation, the historically familiar pattern of booming prices, bubbles, bursting bubbles, panic, and crises was being repeated with increasing frequency.

It was not a coincidence, therefore, that during these years bank of mergers, neoliberalism, and high-tech financial engineering led directly to one of largest financial crises in modern history. For those of us who bothered to look carefully at what was going on as we entered the new millennium, it was becoming clear that the financial system was heading toward something quite dangerous.

The public sector, a functionary in the corporate hegemony, played a critical role in sustaining this pattern. Treasury officials made it their

J. Magnuson, *Financing the Apocalypse*,
Palgrave Insights into Apocalypse Economics,
https://doi.org/10.1007/978-3-030-04720-7_9

business to assure that Wall Street that they would have access to every financial market in the world. They gave investment banks an open field in which to engineer new financial instruments for more speculation in total secrecy. Deregulation allowed for the creation of monstrous leviathan bank holding companies that were able to pool together vast amounts of speculative money and channel that money into extremely risky and poorly understood mortgage derivatives. The Fed made sure that there was plenty of cheap money sloshing around the banking system that could be used for leveraged speculation in these new instruments and real estate. As the Fed institutionalized cheap credit and speculation, it made sure that bubbles in stocks, real estate, and derivatives would be maintained and allowed to inflate as long as technically possible.

These developments along with the hubris and greed of *too big to fail* Wall Street institutions combined to erect an upside-down financial pyramid constructed out of fragile real estate markets, subprime mortgage contracts, dubious securities backed by those same mortgages, massive debt collateralized by those dubious securities, and questionable derivatives that were gambles on an assumption that somehow all of this was low-risk. It was like an upside-down pyramid of bubbles layered on top of each other. At each level, a bubble below would help inflate an even larger one above. It was inevitable that the whole edifice was going to crumble and the costs and the damage to people's lives would be staggering.

Before we get into this story, it is important to return to our central theme of Veblen's secular trend and just how far our economy has drifted from the Deweyan project of social provisioning. Beyond engineering ways to make fortunes off of securities trades, it is hard to explain why any system anywhere would need things like structured investment vehicles, collateralized debt obligations, or mortgage default swaps. They are just variations on a theme of the nearly six-thousand-year-old practice of betting on horses. People and institutions place their bets and then watch with hope, exhilaration, greed, fear, and panic. Such is the major preoccupation of modern finance, yet we would never hear a Wall Street CEO say that this is what they are doing. The outward pretense, as it is with all major corporations, is story that they are doing good things for people and their communities. And as we are all vested in the system in one way or another, it behooves us to believe this story even though so much as a cursory glance at objective reality tells otherwise.

Insurance companies say that they are providing coverage. But anyone who has tried to process a claim or look at the deductibles on their plans know that providing coverage is the last thing insurance companies want to do. They employ every possible stratagem to get out of doing that, and then go yodeling to the government about how being forced to do this is prevent them from making money. Nor do the health care providers that charge insurers want to provide actual care. They provide expensive procedures that may or may not improve people's lives. And pharmaceutical companies do not make drugs, they make patents. Software giants do not really care if their products are stable or useable, they care about having monopolies. Cell phone companies are constantly innovating apps to make sure that people everywhere unable to put them down, not even while driving cars on the freeway. Agriculture has become a kind of alchemy in which, as physicist and mathematician Albert Bartlett once quipped, "Modern agriculture is the use of land to convert petroleum into food."[1] Social media giants have commodified human social relationships and transformed them into electronic surrogates that are open for sale to the highest bidder, and are used for surveillance by corporations and governments alike. Online retail giants have stomped small, local shops into oblivion so that what used to be neighborhood bookstores and boutiques are now empty spaces with "for lease" signs on the glass fronts.

And what about housing? The structures in which we live are instruments that indexed, securitized, and traded in global markets. As most of us buy homes using mortgages, the moment we do this, someone, somewhere is placing bets on whether or not we can keep up with the payments. The bet is made into an instrument and sold to someone else, somewhere else. These *someones* could not care less about how important our homes are to our living, or to social provisioning. They see them only in the financial abstract.

This takes us to the central point. The evolutionary drift of economic society has moved so far away from social provisioning, to suggest that it should not be this way sounds quaint. It simply is not recognizable in that way now. Over the last century, corporate hegemony has pieced itself together like a gargantuan jigsaw puzzle. It continues to commodify, securitize, and financialize everything possible thing because it is in nature to do this. What Walton Hamilton described as the "unbroken web" has become a massless and amorphous tangle of electronic currents from which all expect to see a steady flow of money to magically trickle into our bank accounts. What we call "the economy" exists in an ethereal field, or matrix, surrounding the planet and human beings. It is not difficult to see how everyone is wired in; all we have to do is look around in public spaces and observe virtually everyone is fixated on flat rectangular device in the palm of their hands. When the matrix produces surges of money, there is a dopaminergic spike among the human population, as if everyone simultaneously took a hit off of a crack pipe—Euphoria. When it stops, there is a spike in the fight-or-flight hormones adrenaline and cortisol—Dysphoria.

In a collection of essays titled "In Dispraise of Economists," Veblen wrote a passage intended to mock neoclassical economics and what he saw as a dubious claim to being scientific. He summarized the neoclassical utility theory—that today still lies as the basis of consumer choice theory—as a portrait of an economic human being as someone who can only passively react to pleasure and pain,

> The hedonistic conception of man is that of a lightning calculator of pleasures and pains, who oscillates like a homogenous globule of desire of happiness under the impulse of stimuli that shift him about the area, but leave him intact. He has neither antecedent nor consequent. He is an isolated, definitive human datum, in stable equilibrium except for the buffets of the impinging forces that displace him on one direction or another. Self-imposed in elemental space, he spins symmetrically about his own spiritual axis until the parallelogram of forces bears down upon him, whereupon he follows the line of the resultant. When the force of the impact is spent, he comes to rest, a self-contained globule of desire as before.[2]

After a century of self-envisioning via neoliberal tenets of economic individualism and self-interest, people are being molded in this self-image as a globule of desire—a consumer and speculator in the corporate society. Unless wellbeing is a considered wave-like swings between euphoria and dysphoria, the production and distribution of things that might contribute to wellbeing should be considered as a side effect. Like the wildfires of California that once were considered sporadic events but are now permanent, so too is our general state economic roller coasting. This state is most exemplified in our financial system.

In the last chapter the pattern of financial market instability was firmly established by the end of the twentieth century. Financial market instability is revealed as an institutional phenomenon involving financial, corporate, and government institutions in a hegemonic structure that holds the entire population in its grip and colors everything with neoliberal ideology. At the center of it all is the large publicly traded corporation as a legal and financial entity robotically programed for buying resources, selling products, and trading securities for wealth accumulation.

As the corporate hegemony has expanded to dominate the world, everything it touches gets pulled into that program. Market exchanges, governments, central banks, and financial institutions are part of that hegemonic conquest where everything imaginable becomes transformed into a commodity, a consumer good, or a financial security to be traded for profit. This transformative process began centuries ago and is now globally complete. Every inch of the planet—land and sea—is now some for sale, for consumption, or for trade.

This is financialization for the new millennium and is a manifestation of late-stage capitalism's desperate thirst for profit. The corporation and the other institutions it has pulled into its hegemonic structure provide the institutional medium for financialization and neoliberalism is its ideology. Everything is open season for hunters looking for financial gain. Actual production of wealth is passé; it should be gained by extraction, speculation, and manipulation—not production. As such the economies of the world are destined to become increasingly unstable. We know this because we can objectively observe the historical record and see clearly that wherever there is speculation and a popular race to get to the front of the line for grabbing whatever can be taken, there is instability.

Economic historians and analysts have outlined a process of instability that has formed into a pattern that in its basic structure has been replicated for centuries. The pattern begins when an opportunity for gain captures the interest of "entrepreneurs" who find a way to turn the opportunity into a free market—a market that is largely unfettered and allows business people to jump in or jump out at their pleasure. As such, whatever it is that is of interest has to be financialized and corporations form ventures to facilitate this. If the ventures are successful, the entrepreneurs become wealthier and display their exploits with ostentatious displays as member of the corporate jet set. Others seek to emulate and take their "capital" to the markets. Institutional investors like hedge funds get involved and quickly whatever it was that caught interest becomes a cow to be milked until there is nothing left to take. Once depleted, the entrepreneurs look for another opportunity.

Not surprisingly, this process often includes speculation. As the securities or commodities (instruments) created in these ventures become publicly traded, a boom and bust pattern typically follows. Speculators are drawn to the venture and buy up the instruments causing prices to rise. Higher prices trigger even more speculative buying which drives prices higher yet, and soon a boom is underway. Speculative booms have a way of turning into bubbles, which means the prices have been inflated far above a reasonable value. The bubbles become even more overinflated as speculators use money borrowed from banks to place their bets, and so on until the instrument's price is ridiculously high. Eventually, however, for a multitude of reasons and circumstances market bubbles always burst. The burst causes speculators to sell, and sell commands in the markets cause prices to fall, which accentuates a selloff, and the collective impulses that once drove prices upwards turns to fear-inspired selling and prices fall to some rock bottom level. At that point, speculators are either ruined financially or they got out early and moved their cash elsewhere in search of another instrument that captures their interest. The whole process starts all over again in another location where greed turns into euphoria, euphoria turns into fear, fear turns into anger, and anger turns into amnesia. The process replicates.

With time and much conditioning through neoliberal ideological indoctrination, the collective mind of the population settles into a belief that is all normal. With the rise of market populism, profit-making through speculation has become a normal, expected practice. It influences health care coverage as insurance companies are merged into Wall Street. Retirement plans are entirely dependent on the success of corporate ventures and their nest eggs portfolios are managed by institutional investors. As such, financial markets have become much more important than ever before. The population generally views continuously expanding financial markets as good and natural, particularly if they feel that they might get a share of the takings. But when the promise of gain turns to ruin as it does repeatedly over time, the population becomes angry and demands that the government to fix the problem and restore the markets to boom times, though governments and central banks have become major players themselves. These are recurring crises with the complicity of virtually all major institutions and with the expectations of the population. As such, each crisis is now growing in magnitude bringing more destruction and hardship and the coming crises will continue to grow in magnitude.

Even the crises themselves have become rationalized and normalized as "corrections." Though ironically it would be quite rare to hear the booming side of market bubbles as "incorrections." It is as if we have all come to expect recurring financial instability as just an ordinary part of how economies work, like the occasional bad weather. Stock market numbers are quoted ceaselessly in news reports, and all the while the actual intention of speculation is scarcely mentioned like a secret to which we are all privy. What passes as financial planning is nothing more than tips on how to play the game of speculation. It would be odd to have a fund manager tell people which horse would be the best bet for gambling their nest eggs, but they do regularly with securities. Through one pair of shades it looks like gambling and through another it is financial prudence. If the laws of physics can trace the ontology of everything in the world to particles and waves in motion, in the universe of corporate hegemony the particles are securities and the waves are oscillating sine functions of market booms and busts.

In the world fashioned in the image of the corporation, everything possible thing can be securitized, commodified, and financialized—tulips, governments, railroads, businesses, minerals, forests, water, poverty, ecology—nothing is protected from financialization and the potentially extreme volatility that it brings, not even the homes we live in.

Housing Market Bubbles and the Crises of Unaffordability

In the first decade of the 2000s, the stock market has been tepid and bonds have been paying very low rates of interest. Funds in search of returns are scouring the landscape hoping to find something that produce their always-demanded compounding returns and the speculative cloud of hot money settled on housing.

Prior to the crisis, the fact that the US housing market had been in a speculative bubble was clear. According to a report in *The Economist*, "A study by the National Association of Realtors (NAR) found that 23% of all American houses bought in 2004 were for investment, not owner-occupation. Another 13% were bought as second homes. Investors are prepared to buy houses they will rent out at a loss, just because they think prices will keep rising—the very definition of a financial bubble."[3]

According to the Case Shiller Index (see chart in Fig. 9.1) on housing prices, the market hovered around its benchmark of 100 throughout the century between 1950 and 1980.[4] That represented stability. After the onset of the Greenspan Era, the index began jumping up and down by magnitudes of around 20% in less than 10-year intervals. The housing market was becoming volatile. After the stock market crash at the turn of the millennium, vast amounts of hot money moved away from stocks to real estate, real estate securities, and real estate investment trusts, the index soared to nearly 200 by 2006 and showed an increase of about 77% in about seven years, then lost nearly all of those gains in a few years after.

Though Fed officials refused to acknowledge it publicly, the evidence was clear that by 2005 and 2006 the US housing market had inflated into a bubble. First of all, for most of the decades after World War Two, the entire second half of the twentieth-century housing prices remained stable and increased at a rate that was consistent with price inflation

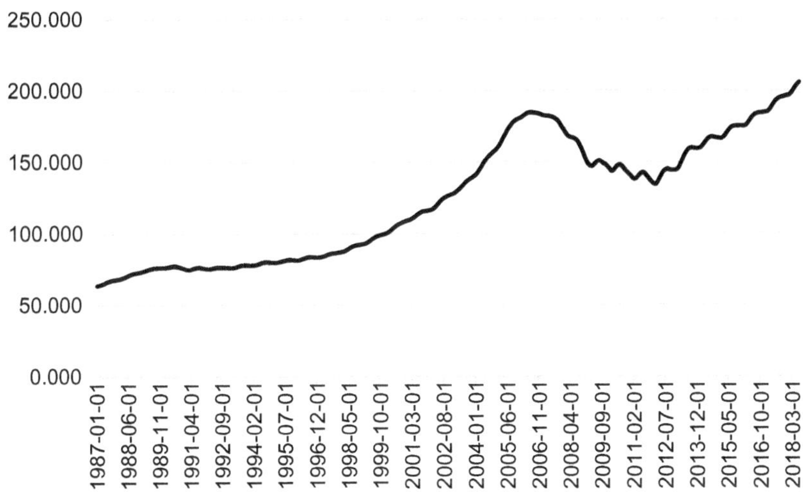

Fig. 9.1 S&P Case-Shiller US National Home Price Index, 1987–2018 (*Source* Federal Reserve Bank of St. Louis and Standard and Poors, S&P/Case-Shiller U.S. National Home Price Index, https://fred.stlouisfed.org/series/CSUSHPINSA)

in general. Throughout those years, the Shiller index of housing prices remained close to the index benchmark of 100. But in the mid-1990s, the housing bubble started to inflate from speculation.

By the 2000s, the housing market had caught the attention of speculators was clearly evident. In 2004, the NAR reported that nearly a quarter of all homes purchased that year were for speculative investments. People and institutions were buying houses in the same way people buy stocks on the speculation that they were going to rise in price.

Also, like other speculative bubbles, as long as enough people believed that real estate prices will always rise, the belief becomes a self-fulfilling prophecy. As more people buy real estate for investment, this drives up prices and their speculation is confirmed. Speculators pumped up the market bubble and the Shiller index soared above 150. Between 2004 and 2005, housing prices in the United States rose 15%, and by 2006, the Shiller index close to 200, which indicated that real estate prices in general were double what would be considered to be normal.

Housing market speculators were also recklessly taking out large "interest only" mortgages to buy property on the gamble that the rate of housing market appreciation will outstretch the finance charges on borrowed funds. Interest-only loans are those that the monthly payments are limited to interest payments only and no principle. Speculators simply measure the cash outflow for interest payments against what they anticipate will be the rate of growth of housing prices. In the premier bubble market in California, over 60% of all new mortgages taken out in 2004 were interest-only loans compared to 2002 when the figure was only 8%.

Between 2004 and 2005, housing prices in the United States overall rose 15%.[5] Such a run-up in prices was triggered by a positive feedback dynamic in which speculators buy property with the intention of owning it for a year and then selling it to make a 15% rate of return. Others get into the game, and by doing so, they drive up prices creating the usual self-fulfilling prophecy of speculation. Prices were also soaring as banks were recklessly lending money to borrowers who could not afford to make their mortgage payments, and everyone was counting on the impossibility that home prices will always appreciate. Speculators have been taking out large mortgages, often through interest-only loans, and buying property on the bet that the rate of appreciation will outstretch the finance charges on borrowed funds. In the premier bubble market of California, over 60% of all new mortgages taken out in 2004 were interest-only loans—in 2002, the figure was only 8%.[6]

As is well known now, the massive housing market bubble burst after 2006. From Case-Shiller data, between 2006 and 2012, the market tanked by about 38%. Since then, private equity has once again surged into real estate with the intention of buying up homes and turn them into investment property. The housing market bubble has reinflated and prices have soared. As of June, 2018 the index has climbed to 204. Housing is far beyond the affordability of most young buyers and the market share of home ownership for first-time buyers has dropped to a 30-year low.[7] One conclusion we can draw from the Case-Shiller long-term trendline is that housing markets have become increasingly unstable, presumably from private equity speculation. Another is that housing is becoming something that fewer and fewer people will ever be able to afford.

The Upside-Down Pyramid and the Crisis of 2007–2009

The housing and mortgage credit industries are inseparable and expand and contract together like a pair of lungs. This is because the demand side of the housing market consists mostly of debt. As credit for mortgages is made available, more potential homeowners and speculators borrow money to buy houses. This borrowed money gets pumped into the housing market and prices start to push upward. If mortgage credit dries up, there will be less demand in the housing market and prices will drop. Bubbles in housing markets will inflate when an excess amount of cash and borrowed money in pumped into the buying or demand side of the market, and that is what happened when The Fed made enormous amounts of credit readily available at low-interest rates throughout the 1990s and well into the 2000s. According to a report in the Boston Globe at the time, "[Our banks] are knowingly approving risky loans to get the feds and activists off their backs… When the coming wave of foreclosures rolls through the inner city, which of today's self-congratulating bankers, politicians, and regulators plans to take the credit?"[8]

After the market crises ran their course in nineties and the dot.com crash at the beginning of the millennium, speculation turned to real estate. Real estate bubbles, debt bubbles, and derivatives constructed out of these bubbles layered on top of one another like an upside-down pyramid—something any two-year-old child could see as an unstable structure. At the narrowest base laid the US housing market and the mortgage industry, which were inflated into speculative bubbles. Part of the gas, so to speak, to inflate the bubbles came from the Fed the rest came from government policy and massive amounts of Wall Street speculative cash. A key segment that became highly unstable was the so-called subprime mortgage business (Fig. 9.2).

As the housing market expands into a bubble, it feeds into the mortgage business. This is inevitable as the housing and mortgage industries are inseparable. Ballooning real estate prices provides more collateral, at least on paper, that can be used to leverage more mortgages.

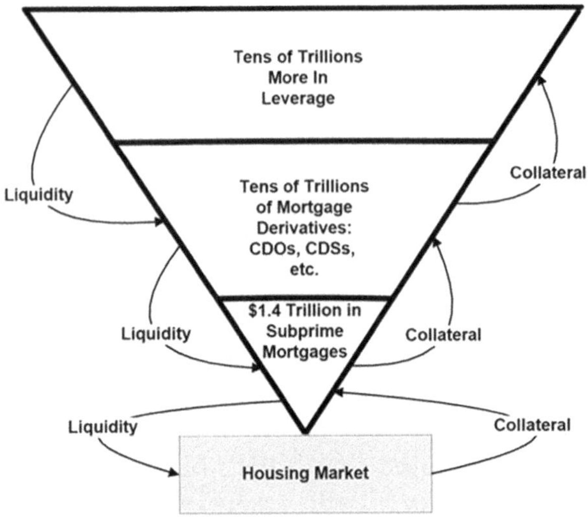

Fig. 9.2 The upside-down pyramid

The money from mortgages comes from various money market sources and from securities markets. When mortgages are securitized, meaning refashioned into something like a bond (mortgage-backed security), and sold for cash. The cash from the sales can be used to finance more mortgages. More mortgages become available and mortgage brokers do everything they can to sell them, even if they sell to borrowers who are unlikely to repay. Mortgage brokers are not overly concerned about risk because they have no intention of holding on to the loans because they can sell to Wall Street investment banks, hedge funds, etc. Speculators are drawn to the market for these mortgage-backed securities and another bubble market is created. Just like in stock market booms, rising bubbles in mortgage instruments catches the attention of speculators who then pour large amounts of money in the market to speculate on these inflating instruments. Many of these speculators were large Wall Street banks borrowing from each other to buy ever larger amounts of these over inflated instruments. Collateral builds up one side the pyramid and money cascades down the other side in a closed feedback loop.

Such a financial structure is an institutional phenomenon. It could not have been built to the gargantuan scale that it did without massive concentrations of money in the hands of Wall Street leviathan banks as well as the support structure of government institutions. The Clinton administration was determined to make home ownership a key part of their economic strategy in the mid-1990s. The Department of Housing and Urban Develop sent a directive to Fannie Mae and Freddie Mac—government sponsored enterprises that specialize in mortgage securitization—that they must devote over 40% of their funds to low-to-middle income households.[9]

The effect of the expansion of home ownership is to also expand bank credit to riskier frontiers. Banks tend to lend to preferred, low-risk borrowers as a no brainers. With the drive to expand home ownership, lending shifts from preferred to riskier borrowers, and eventually to subprime, which carry a likelihood of default. But unlike other risky deals, these loans are collateralized by the underlying property. Even if lenders intended on holding on to the loans, they were less concerned about the risk because if the homeowner defaulted the bank takes ownership of the property, and with market appreciation, they could sell the property and still profit. That was all based on an assumption that the housing market would always appreciate.

This expansion was institutionally facilitated by government sponsored enterprises and their securitization of mortgages. Ginnie Mae, one of the original government sponsored enterprises, created mortgage-backed securities (MBS) and collateralized debt obligations (CDO) with the intention of expanding the availability of credit that can be used to help banks provide loans to people who wanted to buy homes. The process of securitization was fairly simple. Banks would lend borrowers their mortgages to buy homes, and once the banks have collected a number of these mortgages into a portfolio, or pool, they would create securities, MBSs, that represent the principal and interest of all the mortgages. The value and income stream from all the mortgages in the pool were divided equally into securities, like bonds. The investors who buy the securities pay the market price for the MBSs and receive a return from the income stream that flows from the borrowers who make their mortgage payments. The cash from the sale of the mortgages goes back to the banks, which now have more money they can use to make more mortgages. As this structure expands, more money is made available, and home ownership expands.

The structure changed with time as the business shifted from government sponsored enterprises to private sector banks. Private MBSs were divided not equally as they were by Ginnie Mae, but into separate groupings or “tranches” as they came to be called on Wall Street. Each tranche represents a different level of risk and different classes of MBSs would be created and assigned different ratings accordingly—AAA, AA, A, etc.—by credit rating agencies. The riskier groups of mortgages were put into the lower rated tranches and the MBSs were sold to investors with higher interest rates to reflect the risk premiums.

Wall Street continued innovate on the basic structure and produced collateralized debt obligations. These are similar to MBSs except that they added other things to the portfolio besides mortgages such as car loans, credit card debt, and student loans. In addition, the CDOs were structured around equity appreciation as well as income streams from borrowers’ payments. Some of the tranches that were sliced into CDOs were paying interest, but the interest was not derived from mortgage payments, but from home equity.

Alan Greenspan at the Fed saw the financial innovations of creating mortgage-related instruments and the deregulation of their markets as a key to expanding home ownership. And in typical fashion, seems to have ignored the elevation of risk it involves. In a 2005 speech, he said, “Unquestionably innovation and deregulation have vastly expanded credit availability to virtually all income classes. Access to credit has enabled families to purchase homes, deal with emergencies, and obtain goods and services. Home ownership is at a record high.”[10]

As long as the housing market bubble continued to soar, the securitization business was booming and the MBSs and CDOs were selling like hotcakes. Institutional investors such as pension funds that could not make their fixed obligations to pensioners were drawn to these securities because interest on traditional government or corporate bonds was not enough. They were particularly drawn to the riskier tranches because of the higher returns.

Speculator money was pouring in from institutional investors and that money moved down one side of the pyramid as it was used to make more mortgages. With more mortgages available, mortgage brokers could make more deals and collect their fees. Mortgage money flowed further down the pyramid to the housing market as borrowers bought homes and the housing market prices inflated into a massive bubble. More expensive houses meant mortgages needed to be larger. This put greater demand pressure on the securitization business, which forced up the returns on MBSs and CDOs. This incentivized banks to create more of them and incentivized institutional investors to buy more. And so the multiple-bubble structure inflated in a self-reinforcing pattern of expansion.

It was not only pension funds that were buying MBSs and CDOs. Some of the largest investors who bought these instruments were Wall Street giants like Lehman Brothers and Bear Stearns. These large companies were buying massive amounts, not on behalf of their clients, but for themselves on their own accounts. Moreover, they were borrowing money or "leveraging" to do it. In many cases, they borrowed money from the same banks that were selling them the instruments. Bringing this practice under regulatory control was one of the substantive provisions in the financial reform legislation.

Like all speculators, these investment banks love cheap credit and they call it leverage to make borrowing money sound more advantageous and business-like. The enormous debt that Lehman Brothers and many other banks accumulated as leverage for buying these dubious instruments created dangerous levels of risk in the system. High levels of systemic risk imply a high probability that the system will crash. The banks were allowed to do this because in 2004, the U.S. Securities Exchange Commission deregulated the rules regarding the amount of debt banks can take on when they trade on their own accounts. As part of a forty-six-page document issued by the SEC called, "Alternative Net Capital Requirements for Broker-Dealers That Are Part of Consolidated Supervised Entities," the rules for the debt to asset ratio limit were changed so that banks could use a different mathematical model for debt-to-asset ratio. This, in effect, lifted from a maximum of 12–1 as high as 30–1 just by tweaking the model. To put this in perspective, if you own a house worth $400,000, and if you were an investment bank, you now could post your house as collateral and borrow a maximum of $12 million rather than $4.8 million as before the rule change. And banks did that.

If banks use $1.4 trillion of subprime mortgages to securitize $14 trillion in instruments, and if those instruments are used as collateral to borrow at debt to asset ratios that range from 12–1 to as high as 30–1, the result is a debt bubble mounted at the top of the pyramid that expands to between $168 trillion and $420 trillion. All fixed above a shaky and narrow base of subprime mortgages that were doomed to fail.

On top of all of this was yet another layer of innovation: credit default swaps (CDSs).

These are instruments that work as insurance against default on a range of fixed income securities, including standard bonds, MBS tranches, and CDOs. In the case of MBSs or CDOs, the buyer buys the instrument and pays a premium in exchange for a promise from the seller to pay off the debt if the debtor defaults. They became popular in the 1990s with the rise of the Clinton administration's plan to expand subprime lending. It became a convenient way for banks to unload default risk of their loan portfolios. This became more important after the SEC allowed banks to lower their capital requirements relative to debt.

Lenders or bond investors used CDSs to hedge against the risk of default. But the tricky part about these instruments is that they became speculative instruments themselves as something you could buy even though you don't own the debt in question. It would be like buying insurance on your neighbor's house on the bet that house will burn down and you will receive payment. Buyers of CDSs used to hedge against defaults in MBSs were willing to make the premium payments on the gamble that those mortgages packaged in the pools were going to fail.

The efficient market argument in neoliberalism sees CDSs as an economic benefit because, "they make it easier for credit risks to be borne by those who are in the best position to bear them, that they enable financial institutions to make loans they would not otherwise be able to make, and that their trading reveals useful information about credit risk."[11] The master neoliberal himself, Alan Greenspan, frequently wax enthusiastically about such innovation and stated in one of his speeches these derivatives contribute "to the development of a far more flexible, efficient, and hence resilient financial system than existed just a quarter century ago."[12] However, the fact that the credit crisis led him to conclude that the "whole intellectual edifice" which underlies the use of credit derivatives and complex financial instruments "collapsed in the summer of last year" because of risk management mistakes.[13] Greenspan remarkably dismissed the whole nasty business as a mere mistake in assessing and managing risk.

Greenspan used his backhand to dismiss the role played by government deregulation and corporate jet setters' hubris. He dismissed the enormous concentration of money that combined to erect an upside-down financial pyramid constructed out of fragile real estate markets, subprime mortgage contracts, dubious securities backed by those same mortgages, massive debt collateralized by those dubious securities, and questionable derivatives that were gambles on an assumption that somehow all of this was low-risk. He dismissed how obvious it was to most astute observers, even those in his inner circle that the whole edifice was going to crumble and that the costs and the damage to people's lives would be staggering.

The Pyramid Crumbles

The cracks in the edifice began to show when housing prices began to decline and between 2006 and 2009. Home prices, measured by the Shiller Index, fell by a devastating 33%. Home sales plunged by 13% in 2007, which up to that point was the biggest decline in 25 years, then continued plummet by 22–24% in each of the years following.[14] Subprime mortgage payments stopped flowing, equity values collapsed, and soon the trillions of mortgage-backed instruments were collapsing in values. In other words, the bubbles that had inflated the inverted pyramid had finally started their long-awaited burst. Soon banks and investors who borrowed heavily to invest in mortgage-backed instruments discovered that their portfolios of these instruments were being obliterated. The universe of fictional financial value that these institutions created had disappeared back into the thin air from where it came.

Among the first to experience large-scale trouble was banking giant, Northern Rock. As Northern Rock's assets dried up, so did its cash flow and it became incapable of servicing its debt obligations. It eventually turned to the Bank of England for emergency bailout funds. But once the news of the bailout was made public, panic spread among its depositors and run on the bank ensued in which the depositors literally demanded their money out of the bank. This was the first bank run in the UK in 150 years. At the same time, Wall Street giant, Lehman Brothers for the same reasons moved into bankruptcy and broke the record as largest corporate failure in history. Until then, the record bankruptcy had occurred in 2002 with the $104 billion collapse of telecommunications giant WorldCom. Lehman Brothers surpassed that record with a bullet and wiped out $639 billion in assets.[15]

Financial crises like this are commonplace events in the history of capitalism. The basic structure is not much different from the so-called dot.com stock market crash of the early 2000s, or the East Asian and Russian crises of the late 1990s, the Mexican financial crisis in the mid-1990s, the various financial crises of the twentieth century including the stock market crashes of 1987 and 1929, the stock market crashes and the American wildcat banking crises of the nineteenth century, the South Sea and Mississippi Bubbles of eighteenth-century Europe, or the Tulip Mania going all the way back to the early 1600s.[16] What sets this crisis apart, however, is that the scale of it is nearly beyond imagination.

When financial crises become extreme like in magnitude they can set in motion a chain reaction of troubles as every aspect of the economic system is linked to every other. As the crisis spread from the banking sector to other sectors of the economy, the economic machine began grinding gears and falling apart. Business failures and layoffs soared. The numbers revealing the magnitude of the economic crisis that followed were stunning. Foreclosures soared everywhere and were up 55% between the summer of 2007 and the summer of 2008, which was up 76% from the previous year and 1.35 million homes falling into foreclosure during the third quarter of 2008. New home sales collapsed and lending companies were taking over the properties that were collateralized with real estate that the loans now were deeply drowning underwater. Banking business associations reported that the first quarter of 2009 showed record levels of credit delinquencies—the highest since 1974—and they attribute the cause of these delinquencies to mounting job losses.[17]

The U.S. Department of Labor shocked the nation when it announced a 597,000 net job loss for the month of November 2008, which is the worst monthly loss in 34 years. This was then followed by new records with a loss of 681,000 in December, 741,000 in January 2009, 681,000 in February, 652,000 in March, and 519,000 in April, and 322,000 in May. People saw the May numbers and began to sigh with relief that the worst was over. But then Labor reported another 467,000 jobs lost in June. By July 2009, total payroll employment had fallen by 6.5 million jobs in less than about a year and half. Job losses caused more defaults, and foreclosures in the mortgage industry continued to rage hitting hit a record of 2.5 million in 2009. That same year, 1 in 45 mortgages fell into default, which was 21% more than in 2008 and more than double what it was in 2009.[18] The rest of the economic fallout that led to the Great Recession is well documented. This was a Wall Street-Washington Joint Venture in ruin and it is unlikely that either institutions can be relied upon for solutions given that they are both culpable and show no signs of changes to their basic structure aside from glossy patches like Dodd-Frank.

Dodd-Frank Illusions

The corporation has become not only too big to fail and politically connected, it has virtually eliminated all other possible institutional orders besides its own hegemony. Members of the corporate class occupy essentially every institutional chamber of federal government from the White House, to Congress, to the Supreme Court. Members of Congress sit on regulatory committees, and occasionally they express indignation when a corporate executive is caught doing some nefarious thing or another. But most of the indignation is performed to give the appearance that the public interest is being served. Even with a threat that top executives could be sacked if there is trouble, there is no serious institutional threat and is tempered by lush severance packages. Moreover, corporate hegemony has captured the media and educational institutions to such a complete extent that the occasional critic or dissident can only be found standing bashfully like a wallflower on the margins.

The captains and lieutenants of industry are acutely aware that their companies are never going to be allowed to fail because of the massive collateral damage that it would cause to everyone else. This institutional situation did not come to pass willy-nilly. This has been a long time coming in corporate evolution. Grabbing power and making sure that the Fed and Treasury and Congress are there to serve their interests have been carefully executed over a long period of time.

One of the most salient lessons we have learned from this crisis is the extent of institutional capture in corporate hegemony. The federal government had an opportunity, for a brief moment at least, in which it could have used its "resolution authority" over the bank holding companies on Wall Street and other corporations that were queued up in the bailout soup line. Such authority would allow the Fed and Treasury the option of taking over failing companies, let stockholders lose their value, fire executives, and renegotiate their terms with creditors. For banks, this is authority already held by the Federal Deposit Insurance Corporation as it deals with insolvent banks in its program. The most cogent argument in favor of this strategy is that if these financial institutions are indeed *too big to fail*, they should be operated as public utilities rather kept on public assistance. Ellen Brown in her book, *The Public Bank Solution: From Austerity to Prosperity* (2013) argues that governments should have public banks that function in a manner similar to public utilities as they are too important to be left to Wall Street. Brown writes, "By making banking a public utility, with expandable credit issued by banks that are owned by the people, the financial system can be made to serve the people rather than people serving the banks." Brown contrasts a public bank that is chartered to serve the needs of the community rather with conventional banking that she characterizes as parasitic, "The virtues of an expandable credit system can be retained while avoiding the parasitic exploitation to which private banks are prone, by establishing a network of public banks that serve the people because they are owned by the people."[19] The federal government obviously did not choose this path and chose the bailout, technical patch up option instead and left the big banks even more *too big to fail* than they were before.

Since the financial crisis and recession that began around 2007, nothing of any institutional significance has changed. The familiar pattern will continue to rewind and be replayed as it has always done. In a practical sense, well-intentioned government officials see that the best we can hope for are a few technical fixes to problems of instability with largely symbolic legislation. Even so, the new bills are brought out with great fanfare.

On July 21, 2010, Barack Obama signed another piece of legislation that was heralded in the press as "sweeping" and "historic." The bill, *Restoring American Financial Stability Act of 2010*, also known as "Dodd-Frank" named after the bill's sponsors, promises to protect the US economy from further instabilities, prevent the need for more bank bailouts, and safeguard consumers from predatory banking practices. The bill is indeed sweeping in the sense that it is complicated and contains over 1500 pages of text. As the title suggests, some level of financial stability will be restored, and to some degree consumers will be better protected from the sleazy banditry from bankers.

One key provision is that it authorizes the federal government to create the Consumer Financial Protection Bureau. This agency will provide oversight into banking practices on how loans are made, under what terms, and with full disclosure and transparency. The intention is to crack down on predatory practices that contributed to the subprime loan disaster, a key element in the broader crisis. The bill requires that certain complex financial instruments be traded in organized exchanges supervised by the federal government. By forcing derivatives into supervised market exchanges, it is hoped that these instruments will become more transparent, better understood through the flow of information in the markets, and easier for the government to regulate. Sponsors of the bill also created new rules that place limitations on banks using their own capital to trade risky derivatives for their own accounts. It also includes new rules limitations on banks "leveraged trading," that is, limiting the amount banks can borrow to trade these risky instruments.

The banking bill is compromise legislation that was mangled by an army of lobbyists. As such, the bill lacks real substance. For one thing, the enforceability of the new rules that will regulate the trading of mortgage-related instruments are significantly diluted and riddled with of exemptions and technicalities that seem to be tailored for Wall Street companies. Most important, the Restoring American Financial Stability Act does very little to change the circumstances that led to the banking crisis in the first place—the overconcentration of bank assets into the hands of what is now a handful of highly merged *too big to fail* leviathan banks.

The final version of the bill was the product of partisan politics and industry lobbying, and also like the health reform bill, it is little more than a political trophy for the Democratic Party. In future elections, the Democrats can boast of scoring a "historic" political victory by passing "sweeping" legislation and hope that no one looks too closely. Simon and Kwak are critical of the patch up approach to dealing with financial crises as it naively ignores what they call the American Oligarchy, "The idea that we can simply regulate large banks more effectively assumes that regulators will have the incentive to do so, despite everything we know about regulatory capture."[20] That is to say capture by the oligarchy, or as we are describing it here, the corporate hegemony. But oligarchy is fitting in another way as it seems more than fate that Donald Trump's administration is given the keys to the regulatory body, the Consumer Financial Protection Agency, as Trump himself has shown a certain fascination with oligarchical politics.

In light of this, Dodd-Frank has created something that raises serious questions about democratic accountability. The law gives substantial leeway to regulators regarding the specific policies it will pursue. It created the Financial Stability Oversight Council (FSOC), which is chaired by the Secretary of the Treasury and consists of representatives from all the major banking and financial system regulatory agencies, including the Fed, SEC, FDIC, and the Consumer Financial Protection Bureau. As of now, the Secretary of Treasury has executive powers over the FSOC on what to regulate, or how to regulate, or on whose behalf the regulations are being carried out. In other words, this is a fatal weak link. The quality of the safeguards put in place for reasons of stability, sanity, or democracy are only as good as a key member of the executive branch of the government wants it to be, particularly one which dreams of oligarchy.

Notes

1. Albert Bartlett, "Forgotten Fundamentals of the Energy Crisis," *Negative Population Growth Special Report*, 1977.
2. Thorstein Veblen, "In Dispraise of Economists: Why Is Economics Not an Evolutionary Science?", in *The Portable Veblen* (New York: Viking Press, 1948), pp. 232–233.
3. *The Economist.com*, "In Come the Waves," June 16, 2005.
4. *Business Week*, February 11, 2008, p. 41.
5. *Washington Post*, July 21, 2005, D1.
6. *The Economist.com*, June 16, 2005.
7. Danielle Booth, 2017, p. 4.
8. Ibid., p. 22.
9. Wayne Barrett, "Andrew Cuomo and Fannie and Freddie: How the Youngest Housing and Urban Development Secretary in History Gave Birth to the Mortgage Crisis," *The Village Voice*, August 5, 2008. http://www.netadvisor.org/wp-content/uploads/2014/10/2008-08-05-New-York-Andrew-Cuomo-and-Fannie-and-Freddie-Village-Voice.pdf.
10. Alan Greenspan, "Remarks by Chairman Alan Greenspan," lecture given at Federal Reserve Community Affairs Research Conference, April 8, 2005. https://www.federalreserve.gov/boarddocs/speeches/2005/20050408/default.htm.
11. René Stulz, "Credit Default Swaps and the Credit Crisis," Working Paper 15384, National Bureau of Economic Research (NBER), p. 3. http://www.nber.org/papers/w15384, National Bureau of Economic Research.
12. Alan Greenspan, "Economic Flexibility," speech to HM Treasury enterprise Conference, 2004, London, U.K. https://www.federalreserve.gov/boarddocs/speeches/2004/20040126/default.htm.
13. Alan Greenspan, "The Financial Crisis and the Role of Economic Regulators: Testimony of Dr. Alan Greenspan, Committee of Government Oversight and Reform," October 23, 2008. https://www.gpo.gov/fdsys/pkg/CHRG-110hhrg55764/html/CHRG-110hhrg55764.htm.

14. Kathryn J. Byun, "The U.S. Housing Bubble and Bust: Impacts on Employment," *Bureau of Labor Statistics Monthly Labor Review*, December 2010, p. 3.
15. Dan Wilchins, "Lehman Files for Bankruptcy, Plans to Sell Units," *Reuters*, September 15, 2008.
16. Joel Magnuson, *Mindful Economics: How the US Economy Works, Why It Matters, and How It Could Be Different* (New York, NY: Seven Stories Press, 2008), pp. 298–336.
17. *Business Week*, July 11, 2008, p. 66.
18. See the Bureau of Labor Statistics historical employment data at http://data.bls.gov/timeseries/CES0000000001?output_view=net_1mth; see also Byun, "The U.S. Housing Bubble and Bust: Impacts on Employment," pp. 10–16.
19. Ellen Brown, *The Public Bank Solution* (Baton Rouge, LA: Third Millennium Press, 2013), p. 3.
20. Simon and Kwak, p. 207.

References

Barrett, Wayne. "Andrew Cuomo and Fannie and Freddie: How the Youngest Housing and Urban Development Secretary in History Gave Birth to the Mortgage Crisis," *The Village Voice*, August 5, 2008. http://www.netadvisor.org/wp-content/uploads/2014/10/2008-08-05-New-York-Andrew-Cuomo-and-Fannie-and-Freddie-Village-Voice.pdf.

Bartlett, Albert. "Forgotten Fundamentals of the Energy Crisis," *Negative Population Growth Special Report*, 1977.

Booth, Danielle. *Fed Up: An Insider's Take On Why the Federal Reserve Is Bad for America* (New York, NY: Penguin, 2017).

Brown, Ellen. *The Public Bank Solution* (Baton Rouge, LA: Third Millennium Press, 2013).

Bureau of Labor Statistics. https://data.bls.gov/timeseries/CES0000000001?output_view=net_1mth.

Business Week, July 11, 2008.

Business Week, February 11, 2008.

Byun, Kathryn J. "The U.S. Housing Bubble and Bust: Impacts on Employment," *Bureau of Labor Statistics Monthly Labor Review*, December 2010, p. 3.

The Economist.com, "In Come the Waves," June 16, 2005.

Greenspan, Alan. "Remarks by Chairman Alan Greenspan: Economic Flexibility," HM Treasury Enterprise Conference, 2004, London. https://www.federalreserve.gov/boarddocs/speeches/2004/20040126/default.htm.

Greenspan, Alan. "Remarks by Chairman Alan Greenspan," Federal Reserve Community Affairs Research Conference, April 8, 2005. https://www.federalreserve.gov/boarddocs/speeches/2005/20050408/default.htm.

Greenspan, Alan. "The Financial Crisis and the Role of Economic Regulators," Committee of Government Oversight and Reform, October 23, 2008. https://www.gpo.gov/fdsys/pkg/CHRG-110hhrg55764/html/CHRG-110hhrg55764.htm.

Magnuson, Joel. *Mindful Economics: How the US Economy Works, Why It Matters, and How It Could Be Different* (New York, NY: Seven Stories Press, 2008).

Stulz, René. "Credit Default Swaps and the Credit Crisis," Working Paper 15384, National Bureau of Economic Research (NBER), p. 3. http://www.nber.org/papers/w15384.

10

Microfinance and Loan Sharking

As we take into account these stories of recurring financial system instability, it raises the question of if it is even possible to make banking and financial stable and serve the purpose of social provisioning. At every turn there seems to be a new innovation that has become all the rage because it promises great things for people and the environment while generating handsome profits and lucrative careers. Things like socially responsible investing, impact investing, organic food production, fair trade, green energy, and so many other initiatives were cast in the limelight as win-win business models in which entrepreneurs could do right by the world and make big bucks along the way. The main drive of all these business models is that they have been designed to change our economic activities in such a way that the goal of making livelihoods is aligned with broader goals of social and environmental goals of equity, sustainability, and profitable business.

Undeniably this drive is part stems from a growing awareness of impact that widening wealth inequality, climate change, and unserviceable debt is having on the world's poorest populations. These problems are becoming so exigent that they can no longer be ignored. Consumers, businesses, and governments everywhere see a need for

J. Magnuson, *Financing the Apocalypse*,
Palgrave Insights into Apocalypse Economics,
https://doi.org/10.1007/978-3-030-04720-7_10

change direction, though real economic change is complicated, and finding real and lasting solutions remains distant and intractable. As a result, genuine efforts tend to be postponed. Problems get rolled over into the next year, next decade, or next generation. As they do, they become more severe. This is the central issue with mounting debt because it never feels like a real problem as long as we can keep putting off repayment. Sinking into a quicksand of unsustainable debt is unfortunately a familiar circumstance for people the world over. Regardless of how or why people become trapped by debt, their circumstances are made much worse with predatory lending practices, or loan sharking, that deliberately target those who are already economically vulnerable.

Banks or financial companies can have an enormous impact on economy and ecology depending on how it is done and what types of projects are financed. Microfinance was once held in high esteem as an innovative alternative to loan sharking as strategy for poverty reduction in the developing world. The strategy, as it was originally conceived decades ago, is simple. Microfinance, (or microcredit) institutions received source funds largely from international aid agencies. The funds were channeled into underserved communities as small, low-cost loans that could be used for investments in simple capital like a sewing machine or a water pump. The borrowers could then use their investment to create microenterprises that generate income and possibly a surplus to pay back the loans. Under the leadership of Bangladeshi economist, founder of the Grameen Bank, microfinance pioneer, and Nobel Prize recipient Mohammed Yunus, the model became established as a means to help the poor. Microfinance advocates rejoiced that the model was to become a sustainable, self-funded, closed loop of economic development that provides income and contributes to the economic vibrancy of otherwise impoverished communities. Yunus was awarded the Nobel Peace Prize in 2006. The model was celebrated with all the glitter of superstar status and was vaulted internationally as *the* development strategy. That is, until its mission began to morph and fell significantly short of its promise.

The microfinance model had caught the attention of the neoliberals in Washington during the Greenspan Era. While the model was being celebrated, it was changing into something else. As the Washington

Consensus steamrolled around the world, the US government and source fund agencies began pressuring developing countries commercialize their microfinance sectors and reshape them into a neoliberal dream: individualistic bootstrap finance, for-profit entrepreneurship, and the elimination of government aid in the fight against poverty. The reality, however, was a different story. Data showed that by the time of the Greenspan Era, microfinance could not give any indication that it was improving living standards for the people it was supposed to help. What was clear from the data, however, was that commercialization of microfinance resulted in soaring profits for the lenders and soaring inequality. Loan sharks returned in drag, only by then they could take cover behind the popularized image of a neoliberal success story. It was drawn into a cult characterized by a blind slavishness toward innovation and quasi-religious faith in free markets.

In January 2011, Muhammad Yunus reflected on this and lamented in a New York Times editorial that, "I never imagined that one day microcredit would give rise to its own breed of loan sharks…. Commercialization has been a terrible wrong turn for microfinance, and it indicates a worrying 'mission drift' in the motivation of those lending to the poor."[1] Yunus's candid declaration of mission drift is consistent with so many aspects of modern finance that we have explored. At one time the institutions and models were development as part of a mission to improve the lives of people, only to drift toward profiteering, speculation, or gambling.

Seeing this from an institutional perspective, however, there are deeper and more pernicious forces at work that simply allowing greed to derail the mission. Under corporate hegemony and its historical relentless to commodify, securitize, and financialize everything it touches, poverty itself is financialized. In this and the chapters that follow, we shall see how even the things that are almost unimaginable to be subjected to financialization have become just that. The globalization of corporate hegemony and its neoliberal ideology have made financial instruments out of poverty, out of people's desire to help others pull themselves out of poverty, and even out of climate change. In a twist of modern history, the efforts to deal with damage done to people and their habitat by corporate capitalism have become the newest frontiers for corporate profit-making and opportunities for posh careers for the corporate class.

Microcredit and Loan Sharking

Loan sharking has been around for as long as banking itself. Wherever there are people who have fallen onto hard times, which is everywhere, there are lenders who lure them into a trap. The promise quick and easy loans that provide leverage people can use to pry themselves out of financial desperation—maybe to get through a business slump, a bad crop yield, or maybe just to pay a month's rent or buy food. The trap gets laid down as the sharks allow the borrowers to put off paying back the loan principal for a time and roll the accruing interest into a larger future loan. Unpaid principal and interest quickly snowball into a larger debt burden for which the lenders agree to keep rolling forward only at increasingly higher interest rates as compensation for mounting risk exposure. Borrowers find themselves overwhelmed, but they also scramble hard to find ways to make debt payments out of fear of being cut off of credit. The poor sink while the sharks make fortunes.

Traditionally loan sharking was largely confined to mafia type organizations that make predatory loans outside the parameters of banking institutions and government regulations. Sharks used coercion, blackmail, and violence to enforce repayment. But it is largely a matter of degree and method that separates legal banking from sharking. Payday lending in the United States is a $6 billion industry.[2] These are typically small loans or cash advances that are made to borrowers on the single criteria that they have a job with a regular payday. These lenders are considered the most predatory—exploiting the financial vulnerability of borrowers—of the legal financial sector. For this reason, they are regulated in most places with usury laws, or interest rate caps, set somewhere between 30 and 40% annual percentage rate (APR), and with limited origination fees. In places without usury laws, the APR could be several hundred or even into the thousands. The trap is set when the borrow comes through the front door and is presented with an instant loan at what appear to be reasonable rates.

Say a borrower needs a $500 loan. The borrower goes to the payday lender, shows proof of employment or secures it with a postdated check, then agrees to pay back the principal plus say 20% interest within 30 days. If the borrower fails to pay according to terms, then the principal and interest roll into the next 30 days and so on. But even if they pay the loan back on time, the APR is much more than 20%. The terms of the loan were set to be paid in a month, which if annualized could snowball to 800% in a year. Once on the hook, the borrower's liability could soar from $500 to well over $4000 in 12 months. At that point, the mafia lender can use coercive methods to extract thousands from borrowers who are already poor and desperate.

Lending by credit card associations among the large commercial banks is not all that different. Rates are high and each month the banks issue a bill with the minimum payment amount featured prominently with the intention of enticing the cardholder to pay the minimum and thus accruing more interest to the bank and eventually falling into a debt trap. Borrowers are nonetheless compelled to stay current with their payments because of the long-term damage defaults can do to people's credit standing, which can affect their careers, possibility of home ownership, and ability to rent housing.

Sharking aside, small-scale lending, or microcredit, has always been an important aspect of community economic development. The objectives of the microcredit models that are legitimate in terms of social provisioning involve making very small loans to people, often those in communities that are struggling economically, that would allow them to finance small income-generating projects—microfinance. The goals are not to enrich lenders, but to help people develop microenterprises, improve livelihoods, and make them less vulnerable to sharks. Models of microfinance have been around for at least a century as financial cooperatives and savings associations that were originally created to help communities survive troubled economic times.

The model of microfinance that has gained so much attention in recent decades, particularly during the Greenspan Era, is that which has been heralded as *the* solution to problems of poverty in developing countries of Asia, Africa, and Latin America. The origins of the model date back to the early 1960s and the Cold War during which the United States and the Soviet Union were competing for political influence in the developing world. In the decades after World War II, the United States sought to see developing countries pull themselves out of poverty through the capitalist institutions of market system and private enterprise. Under the leadership of president Dwight Eisenhower, the US government used its influence, money, and military strength to pursue that goal wherever possible, at the same time suppressing socialist and popular democratic movements. US aggression was palpable as troops were sent around the world setting up what were often dictatorial regimes as a levy to hold back popular uprisings. The fear in Washington was that such uprisings could form into communist insurgencies and the countries themselves could turn into client states of the Soviet Union. The Americans were discovering, however, that such aggression was backfiring. Populist movements were turning to the Soviets for help as they watched American marines and warplanes invade their countries.[3]

The United States shifted toward a softer policy to gain influence by providing financial assistance and other resources to quell insurgent movements and radical change.[4] The testing ground for this approach was in tried out in Latin America under the leadership of Eisenhower's successor to the White House, John Kennedy. Kennedy initiated a program entitled Alliance for Progress. The program began in 1961 immediately after he became the US president, and a year and a half after Fidel Castro's "26th of July Movement" in which Castro succeeded in overthrowing Cuba's authoritarian regime and established a state socialist government. The program was also put in place in part as a response to the failed American "Bay of Pigs" invasion of Cuba.

Alliance for Progress called for a comprehensive set of social and economic reforms, including redistribution of land, currency stabilization, long-term economic planning, and sustained growth. The US government pledged that in exchange for a commitment to these reforms, it would offer financial assistance. Under this program, the United States provided over four billion per year (in current dollars) in foreign aid to countries in Latin America such as Peru, Bolivia, and Brazil.[5] The money earmarked as foreign aid streamed in from both public and private sources some of which became source funds for the nascent MFI industry in recipient countries. From there microfinance evolved into a network that linked together source funds, donations, aid agencies, non-governmental organizations (NGOs), government institutions, and MFIs. The network was established on the belief that individuals could actively defeat their own condition of poverty by developing livelihoods, as opposed to the belief that they can only stay out of poverty by being passive recipients of charity or public assistance.

The microfinance model was predicated on the assumption that self-help options for the poor were possible and likely to succeed if individuals could obtain a bit of capital to put together a microenterprise self-proprietorship. The strategy was seeming to work for a time in the seventies and eighties, although with mixed results. The majority of the source funds were provided by government agencies and international institutions such as the United States Agency for International Development (USAID) and the World Bank's affiliate the Inter-American Development Banks (IDB). The model expanded from Latin America to Asia, and in particular Bangladesh under the highly charged inspiration of Muhammad Yunus.

The Grameen Bank

After a series of microlending experiments conducted in Bangladesh during the seventies, Yunus became convinced that microloans could go a long way in the effort to eradicate poverty if they were used as start-up capital for small, informal microenterprises as was the case in South American countries. In both South America and Asia such small-scale enterprises constituted self-employment ventures in areas such as food carts, retail shops, basket weaving crafts, pedicabs, or bicycle repair shops. Seeing progress in the enterprises, Yunus became convinced that he grinding poverty that has been so prevalent in his country, particularly among women, could be eradicated in a single generation.[6]

Yunus embarked on a mission to do just that. With the help of Shorebank, a community development bank based in Chicago, Yunus was able to secure a modest grant from the Ford Foundation for research and development. Along with the Ford grant, Yunus also nailed down $3.4 million in grants from the International Fund for Agricultural Development (IFAD) at the United Nations.[7] Finally, with these grants in a portfolio, Yunus was able to persuade the Bangladesh to grant funds matching that of the IFAD government to authorize a bank charter for the Grameen Bank as an MFI entity housed in Bangladesh's central bank. The bank was established, and by 1983 it was privatized to become an independent, for-profit financial institution, and within a couple of years the majority of its shareholders were private investors.

Grameen quickly became the prototype MFI. It worked in conjunction with development NGOs with a mandate to provide services for poor people in rural areas. International aid agencies saw the NGO-MFI connection as more effective in this effort as these institutions were seen less at risk for corruption or misappropriation of funds compared to government. The Grameen model had the potential to become an alternative to government anti-poverty programs and emphasized self-help entrepreneurship, and an open market environment. Yunus appealed to governments and international aid agencies for donor money to help expand MFI outreach and capacity by emphasizing success, "…if poor people can achieve all this through their own efforts within a market environment, why isn't the world doing more of this?"[8] Microfinance economists Milford Bateman and Ha-Joon Chang documented the popularity of the Grameen model, particularly by the onset of the Greenspan Era and globalization of neoliberalism, "The international donor community very much liked what Yunus was saying, and so agreed to underwrite his bold ideas for promoting self-help and individual entrepreneurship among Bangladesh's poor through a dedicated institution—the Grameen Bank."

The bank was also rapidly gaining notoriety in part because of Yunus's public pronouncements of Grameen's success. The momentum was on the Grameen model was soon copied "all over Bangladesh and then all over the world. A new efficient model of poverty reduction and 'bottom-up' development appeared to have been found."[9] It was sublimated as a panacea for poverty elimination everywhere, even though there were growing concerns that the evidence was not confirming this.[10]

Nonetheless, its operations expanded and were replicated in Nepal, Vietnam, various locations in Africa, and back again in Latin America.[11]

One of the hallmark characteristics boasted of the Grameen MFI model was the high loan repayment rate, which according to Yunus was around 98%. A number far greater than conventional banking loan repayment.[12] The key to achieving such high repayment rates rests with the group collateral concept and the focus on women. It is assumed in this model that women in many developing countries lacked collateral of their own names but could be relied on to repay their loans on the basis of group collateral of a community. Individual households rely on the community for assistance when things break down such as flood washouts or drought. But such reliance is also predicated on each household being vested in the community by establishing a positive reputation and goodwill among community peers. In Bangladesh particularly, this was the job of women. Geographer and microfinance expert, Kate Maclean explains, “Women are often charged with maintaining the reputation of the family and with ‘servicing’ community relations.” As it this responsibility falls on women to maintain, it stands to reason that the banking model would tie social collateral and lending practices to women. Maclean also points out that “We should not be surprised that staking a woman’s friends, family, and neighbors against a loan is an effective way of guaranteeing repayment.”[13] It might also be fair to say that there is a difference between gender empowerment and using gender as leverage for repayment.

MFIs effectively financialized a gender-based custom of social cohesion ad transformed it into financial collateral. Such cohesion becomes valueless outside its role as a resource to be used to facilitate the flows of capital. As the push to continue financialization under the expanding corporate hegemony and the global sweep of neoliberalism, the Grameen model took center stage. Other MFIs patterned after Grameen spread everywhere and millions of the world’s poor were pulled into global corporate hegemony through the MFI network. For countries where microfinance initiatives were expanding, neoliberal economists were making bold pronouncements about how financial innovation, government deregulation, and free market capitalism promise to bring poor people out of poverty by financing petite capitalism.

The mystique of microfinance that the American government found so compelling was that it promised to defy history and bring capitalism down to the poor.

The message being cast around the world was that the Cold War was over and capitalism has emerged triumphant. The aid-based model of Kennedy's Alliance for Progress was becoming obsolete and the market-based MFI would take over. The poor would have no excuse not to become small-scale capitalist entrepreneurs and pull themselves out of poverty. As they do, they would not need to rely on any form of public aid, nor should they feel compelled to join social and political movements that challenge the global capitalism market system. The same Washington Consensus economists who pushed the world to deregulate their capital markets, which led to the crises in Thailand and other parts of East Asia, were pushing for MFIs to be the model of a broader move toward privatization. MFIs were seized upon to be used for other purposes beyond financing small-scale entrepreneurs. Microcredit programs began a mission drift toward privatized water reclamation and sanitation projects, thus facilitating the extension of financialization to the commons; to public goods that were shared by all. Governance of public goods and services was being re-evaluated, and wherever we encounter the question of governance we are encountering institutional structures and the rules for control. Privatization involves a shift away from governance by public institutions to private ones; away from social provisioning toward profit opportunity.

Philip Mader from the Institute of Development Studies at the University of Sussex studied the use of microfinance in the neoliberal push to financialization during the Greenspan Era. He noted that MFIs are increasingly being used to "extend the reach of private finance into the governance of traditionally publicly managed goods." This involves the usual elements of forming corporate start-ups, selling securities to investors, and commodifying water services to be sold for profit. The neoliberal vision is that with market incentives, water entrepreneurs are motivated to supply water, making water more available than otherwise would be the case.

As is so popular among well-intentioned models for change that get coopted by neoliberalism, microfinance enthusiasts are quick to celebrate the magic of win-win market scenarios. Once water rights are privatized and sold to a private company, the company sells water to farmers and households to recoup their investment costs and generate a profit. Users of water can apply for microloans to pay for the spendy water and the government is relieved of the burden of having to provide water as a public good. In the win-win narrative, farmers get the water they need with MFI credit, investors make profits, MFIs make interest income, and government is free to focus on other things. Neoliberals rejoice. In the world of corporate hegemony these arguments need not be backed with data. They are considered pious.

As he critically examined this model, however, Mader found that there has been no evidence showing that microfinance helped make water more accessible or qualitatively improved. What he discovered most distinctly instead was that microfinance initiatives were being pushed with cultish fervor, "The processes of groupthink …may help to explain why, despite the lack of proof, so many proponents of microfinance conclude again and again that more microfinance is key to addressing social problems."[14]

Groupthink is similar to cognitive dissonance as it is a social-psychological phenomenon of consensus without critical evaluation. People involved in something big like this are prone to get pulled into a dynamic in which the more powerful voices of devotion to the cause create a group atmosphere in which critics or those who simply raise questions are driven out of the group. The groupthink consensus holds a grip on the imagination of people by rationalizing away evidence suggesting that the mission is vulnerable to failure or is slipping off the rails. Groupthink creates caricatures of its critics as cynical, curmudgeonly, or politically spiteful. It relies heavily on a constant stream of propaganda while strategically undermining opposing views or strategies.

The MFI privatization movement has been saturated with neoliberal narratives on how public services are inefficient, lack profit incentives to be productive, and tangled in government bureaucracy, as expressed by MFI privatization advocate Robert Varley at USAID, "Municipal or state-owned utilities are often inefficient, overregulated, and unable to supply even the formal sector with adequate services."[15] Such statement is regularly rolled out as forgone conclusions along with assumptions that the market can always do better. He argues further that water and sanitation facilities are "attractive to many poor urban and peri-urban [suburban] residents and generate personal economic benefits for which consumers are both willing and able to pay."[16] The neoliberals can make such demand-led arguments with confidence because those who are not able to pay are pushed out of the market, and the win-win scenario applies only to those who have the means to pay private companies a price that covers operations, profits, and interest for the microloans.

Central to Varley's argument is that entrepreneurship stands a better chance of positive impact—a more cost-effective way of supplying water—because free markets are a more open and fluid means to attract finance and to provide competitive services.[17] By having users pay for water directly, the model links cost recovery of the producers to the private benefits of the consumers. The key point in this narrative is cost recovery. If water can be provided in such a way as to internally cover costs without public subsidization, it proves the efficiency of the market system, or so the argument goes. If cost recovery, however, is the main concern here then the market system is indeed a win-win institution. Markets have a built-in rationing function that, if left to the forces of supply and demand, will always eliminate surpluses or shortages of any commodity. If a surplus of water exists, the price falls and producers have a disincentive to supply and they cut back, but demand rises until the surplus is vanquished. If a shortage exists, the price rises, suppliers are incentivized to produce more and demand falls until the shortage is eliminated. For privatized water—like so many other crucial but unaffordable services such as health care and housing—the fall in demand means weeding those who cannot afford to pay out of the market. Being weeded out of markets is consistently the fate of the poor. Yet helping the poor get out of poverty was supposed to be the mission of microfinance. But in cult atmospheres, such critical views are also weeded out of the scene entirely.

After working in microfinance for ten years on three continents, economist Hugh Sinclair published an expose highlighting the cultish nature of the MFI industry. In his book titled, *Confessions of a Microfinance Heretic: How Microfinance Lost its Way and Betrayed the*

Poor (2010) Sinclair writes, "The microfinance community often resembles a religious cult. Criticism is considered heresy and is not tolerated. Impact on poverty is dogmatically claimed but demonstrated in only exceptional cases."[18] His concern is shared by Mader and many others who are veterans in the business who raise the question of why there is such a devotion to microfinance even though, as we will see, there is virtually no evidence that it is helping people get out of poverty.

Does Microfinance Work?

The short answer to that questions is *no*. At least not according to the studies conducted thus far. But the answer depends on how we mean by what works. For the champions of the Grameen model, the litmus test is the high repayment rate. Author and USAID consultant Mohini Halhotra put it succinctly and suggestion that successful MFI passes the test when their "clients, who are paying full price for services, vote with their feet and come back for more. Poor clients are borrowing, saving, repaying, and retuning to purchase additional services at above-market interest rates. That is as honest an impact assessment as I need."[19]

For MFI whistleblowers high repayment possibly tells a different story. In their view, it is more likely a sign of debt trap, the very target of the microfinance movement in the first place. As mentioned above, debt trap is common wherever there are people who need to borrow money because they are struggling, not just in developing countries. If borrowers accumulate so much debt that they deplete their funds to pay the balance due, they must borrow more to sustain their living. They also are compelled to keep up with their debt payments to keep their credit open. More borrowing is a drain because of the accruing interest liability. Unless the conditions that cause the hardship in the first place are changed, trapped borrowers cannot pay down their principal.

Perhaps a question that should be asked is whether MFI programs are pulling people out of poverty in measurable numbers and not just highlighted in apocryphal stories and anecdotes. Maren Duvendack from the School of International Development at the University of East Anglia looked into this. She and her team of researchers located four large-scale independent studies conducted between 1996 and 2011 on the impact of microfinance on poverty in places where MFIs were operating their anti-poverty interventions (programs).[20] The team examined the studies for wellbeing indicators such as positive changes in income, spending trends, holdings of assets, health, education, and other measurements that would signify improvements in people's standards of living. After studying the microfinance reviews, they found significant problems with the methodologies of the studies and concluded that, "Despite the apparent success and popularity of microfinance, no clear evidence yet exists that microfinance programmes have positive impacts. There have been four major reviews examining impacts of microfinance. These reviews concluded that, while anecdotes and other inspiring stories purported to show that microfinance can make a real difference in the lives of those served."[21]

The Duvendack group decided microfinance needed to be re-investigated with improved methodology with random control trials, and because the industry has since undergone much development and is bolstered with new technologies since the original studies. They conducted a thorough investigation in academic databases, aid organization archives, books, and journal literature, and found 58 studies that were suitable for detailed study. Their conclusion from their rigorous re-examination was the same as before—zero impact.[22]

As the MFI had become such a high profile, celebrated phenomenon, the discourse surrounding their findings were peculiar and consistent with the phenomena of groupthink and cognitive dissonance. Instead of accepting that perhaps MFIs are not living up to their legends, industry devotees were inclined to interpret the null results as a *not-not-positive* indication.[23] That is to say that it is a priori assumption that microfinance does have positive results, and this conclusion shall remain orthodox until it is proven unequivocally otherwise. But even so, the question remains as to why the steadfast adherence to MFI if there is no evidence to support its efficacy.

There is a deeper level of critical analysis here that is connected to the broader situation of financialization. The vast majority of those are impacted by MFI programs and payday lenders are people who perform labor to make their livelihoods. If they ever want to rise above debt trap, they have to do even more work to earn the extra income to pay off their debts and interest. In Marxian terms, this extra work is labor performed beyond what is socially necessary for living, which gets expropriated by owners of capital—the MFIs and their investors. Financialization in this case is the process of converting poverty and hard times into a market—the financialization of poverty. Malcolm Harper, author and former microfinance enthusiast summarizes, "Microfinance offers a more subtle and potentially more durable means whereby those who control capital can exploit those who have only their labor to sell… Capitalists no longer have to organize and manage labor. They can extract a higher return on their capital not by directly employing people, but by financing their petty businesses under the use of assisting them to become entrepreneurs."[24] Duvendack and her group put numbers behind this assertion. The global MFI industry is expanding and is in excess of $100 billion annually. Looking at the aggregate MFI loan portfolios between 2003 and 2010, they estimate about somewhere between $88.8 billion and $124.6 billion in yields was paid from borrowers to MFI companies and their investors.[25,26]

Returning to the question of why all the microfinance hype if it is exploitative and shows to have no impact on wellbeing of the poor. A partial answer to that is given by Duvendack's research: it's profitable. It represents a frontier in the corporate hegemony's broader quest for emerging markets and opportunities.

Institutions Matter: The Washington Consensus and Microfinance

Hugh Sinclair reflected on his experience observing how microfinance shifted from a model that was intended to help the world's poor to a model that exploited them, "Good, honest, hardworking microfinance practitioners were gradually replaced with a single motivation: profit"[27] The win-win gimmick was wearing thin as recipient countries were increasingly pressured by the Washington Consensus to push MFIs into a for-profit, self-funded, commercial industry. The source funding institutions based in Washington DC such as USAID and the World Bank and their affiliates in Europe attached strings to their continued support of MFIs. Through these institutions the corporate hegemony flexed its muscles and pressed MFIs transform into an image mirroring Wall Street.

In the mid-nineties, the World Bank under the new leadership of James Wolfensohn established a new body called The Consultative Group to Assist the Poorest (CGAP). The body was given the mandate to coordinate microlending programs among donor-institutions, which meant pressuring all the institutions to conform to its neoliberal plans. Wolfensohn was an experienced Wall Street investment banker and had also worked closely with the Federal Reserve to orchestrate the bailout of Chrysler Corporation in 1979 (see Chapter 7). He was no stranger to neoliberalism or to working as a servant to corporate hegemony.

CGAP produced a rule book designed to provide guidelines on how to make MFIs more commercially viable institutions. The book, titled Good Practice Guidelines for Funders of Microfinance, which came to be known as the "pink book" from its cover, laid out strictures for source funding, the most important of which is "to complement private capital and to accelerate innovative domestic market solutions."[28] In a phrase, neoliberalism is thus encapsulated: private capital, efficient markets, and the idolatry of financial innovation. Ultimately what this meant for the poor was higher and higher interest rates and a return to the good old days of loan sharking. The push for this innovation, as we will see shortly, had more to with the survival of MFI institutions than it did with serving the poor.

According to the Microfinance Information Exchange, some MFIs in Mexico for example were charge as much as 82% interest on loans. Exploitative rates triggered a backlash and some branches were set on fire while people chanted "We're not paying."[29]

The commercialization of MFIs was top-down institutional pressure. It was the very same pressure, even the same people—Greenspan, Rubin, Summers, and Wolfensohn—that pressured countries everywhere to liberalize their capital markets to make way for wild instabilities in the nineties (see Chapter 8). Neoliberalism provided the ideological window dressing for shaking corporation loose to do what they do best—to scour the planet in the hunt for new profit opportunities and emerging markets. Despite that, and despite the fact that neoliberalism had piloted the global economy into an abyss of speculative bubbles, crises, and economic ruin from Mexico to Thailand to Iceland to Wall Street, and despite that it has failed the majority of people in the world, it remains a cult favorite. Bateman and Maclean write, "The notion that microfinance emerged and was subsequently promoted because it is an intervention that can successfully address poverty and underdevelopment is not just simplistic, as even most microfinance advocates now accept, it is largely false."[30] Sinclair, too, blows the whistle, "Some microfinance is extremely beneficial to the poor, but it is not the miracle cure that its publicists would have you believe. Microfinance has been hijacked by profiteers, and we need to reclaim it or the poor."[31]

In the microfinance world, profiteers are loan sharks. Under pressure from the Washington Consensus and under the rubric of neoliberal ideology set forward in the Pink Book, microfinance reverted to the very loan sharking enterprise it was created to work against. Yunus laments,

> To ensure that the small loans would be profitable for their shareholders such banks needed to raise interest rates and engage in aggressive marketing and loan collection. The kind of empathy that had once been shown toward borrowers when the lenders were nonprofits disappeared. The people whom microcredit was supposed to help were being harmed… Commercialization has been a terrible wrong turn for microfinance, and it indicates a worrying 'mission drift' in the motivation of those lending to the poor. Poverty should be eradicated, not seen as a money-making opportunity.[32]

This message, along with those of Bateman, Maclean, Sinclair, Duvendack, all point to the same conclusion that microfinance has had no measurable benefit for the poor, ignores the structure causes of poverty in the first place, has reverted to loan sharking, and represents mission drift far from its original intentions. It stands as an extension of corporate hegemony and facilitates the financialization and exploitation of poverty and the social collateral of poor women, and it does all of this behind the ideological shield of neoliberalism. It is institutionally and ideologically fixed into the structure of corporate hegemony, and as such it stubbornly prevails.

Not only does microfinance prevail in this way, it is evolving and proliferating. Microfinance if anything exemplifies the adaptability of corporate capitalism and its ability to survive. In the wake of so much criticism, MFIs morphed to fit itself into new ecological niches. In the 2006 edition of the Pink Book spells out a broader mission, "Poor people need a variety of financial services, not just loans. In addition to credit, they want savings, insurance, and money transfer services."[33] With much fanfare and yuppie TED talks sublimating new MFI "products" microfinance innovated and rebranded.

Among the most remarkable strokes of MFI innovation is the "financial inclusion" movement. As data poured in and it became increasingly clear that microfinance was debunked, the industry suddenly recreated itself in the image of Wall Street universal banks—one stop financial shopping center. The spin was that poverty eradication was not able to be realized because the MFIs were not yet fully developed. They needed to expand into a broader array of financial services.[34] Microfinance shifted to a wider focus to include microsavings plans and investment strategies, microinsurance, microleasing, digital payment opportunities, and even forays into cryptocurrencies.[35] The argument for financial inclusion was identical to those of Wall Street banks that argued for deregulation and consolidation of commercial banking, investment banking, and insurance—competitiveness and diversification as a strategy to mitigate risk. The mission of poverty eradication—social provisioning—was drowned out by the feverish buzz of yuppie hype.

Microfinance institutions distanced themselves from microcredit, changed their mission statements, and even some changed their names of their companies and wrapped themselves in happy talk. As we will see in the next chapter, another dimension to the MFI is the peer-to-peer models in which small-scale donors can be involved by "directly" providing donation funds through internet portals.

Rebranding and product differentiation are tried and true methods of staying alive amidst the corporate capitalist survival of the fittest. At one time coffee shops just sold coffee along with some scones or doughnuts. Such shops are either long extinct and replaced Starbucks or have adapted by offering lattes, hazelnut lattes, frappucinos, and caramel macchiatos. So too has become the menu of microservices. As for poverty, though, let them drink lattes.

Notes

1. Muhammad Yunus, "Sacrificing Microcredit for Megaprofits," *The New York Times*, January 14, 2011.
2. https://files.consumerfinance.gov/f/201403_cfpb_report_payday-lending.pdf.
3. Martin Gilens and Benjamin Page, "Testing Theories of American Politics: Elites, Interest Groups, and Average Citizens," *Perspectives on Politics*, Vol. 12, No. 3, pp. 564–581.
4. For a complete story of soft power in American political strategy, see Joseph Nye, *Bound to Lead: The Changing Nature of American Power* (New York, NY: Basic Books, 1990).
5. Ronald Scheman, *The Alliance for Progress: A Retrospective* (New York, NY: Praeger, 1991), pp. 10–11.
6. Milford Bateman and Ha-Joon Chang, "Microfinance and the Illusion of Development: From Hubris to Nemesis in Thirty Years," *World Economic Review*, Vol. 1, 2012, p. 14. http://wer.worldeconomicsassociation.org/files/WER-Vol1-No1-Article2-Bateman-and-Chang-v2.pdf.
7. Ford Foundation Annual Report 1980. New York: Ford Foundation, 1980, p. 21. Retrieved from http://www.fordfound.org/elibrary/documents/1980/normal/low/1980norm-low.pdf. See also the Duke Sanford School of Public Policy, "The Ford Foundation and the Grameen Bank," 2012, p. 14.
8. http://www.thecommonwealth.org/document/34293/35178/152062/37474/commonwealth_lecture_2003.htm.
9. Bateman and Chang, 2012, p. 3.
10. Lamia Karim, "The 'Scandal' of Grameen; The Nobel Prize, the Bank, and the State in Bangladesh," in Milford Bateman and Kate Maclean (eds.), *Seduced and Betrayed: Exposing the Contemporary Microfinance Phenomenon* (Albuquerque, NM: University of New Mexico Press, 2017), p. 204.
11. "The Ford Foundation and the Grameen Bank," 2012, p. 17.

12. Muhammad Yunus and Alan Jolis, *Banker to the Poor: Micro-Lending and the Battle Against World Poverty* (New York, NY: Public Affairs, 1999), p. 58.
13. Kate Maclean, "Microfinance and the 'Woman' Question," *Seduced and Betrayed*, 2017, p. 257.
14. Philip Mader, "Public Goods Provision Aided by Microfinance," *Seduced and Betrayed*, 2017, p. 184.
15. Robert C.G. Varley, "Financial Services and Environmental Health: Household Credit for Water Sanitation," USAID, January 2, 1995, p. ix. https://www.gdrc.org/icm/environ/usaid.html.
16. Ibid.
17. Ibid.
18. Hugh Sinclair, *Confessions of a Microfinance Heretic: How Microfinance Lost Its Way and Betrayed the Poor* (San Francisco, CA: Berrett-Koehler, 2010), p. 20.
19. Mohini Malhotra, "Comments: Microfinance Impact Evaluation: Going Down Market," in Feinstein, Picciotto, and Wolfensohn (eds.), *Evaluation and Poverty Reduction; Proceedings from a World Bank Conference* (Washington, DC: World Bank, 2000), p. 204.
20. Maren Duvendack, et al., *Systematic Review: What Is the Evidence of the Impact of Microfinance on the Well-Being of Poor People?* 2011. https://www.givedirectly.org/pdf/DFID_microfinance_evidence_review.pdf.
21. Ibid., p. 2.
22. Ibid.
23. *The Economist*, "Froth at the Bottom of the Pyramid: Is Microfinance Going the Same Way as Subprime Mortgages?" August, 2009.
24. Malcolm Harper, "Microfinance and Farmers: Do They Fit?" in Thomas Dichter and Malcolm Harper (eds.), *What's Wrong with Microfinance?* (Rugby, UK: 2007), p. 59.
25. Maren Duvendack and Philip Mader, "Poverty Reduction or the Financialization of Poverty?" *Seduced and Betrayed*, 2017, p. 41. The difference in the two figures is the difference between only the portfolios that are reported and what is estimated to include those that are not reported.
26. The difference in the two figures is the difference between only the portfolios that are reported and what is estimated to include those that are not reported.
27. Sinclair, 2010, p. x.

28. Consultative Group to Assist the Poorest (CGAP), *Good Practice Guidelines for Funders of Microfinance: Microfinance Consensus Guidelines* (Washington, DC: World Bank, 2006), p. viii.
29. Neil MacFarquhar, "Banks Making Big Profits from Tiny Loans," *The New York Times*, April 13, 2010.
30. Bateman and Maclean, "Conclusion," *Seduced and Betrayed*, p. 298.
31. Sinclair, *Confessions of a Microfinance Heretic*, p. xi.
32. Muhammad Yunus, *The New York Times*, 2011.
33. CGAP, 2006, p. viii.
34. Asli Demirguc-Kunt, Leora Klapper, Dorothe Singer, and Peter Van Oudheusden, "The Global Findex Database 2014: Measuring Financial Inclusion Around the World," (Washington, DC: World Bank Policy Research Group, 2015). http://documents.worldbank.org/curated/en/187761468179367706/The-Global-Findex-Database-2014-measuring-financial-inclusion-around-the-world.
35. Ibid.

References

Bateman, Milford, and Ha-Joon Chang. "Microfinance and the Illusion of Development: From Hubris to Nemesis in Thirty Years," *World Economic Review*, Vol. 1, 2012, p. 14. http://wer.worldeconomicsassociation.org/files/WER-Vol1-No1-Article2-Bateman-and-Chang-v2.pdf.

Bateman, Milford, and Kate Maclean, eds. *Seduced and Betrayed: Exposing the Contemporary Microfinance Phenomenon* (Albuquerque: University of New Mexico Press, 2017).

Burke, Kathleen, Jonathan Lanning, Jesse Leary, and Jialan Wang. "Consumer Financial Protection Bureau Data Point: Payday Lending," March 2014. https://files.consumerfinance.gov/f/201403_cfpb_report_payday-lending.pdf.

Consultative Group to Assist the Poorest (CGAP). *Good Practice Guidelines for Funders of Microfinance: Microfinance Consensus Guidelines* (Washington, DC: World Bank, 2006).

Demirguc-Kunt, Asli, Leora Klapper, Dorothe Singer, and Peter Van Oudheusden. *The Global Findex Database 2014: Measuring Financial Inclusion Around the World* (Washington, DC: World Bank Policy Research Group, 2015). http://documents.worldbank.org/curated/en/187761468179367706/The-Global-Findex-Database-2014-measuring-financial-inclusion-around-the-world.

Duke Sanford School of Public Policy. "The Ford Foundation and the Grameen Bank," 2012. http://cspcs.sanford.duke.edu/sites/default/files/FordGrameenfinal.pdf.

Duvendack, Maren, et al. *Systematic Review: What Is the Evidence of the Impact of Microfinance on the Well-Being of Poor People*? 2011. https://www.givedirectly.org/pdf/DFID_microfinance_evidence_review.pdf.

The Economist. "Froth at the Bottom of the Pyramid: Is Microfinance Going the Same Way as Subprime Mortgages?" August 2009.

Ford Foundation Annual Report 1980. New York: Ford Foundation, 1980, p. 21. Retrieved from http://www.fordfound.org/elibrary/documents/1980/normal/low/1980norm-low.pdf.

Gilens, Martin, and Benjamin Page. "Testing Theories of American Politics: Elites, Interest Groups, and Average Citizens," *Perspectives on Politics*, Vol. 12, No. 3, 2014, pp. 564–581.

Harper, Malcolm. "Microfinance and Farmers: Do They Fit?" in Thomas Dichter and Malcolm Harper (eds.), *What's Wrong with Microfinance?* (Rugby, UK: 2007).

MacFarquhar, Neil. "Banks Making Big Profits from Tiny Loans," *The New York Times*, April 13, 2010.

Malhotra, Mohini. "Comments: Microfinance Impact Evaluation: Going Down Market," in Osvaldo Feinstein and Robert Picciotto (eds.), *Evaluation and Poverty Reduction; Proceedings from a World Bank Conference* (Washington, DC: World Bank, 2000).

Nye, Joseph. *Bound to Lead: The Changing Nature of American Power* (New York, NY: Basic Books, 1990).

Scheman, Ronald. *The Alliance for Progress: A Retrospective* (New York, NY: Praeger, 1991), pp. 10–11.

Sinclair, Hugh. *Confessions of a Microfinance Heretic: How Microfinance Lost Its Way and Betrayed the Poor* (San Francisco, CA: Berrett-Koehler, 2010).

Varley, Robert C.G. "Financial Services and Environmental Health: Household Credit for Water Sanitation," USAID, January 2, 1995, p. ix. https://www.gdrc.org/icm/environ/usaid.html.

Yunus, Muhammad. "Sacrificing Microcredit for Megaprofits," *The New York Times*, January 14, 2011.

Yunus, Muhammad, and Alan Jolis. *Banker to the Poor: Micro-Lending and the Battle Against World Poverty* (New York, NY: Public Affairs, 1999).

11

Will Peer-to-Peer and Equity Crowdfunding Be Different?

In the discourse on climate change, resource depletion, and political instability arising from widening inequality, there is a tendency to hitch a happy ending to the stories. There is an unwritten rule that one is not allowed to engage in this discourse unless one has a solution in hand, even if it is completely delusional. Most advocates of social change in America demand a happy ending, particularly one that arises from individual choices and initiatives, technological innovation, and win-win scenarios in which people can simultaneously do good and do well. That is, even the most progressively minded are more likely to get behind a model for change if it includes promises of making money while saving the world through entrepreneurship, shopping strategies, and no real change to already long-established habits and expectations. Stories of getting rich while saving the world have been passed around for decades and are particularly a feature of the Greenspan Era of neoliberalism in which corporate capitalism is continually refashioned with new costumes to make it greener, more equitable, and equipped with revolutionary new technologies.

In terms of basic sanity, technology would have to be a part of the progressive change or a move toward genuine sustainability if our

J. Magnuson, *Financing the Apocalypse*,
Palgrave Insights into Apocalypse Economics,
https://doi.org/10.1007/978-3-030-04720-7_11

economic system were to prioritize such things. But for that to happen there would have to be an equal amount of emphasis on creating the appropriate institutional environment along with the new technologies, because technology is spawned within an institutional context.

Absent from the win-win narrative is any mention of institutions because there is a generally accepted and pious conclusion that there is no alternative to a market-driven, for-profit approach to any problem related to economics. Win-winners hold on to the belief that the same institutions and ideologies that have brought the world to apocalyptic conditions in the first place are the solution. All that is needed is a tweak of new technology. It is a bizarre twist of logic that would be like arguing that the only way to deal with a humanitarian crisis created by war or slavery is with more war slavery. Microfinance is sewn into the cloth of that narrative. As it pushes on, microfinance has assimilated morphed into financial inclusion, is accessible through internet portals, and has adopted some new gimmicks such as the peer-to-peer (P2P) model and equity crowdfunding models of finance.

Peer-to-Peer (P2P)

As the name suggests, P2P formats are lending facilities that directly link lender and borrower. By stepping around traditional financial intermediaries, P2P companies stand as an alternative to the practice of taking deposits and making loans, and rather provide a matchmaking and credit checking service facilitating credit for personal and business financing, and the borrowing can be large or small, collateralized or not.

One of the main principles underlying P2P is the notion of market competition among lenders. In a manner similar to other internet trading models, P2P companies find borrowers, check their credit standing and set down lending and repayment terms, then offers the loan to individuals who compete with each other for the contract. Supporters of P2P argue that one of its principal advantages is disintermediation, which is another way of saying eliminating the middleman or financial intermediary. The advantage presumably is to lower transaction costs and pass those cost savings on to the borrowers. Another argument is that it allows finance to bypass Wall Street, which has had much popular appeal in the aftermath of the Banking Crisis of 2007–2009. According to P2P blogger Peter Renton, "Peer to peer (P2P) lending was always an idea with great potential. It is a simple concept. Match people who want to borrow money with people who want to invest money. Cut the banks out of the equation and everybody wins."[1]

Everybody except those bankers who are cut out of the equation, that is.

Among the largest P2P businesses are companies like Lending Club and Prosper Marketplace, which are now publicly traded corporations collecting about a half billion in revenues annually.[2] Lending Club and others launched their operations right at the cusp of the banking crisis in 2007. In the last few years, P2P loans have added up to about $72 billion in the U.S., U.K., and E.U., and about $100 billion in China, which is very small compared to the conventional banking industry but is growing.[3] The interest rates in the P2P facilities run between 5.6 and 35.8% depending on risk, which are rates that are higher than conventional loans but less than what one would pay on credit cards.[4] By 2014, Lending Club went public with its stock, and 2016 it had originated over $19 billion in loans, which made it the largest P2P corporation in the world.[5]

As the industry matured, P2P like microfinance became absorbed into the sphere of corporate hegemony and quickly lost their peer connections. The majority of loans initiated in the larger P2P platforms in the United States are increasingly packaged, securitized, and sold to hedge funds and other institutional investors.[6] P2P started to lose its appeal as it became known that the investor peers turned out to be Goldman Sachs and billionaire hedge fund managers. In 2014, the New York Times reported that, "Today big financial firms, not small investors, dominate lending on the two platforms,"[7] Lending Club and Prosper. This means that in the auction environment where P2P was originated, the big corporate players dominate and the small individual players are squeezed out. Although industry insiders claim that having large institutional players gives P2P access to deep lending pockets that would not exist otherwise.

Notwithstanding, as they began to work in a manner resembling Wall Street institutions involving large institutional players P2P companies came under the close scrutiny of the Securities Exchange Commission and the U.S. Department of Treasury. In 2016, Lending Club was thrust into turmoil after the feds launched an investigation into its business practices. The investigation found that in 2014, Lending Club had originated over $22 million in loans by selling them to Wall Street investment banking firm, Jeffries Financial Group. Jefferies had a set of criteria established for buying P2P loans, but some of the loans brokered by Lending Club did not meet that criteria and were given a makeover to give the appearance that they did. Lending Club was caught, its CEO was ousted, and its share prices plunged over 20% in a single day of trading.[8] Hedge funds and investment banks quickly moved to cut off P2P companies of source funds, which forced them to either use their own cash or look to other sources.

By 2017, share prices of Lending Club continue to fall as the company continued to report losses. The industry overall has continued to struggle since but has recently shown signs of revival after large online financial services companies like Square, Inc have stepped into the arena. Such an industry now can only be considered P2P if we choose to consider large publicly traded corporations as "peers," which for corporate hegemony is not far-fetched considering that corporations are seen as fictitious "persons" in the framework of law.

Kiva

Kiva is a 501(c)3 US nonprofit P2P lending enterprise founded in 2005 and is popularly considered a pioneer in social entrepreneurship. According to its website, its mission is social provisioning and "to connect people through lending to alleviate poverty. We celebrate and support people looking to create a better future for themselves, their families and their communities."[9] What makes it original compared to other P2P formats is that it melds a P2P online platform design in such a way as to facilitate individual direct sponsorships—interest-free donations—with other individuals seeking microfinancing. Like microfinance in general, Kiva has been upheld in popular media as a model of financial innovation and philanthropy and won the accolades from celebrities such as Oprah Winfrey and Bill Clinton. New York Times columnist Nicholas Kristof esteemed Kiva as a model that connects "the donor directly to the beneficiary, without going through a bureaucratic and expense layer of aid groups."[10] Kiva is highlighted as a win-win model, "praised for leveraging technology and entrepreneurial know-how and making high impact P2P charity and reality."[11] According to the tax records for 2015, about 17% of Kiva's functioning expenses goes for executive compensation. The records show that of the twenty-five officers, directors, trustees, and key employees, twenty-four are listed as full time and all bring in annual salaries ranging between $106,748 and $292,358. These salaries do not measure up to Wall Street leviathan bank executives, but nonetheless remarkable for an organization that operates on less than $20 million in annual revenues. The bulk of the revenue used to pay these salaries derive from contributions and grants.[12] Part of the win-win is to have 501(c)3 US nonprofit, tax-exempt status, which does not preclude securing lucrative careers for its own members of the corporate class.

Aside from that, some investigators such as David Roodman have found while scratching the surface is that "Kiva is Not Quite What it Seems."[13] Kiva markets its service by suggesting to donors that they can directly fund specific people or projects profiled on Kiva's website. Donors are drawn to borrower profiles under the slogans such as "loans for entrepreneurs doing amazing things"[14] and are led to believe that the money they donate goes directly to the people who they select to sponsor. Each profile has a completion metric that specifies how much is needed to complete the loan. Roodman found, however, that the loans have already been made by way of MFIs before the donors put up their donations. The concept of intermediation is distorted in this way because Kiva is using MFIs as financial intermediaries.[15] Instead of P2P financing, donors are in effect donating free source funds to capitalize for-profit MFIs using Kiva as a go-between.

Kiva lenders or donors, also called Kivans on the website, are largely assuming that because they make interest-free donations to the platform, the cost savings are passed on to the borrowers. This is rarely the case, however. MFIs benefit from having low-cost source funds on the input side and charging premium rates on the output side.[16] Data on Kiva-funded projects show that the benefits of having low-cost or no-cost source funds accrue to MFI shareholders.

For years after Roodman unveiled this aspect of Kiva, criticisms of the nonprofit began to stream out on the web along with other troubling stories. One story in particular was regarding an MFI known as Life Above Poverty Organization (LAPO) based in Nigeria, which had been on the Kiva network. Kiva has disclaimers that they refuse to work with MFIs that are charging sharking rates alongside statements that there may be variations between estimated rates and actual rates charged borrowers. Kiva had advertised a rate of 57% for LAPO but when journalists began to investigate, Kiva changed the rate to 83%.[17] The same journalists found that LAPOs rates were being reported as between 114 and 126%.[18] It raised concerns that Kiva was not forthcoming about its affiliates using sharking rates. Other criticisms were raised regarding some profiles being duplicated suggesting that there was more than one particular borrower who was applying for funds, but turned out to be the same individual.[19] Many of the insights and criticisms of Kivans derive from their own donors who see things that give them pause.

One Kiva sponsor Kiva received a painful black eye when it was revealed that it was sponsoring a cockfight loan. Those who discovered took action and set up a web page titled "Kivans Against Cock-Fighting" after seeing an MFI in Peru using Kiva source funds to finance a cockfighting venture.[20] Kiva and its affiliate Finca Peru closed the loan, but it stirred a lively debate among Kivans as some see it as appropriate for Kiva to refuse funding projects that encourage blood sports, whereas others see a "slippery slope" problem in which Kiva is put in a position to be ideological police. Important questions were raised about whether an organization like Kiva should be imposing culturally specific values on the borrowing public among populations everywhere.[21] The Kiva chat thread on cockfighting turned into an ethics debate and extended to whether Kiva should do redlining based on other potentially ethical concerns regarding animal testing, child safety, nutrition, reproductive rights, whether alcohol is produced, the use of pesticides, and so on. Still others contend that their choice to boycott Kiva over ethical concerns is still an exercise to vote for or against something in the market.

In blog commentary Kiva co-founder Matt Flannery weighed in emphasizing that, "The real question is whether or not permitting these loans is a good strategic choice. In particular, does this somehow help Kiva achieve its mission of connecting people to alleviate poverty? It's debatable." Flannery, like some of Kivans resist the idea that Kiva should be paternalistically imposing moral imperatives on the rest of the world, and "Kiva, the organization, should not be making those decisions. Our lenders should be the ones voting with their dollars."[22]

This sensibility from Kiva caught the attention of a Kivan who pointed out that Kiva focusing on lenders, "not only are we worried about interfering in 'cultural issues' in the borrowers [sic] country… the MFI appears to be worried about 'the lenders cultural issues' kind of makes me blink – twice."[23] Scandals and ethical debates aside, this is the point of interest here. Flannery shifts the focus, perhaps unintentionally, from the people and their projects to be funded to the lenders—the Kivans. It is here that critics of microfinance and organizations like Kiva find problems. The projects have become more about the Kivans' thrill sensations than economic development. And as many of the MFI critics have pointed out, there is no exploration or discussion about the causes of poverty and underdevelopment in the places where they operate.

The Financialization of Humanitarianism

New York Times journalist and Kivan Nicholas Kristof tweeted about his Kiva experience, "Just made a new microloan on www.kiva.org to a Nicaraguan woman. Great therapy. Always makes me feel good." This emotional investment and the feel-good vibe is part of the draw of P2P models. As we saw in the last chapter, the social psychological phenomenon of groupthink runs strong within MFIs and it is also true in these lending portals. They have achieved an unassailable, cult status in which many followers and members of the development community have become so attached to the vibe that they will turn away from criticisms of ethical transgressions or deception. Ideology also plays a role in this. Kiva fits comfortably within the tenets of neoliberalism so that donors are already preconditioned to appreciate the self-help, market-based, entrepreneurial model of economic development. Kiva accentuates this with compelling marketing imagery and atmosphere of thrill on the website so that Kivans experience a hedonic rush and the familiar dopaminergic sensations experienced by cell phone and social media addicts.

Some Kiva members have opened up about the strange phenomenon of kivamania and share stories about going online and scanning Kiva profiles looking for people who "hook" them because of the stories and pictures.[24] They are drawn to Kiva's rousing atmosphere of fun and entertainment like children to video games. As an example, Kiva has lending teams that compete with each other like sports teams that aggressively seek a victory by accumulating borrowers as if they were numbers on a scoreboard. As one Kivan admitted, "I am a Kivaholic… At the moment I'm still 'collecting' countries and borrowers with cheerful smiles—how shallow is that, but in the presence of other addicts maybe I shouldn't be too embarrassed to confess a frisson of excitement at being able to bag a new one."[25] The word choice is remarkable as "bagging" connotes hunting prey. Kiva intentionally creates this aggressive environment in which Kivans are hunting down and bagging borrowers for sport and thrills.

The focus on donor fun and recreation clouds over the mission of economic development. A Kivan shared their concern with the candor of someone speaking to an A.A. group that the competing lending teams made the whole experience about the lenders, and that Kiva lost touch with poverty its mission. The Kivan reflects, "The lending teams, didn't cause Kiva to lose their way, they were a sign of the way becoming lost…. Teams battled one another to see which could make the most loans. That was my realization that the folks at Kiva don't look at it the same way I do. It was like I was talking to Mars Candy trying to figure out how to get people to buy more M&Ms. Kiva came off as just another business."[26]

That a Kivan would compare a presumably philanthropic organization to a for-profit, publicly traded corporation is evidence of the omnipresence of corporate hegemony. Recall Dugger's model of corporate emulation in which organizations of all kinds, even philanthropic or regulatory ones, are ensnared in the hegemonic culture of the corporate institution. As such, it creates a schism between what organizations or agencies were created to do and what they became preoccupied with as they became institutionalized under corporate hegemony. Such mission drift is everywhere in the world of finance, not just in developing countries.

Domen Bajde from the department of marketing and management at the University of Southern Denmark sees the Kiva marketplace that has little to do with the humanitarian mission of microfinance, and is rather "a consumption playground where the poor are objectified and consumed, rather than empowered… Such appropriation feeds donors' needs for self-expression, voyeurism, and play in the name of poverty alleviation."[27] There is a financial need to keep Kivans drawn in and entertained. They are the customers.

Mission drift is endemic in the financial sector. The original intention of all forms of finance was a legitimate economic function. It was to aggregate financial resources so that they could be used for economic development, home ownership, or infrastructure, but instead became preoccupied with underwriting speculation and hunting down emerging markets and opportunities for financial gain. P2P portals and microfinance were supposed to be about helping people in developing countries pull themselves out of poverty. It may be achieving that to some degree, but the data compiles by Duvendack and others suggestions otherwise. What is unambiguous, however, that these portals and MFIs have facilitated the expansion of the finance industry with its endless obsession with capturing emerging markets. To that end they have captured the humanitarian instincts of people who seek to make positive changes and to genuinely help others, and turned it into a marketing gimmick to help spread loan sharking. Yunus lamented such mission drift that has overtaken microfinance as do some Kivans who express concern, "In short, some started to have a second agenda for lending which in my view diminished the original commonly shared cause and idealism… now we are fractured and by Kiva turned into consumers in a marketplace."[28]

Equity Crowdfunding

Equity crowdfunding is a kind of Jeffersonian model that allows for smallish businesses to capitalize using internet-based crowdfunding platforms as intermediaries, or "portals." In one sense, the model is not substantially different from any other mode of capitalization by way of selling securities. What is innovative is that this model hitches securities trades onto established, donor-based crowdsource infrastructure that was originally a place where starving artists could find patrons through internet portals. The idea of using this infrastructure for business capitalization got a tremendous boost through yet another government financial market deregulation plan. The upshot is that it moves in the direction of allowing small businesses to act as their own investment banker. Like most novelties in financial innovation, equity crowdfunding got a boost from neoliberal government deregulation.

In 2012, the federal government passed a piece of legislation titled, *The Jumpstart Our Business Startups Act* (JOBS). The legislation allows for certain exemptions from securities laws in order to facilitate the expansion of small business capitalization and was strongly supported by tech sector heavy hitters such as Google. But the deregulation also caught the attention and support of some progressives who saw it as a possible financial model for real, practical alternatives to business as usual.

In that spirit, the legislation contains certain small-is-beautiful restrictions. For example, the total amount of capitalization a startup can generate through equity crowdfunding portals cannot exceed $1 million in a year's time. It is also designed to sweep together capital scattered among a multitude of small investors such that no individual investor can purchase more than $2000 worth of a company's securities, or an amount equal to 5% of their annual income or net worth, provided that either their income or net worth is less than $100,000, whichever is lesser. If their income/net worth is equal to, or greater than $100,000 the restriction caps at 10%. In either case, the maximum an individual can pony up for capitalizing a startup cannot exceed $100,000.

To put it plainly, the legislation makes it such that a company can raise up to a million in capital annually by selling securities to investors up to $100,000 per person without going through the traditional channels that are regulated by the Security Exchange Commission (SEC). The legislation has other provisions such as requiring the internet portals to register with the SEC, though they do not have to be licensed as "broker/dealers." It also requires that the portals establish safeguards against fraud, requires financial reviews and audits for investor transparency, and places restrictions on marketing strategies that portray equity crowdfunding as public offerings.

The models that were spawned by this legislation are still in their infancy as the SEC had set the new rules to go into effect in May 2016. But like so many adventures in financial innovation, the devil is in the details. The provisions of the legislation presumably were put in place with the intention of creating a new model of finance that would constitute a break from established securities trading. Entrepreneurs can initiate a business plan, sign up with a crowdfunding portal or P2P platform and sell shares or debt instruments without going through registered dealers. Small-scale entrepreneurs meet small-scale investors. The model is seen by many to be initial baby steps for startups that are not ready to make initial public offerings of stocks.

So far, however, there has been little capital raised this way. Joyce Rosenberg, business writer for *Inc* reports that equity crowdfunding is not living up to the hype.[29] According to Crowdfund Capital Advisors, between 2016 and 2018 equity crowdfunding has only aggregated a bit over $100 million for about 438 companies.[30] Nick Tommarello, CEO of Wefunder complains that "Some of what's held crowdfunding back are legal limitations and requirements, designed to protect investors who may be unfamiliar with the risks of committing money to young companies without proven track records."[31]

The legal complexity of side-stepping long-standing SEC regulations is a daunting obstacle for small startups. The consulting, legal, and accounting fees alone can easily soar into the tens of thousands before even raising a dime from the portals. And indeed, like payday and microfinance lenders, sharks have already been sighted in these shallow waters. Surrounding the hype and buzz of equity crowdfunding are entrepreneurs who are aggressively pushing this model in hopes of garnering lucrative consulting fees at the expense of small business. Evidence of mission drift is surfacing as the models are hustled away from small-is-beautiful to a professional services bonanza. The bulk of equity crowdfunding advocates are consultants, certified public accountants, lawyers, and other professionals who see an emerging market for their services.

One highly energized supporter of equity crowdfunding is another nonprofit and consulting enterprise, Hatch Innovation. Hatch offers equity crowdfunding "accelerator" workshops for microenterprise entrepreneurs who seek to capitalize. The workshops are eight sessions for a total of $3000, which does not include legal counsel, financial services, or anything else beyond sharing information about the new legislation and how to profit from it.[32] But much of what defines crowdfunding still holds to a tradition of people funding something of that is of personal interest to them rather than a business venture. They use the platform to help fund a small brewery that makes their favorite beer, or a music recording project, or a small bakery. Moreover, deregulation has removed strictures that have been in place to protect those who are not experienced financiers. For these microenterprises to pony up tens of thousands in legal and professional services fees is cost prohibitive.

The trend, however, is to push crowdfunding into a micro-investment banking industry. Many of those in the business are pushing for further deregulation to raise the cap of one million or eliminate it entirely. As a business must comply with SEC regulations and disclosure documentation, the legal costs can soar into the tens of thousands, which would be manageable if the companies could raise more than a million dollars per year. Rosenberg reports that "The crowdfunding industry is hoping that Congress and the SEC change some of the rules… bills have been proposed in Congress to modify some of the requirements and allow companies to raise more than $1 million."[33] But these restrictions were put in place to protect small investors who are not necessarily familiar with hedging against the risk of putting money into businesses that do not have an established and publicly disclosed track record.

As of this writing, further deregulation has not materialized. If it were and the caps were lifted, it would be certain that equity crowdfunding would transform into a something darkly familiar—an opaque frontier of finance with untested instruments that would be traded in newly deregulated markets under the slogan of innovation, beckoning the involvement of hedge funds and institutional investors—though now glossed with small-is-beautiful imagery. It would be following the same route as microfinance. When that happens it would be another instance for mission drift and it would trample on that which brought people to crowdfunding in the first place: the ability to personally capitalize a project that has meaning beyond the expectation of financial returns.

Gimmickry abounds in the world of hipster finance. Portal-based finance is breeding new buzzwords and gimmicks almost daily. The race to get in front of the crowd pushes innovation before anyone can clearly grasp their implications. But to question innovation is heresy. It is not enough to have portals to fund ventures in social entrepreneurship that promise to save the world and to get rich. For decades we have been hearing promises coming from progressives about win-win scenarios like new bottles for the same wine. Socially responsible investments, impact investments, green capitalism, corporate social responsibility, benefit corporations, social benefit enterprise, impact entrepreneurship, social entrepreneurship, and now the latest buzzword is "accelerator." Product differentiation and marketing are alive and well in the corporate capitalist world.

For an enterprise now to be considered truly impactful, innovative, and socially or environmentally beneficial it needs to be called a "social entrepreneurship accelerator" and affixed to cryptocurrency. Common Cents is a new business model that promises to help companies do just that.[34] Founded in 2011 by advertising industry professionals, the idea is to provide an online platform for helping people with marketing strategies and sales pitches, particularly targeting social entrepreneurs. Part of the business model is the facilitate what they call "Maniacal Business Attacks," for sharing thoughts and ideas on how to keep tapping into anything new or prototypical. They are structuring the social entrepreneurship environment within a cryptocurrency environment that, presumably, will help maintain a close network of businesses who want to share information and capital. Though it is unclear why people would need the cryptocurrency for this other than to create what one of the co-founders declared as "a voice for a new kind of capitalism."[35]

What a statement it is to say that capitalism needs a voice for renewal, as if it has been drowned out and marginalized by something else. In the world of corporate hegemony, it is the only voice, and since the hegemony covers everything and every possible scrap of value under the sun, the voice is everywhere. The digital-portal universe is clogged with its expressions of "collaboration sites," "project management platforms," "strategic consultancy networks," "peer-to-peer," and "financial inclusion."

The oldest gimmick in the history of capitalism is to pitch the old wine in a new bottle and call it innovative, advanced, cutting-edge, next generation, revolutionizing; and then also claim that it is part of a new era, new world economic order, or new economy. Tweak the words and it is no longer cliché and an emerging market is born. With new markets come new investment opportunities, speculation, and instability. We know this because this is a salient characteristic of the historical record of capitalism. If historical patterns still have meaning, such financial gimmickry successfully draws multitudes of dupes into some schemes that result in crisis and instability. But with each round of innovation there is a built-in fail-safe device that deflects critical scrutiny. The device is the assertion that because this one is the newest and latest, this time will be different.

Economists Carmen Reinhart and Kenneth Rogoff chronicle several centuries of financial crises in their book, *This Time Is Different: Eight Centuries of Financial Folly* (2009). The central message of their book they say is simple: "We have been here before. No matter how different the latest financial frenzy or crisis always appears, there are usually remarkable similarities with past experience from other countries and from history… We hope the weight of evidence in this book will give future policy makers and investors a bit more pause before next they declare, 'This time is different.' It almost never is."[36]

Notes

1. Peter Renton, "Peer to Peer Lending Crosses $1 Billion in Loans Issued." https://techcrunch.com/2012/05/29/peer-to-peer-lending-crosses-1-billion-in-loans-issued/.
2. https://www.lendingclub.com/.
3. Noah Buhayar, "Peer-to-Peer Lending," *Bloomberg*, June 6, 2017. https://www.bloomberg.com/quicktake/peer-peer-lending.
4. Consumer Action, "Peer-to-Peer Lending Survey" (June 2012). https://www.consumer-action.org/news/articles/2012_p2p_lending_survey/.
5. Oscar Williams Grut, "After Firing Its CEO, Lending Club Is Facing a Crisis," *Business Insider*, May 17, 2016. https://www.inc.com/business-insider/inside-lending-club-scandal.html.
6. Amy Cortese, "Loans That Avoid Banks? Maybe Not," *The New York Times*, May 3, 2014.
7. Ibid.
8. Oscar Williams Grut, 2016.
9. Kiva website https://www.kiva.org/about.
10. Nicholas Kristof, "You, Too, Can Be a Banker to the Poor," *The New York Times*, March 27, 2003.
11. Domen Bajde, "Kiva's Staging of 'Peer-to-Peer' Charitable Lending: Innovative Marketing or Egregious Deception?" in Milford Bateman and Kate Maclean (eds.), *Seduced and Betrayed: Exposing the Contemporary Microfinance Phenomenon* (Albuquerque: University of New Mexico Press, 2017), p. 91.
12. See tax records posted on Pro Publica: Nonprofit Explorer Research Tax-Exempt Organizations, for 2015, IRS Form 990, Kiva Microfunds. https://pp-990.s3.amazonaws.com/2016_09_EO/71-0992446_990_201512.pdf?X-Amz-Algorithm=AWS4-HMAC-SHA256&X-Amz-Credential=AKIAI7C6X5GT42DHYZIA%2F20180828%2Fus-east-1%2Fs3%2Faws4_request&X-Amz-Date=20180828T144020Z&X-Amz-Expires=1800&X-Amz-SignedHeaders=host&X-Amz-Signature=445087ae33d05e0d199590a4b973e8eb8e9ac731c2b95d7debc65a6ab707b9e2.
13. David Roodman, "Kiva Is Not Quite What It Seems," Center for Global Development, October 2, 2009. https://www.cgdev.org/blog/kiva-not-quite-what-it-seems.

14. Kiva website https://www.kiva.org/about.
15. Roodman (2009).
16. Hugh Sinclair, *Confessions of a Microfinance Heretic*, pp. 262–270.
17. Ibid., p. 256.
18. Neil McFarquhar, "Banks Making Big Profits from Tiny Loans," April 13, 2010 and Stephanie Strom, "Confusion on Where Money Let via Kiva Goes," November 8, 2009, *The New York Times*.
19. Sinclair, 2012, pp. 250–260.
20. http://www.microfinancetransparency.com/evidence/PDF/11.11%20Kivafriends%20on%20cockfighting%20loans.pdf.
21. Ibid.
22. Matt Flannery, "Cockfighting," Skoll Foundation Archives, March, 2008. http://archive.skoll.org/2008/03/30/cockfighting/.
23. http://www.microfinancetransparency.com/evidence/PDF/11.11%20Kivafriends%20on%20cockfighting%20loans.pdf.
24. Bajde, 2017, p. 95.
25. Ibid., p. 96.
26. Ibid., p. 97.
27. Bajde, 2017, p. 100.
28. Ibid.
29. Joyce Rosenberg, "Why Equity Crowdfunding Is Not Living up to the Hype," *Inc*, May 9, 2018. https://www.inc.com/associated-press/equity-crowdfunding-investing-business-not-working-hype-investors-regulations-sec.html.
30. Ibid.
31. Ibid.
32. See Hatch Innovation website and workshop information at https://hatchoregon.com/accelerator/.
33. Rosenberg 2018.
34. Anne Field, "A Social Enterprise Accelerator Launches a Cryptocurrency for Its Community," *Locavesting*, June 12, 2018. https://www.locavesting.com/new-economy/social-enterprise-accelerator-launches-cryptocurrency-community/.
35. Ibid.
36. Carmen Reinhart and Kenneth Rogoff, *This Time Is Different: Eight Centuries of Financial Folly* (Princeton, NJ: Princeton University Press, 2009), pp. xxv and xxxv.

References

Bajde, Domen. "Kiva's Staging of 'Peer-to-Peer' Charitable Lending: Innovative Marketing or Egregious Deception?" in Milford Bateman and Kate Maclean (eds.), *Seduced and Betrayed: Exposing the Contemporary Microfinance Phenomenon* (Albuquerque: University of New Mexico Press, 2017).

Buhayar, Noah. "Peer-to-Peer Lending," *Bloomberg*, June 6, 2017. https://www.bloomberg.com/quicktake/peer-peer-lending.

Consumer Action. "Peer-to-Peer Lending Survey" (June 2012). https://www.consumer-action.org/news/articles/2012_p2p_lending_survey/.

Cortese, Amy. "Loans That Avoid Banks? Maybe Not," *The New York Times*, May 3, 2014.

Flannery, Matt. "Cockfighting," Skoll Foundation Archives, March 2008. http://archive.skoll.org/2008/03/30/cockfighting/.

Field, Anne. "A Social Enterprise Accelerator Launches a Cryptocurrency for Its Community," *Locavesting*, June 12, 2018. https://www.locavesting.com/new-economy/social-enterprise-accelerator-launches-cryptocurrency-community/.

Grut, Oscar Williams. "After Firing Its CEO, Lending Club Is Facing a Crisis," *Business Insider*, May 17, 2016. https://www.inc.com/business-insider/inside-lending-club-scandal.html.

Hatch Innovation. https://hatchoregon.com/accelerator/.

Kiva. https://www.kiva.org/about.

Kiva.org. "Cockfighting." http://www.microfinancetransparency.com/evidence/PDF/11.11%20Kivafriends%20on%20cockfighting%20loans.pdf.

Kristof, Nicholas. "You, Too, Can Be a Banker to the Poor," *The New York Times*, March 27, 2003.

The Lending Club. https://www.lendingclub.com/.

McFarquhar, Neil. "Banks Making Big Profits from Tiny Loans," *The New York Times*, April 13, 2010.

Pro Publica: Nonprofit Explorer Research Tax-Exempt Organizations, for 2015, IRS Form 990, Kiva Microfunds. https://pp-990.s3.amazonaws.com/2016_09_EO/71-0992446_990_201512.pdf?X-Amz-Algorithm=AWS4-HMAC-SHA256&X-Amz-Credential=AKIAI7C6X5GT42DHYZIA%2F20180828%2Fus-east-1%2Fs3%2Faws4_request&X-Amz-Date=20180828T144020Z&X-Amz-Expires=1800&X-Amz-SignedHeaders=host&X-Amz-Signature=445087ae33d05e0d199590a4b973e8eb8e9ac731c2b95d7debc65a6ab707b9e2.

Reinhart, Carmen, and Kenneth Rogoff. *This Time Is Different: Eight Centuries of Financial Folly* (Princeton, NJ: Princeton University Press, 2009).
Renton, Peter. "Peer To Peer Lending Crosses $1 Billion in Loans Issued." https://techcrunch.com/2012/05/29/peer-to-peer-lending-crosses-1-billion-in-loans-issued/.
Roodman, David. "Kiva Is Not Quite What It Seems," Center for Global Development, October 2, 2009. https://www.cgdev.org/blog/kiva-not-quite-what-it-seems.
Rosenberg, Joyce. "Why Equity Crowdfunding Is Not Living up to the Hype," *Inc*, May 9, 2018. https://www.inc.com/associated-press/equity-crowdfunding-investing-business-not-working-hype-investors-regulations-sec.html.
Sinclair, Hugh. *Confessions of a Microfinance Heretic: How Microfinance Lost Its Way and Betrayed the Poor* (San Francisco, CA: Berrett-Koehler, 2010).
Strom, Stephanie. "Confusion on Where Money Let via Kiva Goes," *The New York Times*, November 8, 2009.

12

The Neoliberal Oxymoron of Green Capitalism

In the mid-eighties a group of scholars convened for two conferences aimed at building a New Economics paradigm. The first was held in London in 1984 and the second, was held in Bonn the following year. The goals set out for the new paradigm were to develop and promote an economic system that is centered on social justice, the satisfaction of a wide range of human needs, sustainable use of resources, and environmental conservation. The meetings were called The Other Economic Summit (TOES) to symbolize a clean break from the business-as-usual Group of Seven meetings or World Economic Forums. TOES addressed a spectrum of economic issues that were becoming increasingly exigent such as the problem of trying to achieve endless economic growth within the confines of a finite planet, the widening income and wealth gap between the world's rich and poor, the need for economic indicators that could better assess human wellbeing than gross domestic product (GDP),[1] chronic unemployment, access to education and health care services for the world's population, alternative business models, alternative systems of finance and trade, gender equality, and tax policies. The conference presentations were compiled, edited by conference organizer and economist Paul Ekins, and a year later published in a book titled,

J. Magnuson, *Financing the Apocalypse*,
Palgrave Insights into Apocalypse Economics,
https://doi.org/10.1007/978-3-030-04720-7_12

The Living Economy: A New Economics in the Making (1986), right at the dawn of the Greenspan Era.

The book contains almost 350 pages of creative thinking on the continuing project of building an economic paradigm that is human-centered and earth-friendly. Remarkably a discussion of corporate power, corporate hegemony, or the corporation as an economic and social institution was nearly non-existent. From an institutionalist perspective this is analogous to having world-class conferences on transitioning from state socialism to market capitalism with scarcely any mention of the state as an institution. This omission is perhaps evidence that the new economy was never really intended to be new, but rather was intended to apply a few tweaks to the old.

The only mention of the role of corporations was in the very last two pages by new age futurist Willis Harman. Harman contemplates a promising economic future that will be shaped by an ascendant, transformative, human consciousness he calls "universal transcendentalism."[2] He anticipates "increasing concern with strengthening commitments to the humane, ecological, and spiritual values necessary to mediate the awesome economic, technological, and military power of modern industrial societies."[3] For Harman, this new consciousness is a kind of awakening to people power and from this power a New Economy will spring forth. He looks to the American Declaration of Independence as an example of political governance by virtue of the consent of the governed. So, too, will be the fiduciary responsibility of corporation as it "will be increasingly judged on 'multiple bottom lines,' social in addition to financial, and the public will be quick to recognize social-responsibility 'window-dressing' and to distinguish it from genuine change."[4] The corporation's long tradition of a single-minded pursuit of profit will give way to the demands of a spiritually and ecologically woke population of consumers and investors. It brings to mind dreams of a counterculture from the sixties in which war protestors were planning a "mystic revolution" in which "superhumans" were going to perform exorcisms of the Pentagon and "long-haired warlocks who 'cast mighty words of white light against the demon-controlled structure,' in hopes of levitating that grim ziggurat right off the ground."[5]

It is preferable to think that by now we have become more sophisticated in our expectations on how we bring about real change. Making categorical assumptions about consciousness-driven transformation of the behavior of capitalism is not it. The TOES did not open a serious dialog about the role of corporate power, but yet the concept of the multiple bottom line caught on and has stood the test of time as central theme New Economy economics. Corporate capitalism should be allowed to keep doing what it does best: making and accumulating profits and people power expressed through consumer goods and financial markets will assure that it toes the line of social and environmental accountability. The win-win of doing well and doing good became the gold standard for neoliberal green economics. That very fact attests to the extraordinary ability of corporate hegemony to co-opt all that it encounters in its path. For the corporation, the New Economy represented new opportunities for investment, growth, and profits with green coloring.

New age visions of an aquarian groundswell of change bubbling upward from a woke population expressing itself in markets remains vague. Corporate gurus have TED talks and open forums in which they wax endlessly and prophetically about how the people at their company or their customers are "witnessing a revolution," or are the "innovators" at the "cutting edge." All nod piously to the fait accompli of the corporate class who can always corral mass consciousness as it pleases with dreamy propositions of success and progress.

Getting Americans to buy into win-win proposals is not difficult. Buried deep in the American psyche is the neoliberal notion that capitalism and democracy are the same thing. Free enterprise and free choice-making in the marketplace are conflated as popular enfranchisement. The notion that markets give people a say in how the economy is governed fits well with a notion that institutions or social structures of power do not exist. But it does not take much effort for any of us to see that people power in the marketplace actually means purchasing power, and there is no *person* more powerful than the corporation and no one more powerless than the average member of the working class struggling to make ends meet.

After decades of corporate hegemony and neoliberal propaganda, that truth gets blurred into oblivion. Popular opinion has been machine-tooled into a corporate-friendly version of things, even for those who seek to repair the social and environmental damage done by corporate commodification and financialization and the growth imperative of capitalism.

The process of coopting alternatives extends far beyond bottom lines. It is about survival of the corporate species. Capitalism has been around for at least four centuries and the corporate version of that has been around for about a century and a half. Compared to the two hundred and forty million years of the species life of a beetle this is but a temporal blip. But in human years it is a good stretch of time. During that time corporate capitalism, like any other complex system, has evolved. Its success is largely attributed to its ability to change and adapt to new environments and survive while keeping its essential nature intact.

The corporation and its social classes are remarkably resilient in this regard. Around the same time C. Wright Mills was unleashing his critique of the *power elite* Herbert Marcuse and observed the strategic ability of corporate capitalism to coopt its opposition. Marcuse noted with concern that in the immediate aftermath of the mass student protests in France and Germany in 1968, his work criticizing the cultural and social repression of contemporary capitalism was becoming a sensation among the bourgeois elite, "I'm very much worried about this. At the same time, it is a beautiful verification of my philosophy, which is that in this society everything can be co-opted, everything can be digested."[6] Fifty years later, Marcuse's message still applies. Cultural production and ideas specifically made in rebellious opposition to cultural hegemony is rendered into corporate media, commercials, and marketing as cool.

In his most renowned work *One-Dimensional Man* (1964), Marcuse extends Gramsci's conception of hegemony by asserting that there have always been multiple dimensions to human existence and experience, but in time all become absorbed into a single corporate-controlled dimension. This becomes forgiven because, frankly, people are lulled into complacency by the "good life" promised by corporate capitalism. He writes, "If it assimilates everything it touches, if it absorbs the opposition, if it plays with the contradiction, it demonstrates its cultural superiority. And in the same way the destruction of resources and the proliferation of waste demonstrate its opulence and [quoting John K. Galbraith] the 'high levels of well-being'; 'the Community is too well off to care!'"[7] Whether real or imagined, the real power of corporate cultural hegemony lies with its ability to raise concerns that commitments to social or environmental change come at the cost of our well-off-ness. Accordingly, the power of green economics is to promise that there is no such cost.

The Oxymoron of Green Capitalism

In the first TOES summit the work of Herman Daly was revered. At the time Daly, former World Bank economist and co-founder of the journal *Ecological Economics,* was already well known for his work on steady-state economics.[8] Daly was recognized for articulating the concept of balance or imbalance in throughput: the production chain links between resource inputs and final outputs, including waste. The central idea of steady-state economics is that output needs to be scaled in line with the regenerative capacity of inputs, and with natural environment's ability to reabsorb waste and pollutants, including carbon dioxide. Maintaining the habitability of the planet is the most significant aspect of the steady-state model. The opposite of steady-state is resource depletion and the systematic accumulation of toxin such as carbon dioxide in the ecosphere, which is our current state. Given the limitations of resources and the toxifying condition of concentrating atmospheric carbon dioxide, Daly argues that the way to move toward steady-state is by slowing output growth to bring it into throughput stasis, or to enhance our resource with technological efficiency, or some combination of both. Daly asserted that capitalism could be retrofitted to make this happen. At this, the corporate world rejoiced.

One of the participants at the London TOES summit was journalist and then editor of the Guardian Hartford Thomas. Thomas gushed on the possibility of steady-state capitalism as it "treats the money-values of profit and loss balance sheets and income and expenditures budgets as secondary to resource accounting, which makes a sustainability assessment of use, conservation and future availability."[9] The messages from Daly and the TOES generation laid the foundation for the "triple bottom line" principle of corporate governance. This, like microfinance, equity crowdfunding, and peer-to-peer models, became a neoliberal dream.

The basic premise of triple bottom line governance is the idea that corporations can be governed in such a way that its mission is to maintain a balance between equity, ecology, and economy, or the so-called "Three Es." Sustainability began to move away from the slower balanced throughput concept put forward by Daly to something more like a canon salute to profit maximization making the biggest boom and lip service to the other goals. As the Greenspan Era and market populism were well underway by the early nineties, a green economics bandwagon was formed. Among the first to jump on were Paul Hawken, Frances Cairncross, Amory Lovins, Hunter L. Lovins, Jonathan Porrit, Lester R. Brown, James "Gus" Speth, and others. Of the next two decades the green capitalists launched a series of books, some of which with oxymoronic titles: *Costing the Earth* (1992), *Ecological Commerce* (1993), *Natural Capitalism* (1999), *Eco-Economy* (2001), *Capitalism as If the World Mattered* (2005), and the *Green Collar Economy* (2009). Yale economist and founder of the National Resource Defense Council Gus Speth articulated the greening of corporate capitalism succinctly,

> The market can be transformed into an instrument for environmental restoration; humanity's ecological footprint can be reduced to what can be sustained environmentally; the incentives that govern corporate behavior can be rewritten; growth can be focused on things that truly need to grow and consumption on having enough, not always more; the rights of future generations and other species can be respected.[10]

Collectively they set forward an agenda to green up the capitalist mode of production. From a historical perspective the agenda seems like a bizarre assertion given capitalism's long-standing reputation for clobbering the resource base and human beings—deforestation, toxic waste dumping, strip mining, land grabs, oil spills, child labor, compulsive consumerism, marketing gimmicks, worker exploitation, banking meltdowns, stock market booms and busts, and oceanic separations between the rich and the poor—is now going green.

Nonetheless, green economics pushed on with an impressive array of ideas such as tax shifts and incentives, new metrics for leading economic indicators, product labeling, education programs, and of course a deep faith in technology. Government officials, educators, media, and every other institution within the sphere of corporate hegemony were riding this bandwagon. "Do good and do well" became the mantra and corporations and consumers alike found it irresistible. Daly's caution of limits to economic growth was thrown to the wind. It was as if capitalism found a loophole in the laws of nature, and loopholes have a way of becoming the rule rather than the exception when there is money to be made.

The environmental movement made a robust commitment to neoliberalism with new markets and investment opportunities. Over three decades the eco-entrepreneurship continually expanded, differentiated its product identities, and rebranded to stay a step ahead of market saturation. Socially responsible investments, or SRIs, morphed into impact investing. Renewable energy, particularly solar, became a global industry with China leading the world in solar panel production. National grocery chains built retail empires on organic food and fair trade labeling. Green business established itself as an economic force in the world. Businesses continued performing for the bottom line as always, and widely dispersed the message to consumers that saving the planet is fun, easy, and they don't have to a change their ways of life or expectations.

Workers were promised that now in addition to becoming information workers, they were also going to secure lucrative green collar jobs. As they make big money, they green collar professionals who can afford to buy high end organic, sustainable, certified consumer goods, and the businesses that successfully market those goods will be plowing their profits back into even greener economic development. Magically everybody wins: producers make profits, workers get jobs, and consumers save the planet by shopping. The very same growth-driven corporate institutions and consumer culture that have brought the world into climate hell is also the go-to solution for restoration.

The only problem is that none of this made any difference. We are now in the Trump Era and as we have seen throughout these pages, in the ways that matter most—climate change, resource depletion, financial system instability, and extreme income and wealth polarization, and mounting debt—the crises we face are more extreme and more intractable than they were at the beginning of the Greenspan Era.

It is perhaps safe to say that climate change is the most pressing ecological issue of our time. The basic scientific reality of it is uncomplicated: too much carbon dioxide and other heat-trapping chemicals have accumulated in the atmosphere. This is something scientists have been studying and warning about for at least fifty years, yet there has been more carbon spewed into the air since the first TOES summit than during the entire span of human history preceding it. Humans were discharging about 20 billion metric tons of carbon dioxide into the air each year at the beginning of the Greenspan Era and by 2017 that figure has risen to 32.5 billion—a new record.[11] That same year recorded record wildfire damage in California, and as of this writing 2018 will be number one.

The green economics are quick to point the finger of culpability at politics, "the knowledge, expertise, and resources for the economic transformation to sustainability are amply available. What is lacking is the political will to deploy them."[12] The message suggests that politicians lack of will to pursue real change is something that they have acquired independently of their corporate patrons. This only makes sense if we choose to pretend that institutions and corporate hegemony do not exist. Aside from that there are glaring contradictions in the green economics movement. Bringing these contradictions out into the open might shed some light on why green economics has not brought the ecological miracles we were promised.

Win-Win Solutions Become Contradictions

Paul Hawken, among the most prominent green economics advocates, expressed concern that a continuation of current corporate practices will potentially destroy life on earth.[13] But he qualified his expression by saying that this destruction is not something that is "inherent nature of business, nor the inevitable outcome of a free-market system," but rather extends from a fundamental problem of pricing and the fact that "the expense of destroying the earth is largely absent from the prices set in the marketplace. A vital and key piece of information is therefore missing in all levels of the economy."[14] Hawken is referring to what environmental economists call "full-cost accounting" or "true-cost pricing."

The basic concept of true-cost pricing is that there are costs associated with producing things that are not included in the market price of things. Some costs are externalized. When we talk of anthropogenic climate change, most of it is attributable to burning fossil fuels. When we burn gasoline or coal the carbon effluents contribute to climate change, which leads to damage such as soil ruination, floods, and wildfires. These disasters are costly, yet those costs are not included in the prices we pay for these fuels. In this view, they are artificially inexpensive. True-cost pricing, therefore is an argument to internalize these costs and so that they are reflected in the final prices. Economist and journalist Frances Caincross was one of the first generations of green economists to advocate for a comprehensive program for true-cost pricing and her market-based solutions ranging from green consumerism to the use of fossil taxes for true costing. Using tax shifts to have a positive impact on the environment has always been popular in the green economics movement.

In her widely recognized book, *Costing the Earth: The Challenge for Governments, the Opportunities for Business* (1992), she argues that people and businesses need to pay for the environmental damage that results from their consumption of energy. One way to make them pay is with a true-cost excise tax on gasoline and other fuels.[15] To the extent businesses burn these fuels like utilities, the tax incentivizes investment in energy-saving technology and equipment. She goes on to argue in a manner echoing those of Willis Harman that "Perceptive firms realize that environmental regulation creates opportunities to compete and to innovate. This is not just a narrow calculation of commercial interest. The attitudes of corporate managers are formed by the same forces that molded the rest of society…to do right by the environment."[16]

Allan Thein Durning and Yoram Bauman from the Northwest Environment Watch make a case for taxing the "bads" and reducing taxes on the "goods," by using government tax policy to encourage good things like work and entrepreneurship by phasing out income taxes, and at the same time discourage bad things with excise taxes. They submit the argument that, "We could tax emissions of deadly fine particles, greenhouse gases, and other air pollutants; discharges of toxic heavy metals and other water pollutants; and the manufacture and use of pesticides and other hazardous chemicals."[17] When they say "we" here, they are referring to government. Their arguments extend the tax shift plan to things like traffic and fresh water, "We could tax away most traffic jams, by charging drivers for use of major routes at rush hour… taxing the pumping of fresh water, impounding rivers behind dams, and the felling of virgin timber."[18] Presumably if the idea is to tax these things away, there would be no hydroelectric energy, no commuter traffic, no use of fresh water, no pollution—no consumption to speak of. The sentiment is that consumers are ultimately responsible for environmental problems and they should pay.

The editors of E Magazine's make a similar argument in *Green Living: The E Magazine Handbook for Living Lightly on the Earth* (2005) in that consumers can do their part to help preserve the natural environment by simply making better choices. They argue that consumers can choose to cut back on consumption (bad) and instead save their money (good).

> …most environmentalists know that 'doing without' is good for the planet. But they may not realize just how good it is for their savings account… After all, money one might spend on an impressive SUV, a large engagement ring, or even a regular habit of junk food snacks, leaves you with less money to invest… If, for example, from the ages of twenty-three to sixty-seven you bypassed the popular American habit of buying a new mid-size car every two years and instead… invested your savings, you'd end up with an extra $869,638. Manage without a car altogether, invest the savings, and that money alone can make you a millionaire.[19]

There are a number of serious logical failures and conundrums with neoliberalist green economics. Going back to true-cost pricing. If the government did implement a fossil tax in gasoline that reflects the true cost in each gallon, what would it have to include. Certainly all the costs of exploration, drilling, refining, distribution, storage, and retailing. But true costing would add externalities by assigning dollar values to the deaths and extinctions of all living species, both known and unknown, that result from climate change, oil spills, and other damages. The calculations would have to take into consideration all future costs as long as the concentrations of carbon dioxide remain in the atmosphere over a certain threshold. That could extend into centuries from now, which implies that true costing would have to calculate all of these future costs of hundreds of years of melting ice caps, hurricanes, floods, drought, and wildfires, then discount them to a present value and add them to the price of each gallon. And with every additional gallon, a new present value would have to be calculated because the future costs are certain to be progressive and cumulative.

If we are serious about true costing all the things we would consider bad, this methodology wouldn't stop at oil. Sustainability under green capitalism would have to be achieved with the true costing of all resources, not just oil and coal. There would have to be true costing of fresh water and mineral use, timber harvests, nuclear power, and even renewable energy sources that require ever-expanding resources for new wind, solar, and geothermal infrastructure construction. It would have to apply to every commodity produced that does not currently include full cost accounting in its market price, which would probably be everything imaginable. To actually achieve this would require God-like omniscience. In other words, it would be impossible, and this is what economists call "market failure." The fault line between what is included in the final price and what is not included would be more or less arbitrary. There is no real science backing true-cost pricing, and markets fail to achieve the neoliberals cherished equilibrium condition where all prices settle at optimum efficiency, except in the realm of imagination.

The mathematical conundrums notwithstanding, there is a normative aspect to true costing. Aside from their commitment to neoliberal ideology, there is an underlying desire to punish consumers. Making people pay by taxing the hell out of everything they buy is an exercise in economic punishment. It is intended to be inflicted on consumers, but ironically it is punishment for doing exactly what is expected of them in the profit-seeking, growth-driven, commodity-producing world of corporate capitalism. This leads to a logical contradiction. In the green economics world, we would give the lash to people for shopping and buying stuff, and at the same time spend billions on corporate advertising to encourage them to buy more. Green economics would function like an economic auto immune disorder in which the system would be attacking itself. Our economic system is built on mass production and mass consumption, and if people are consuming fossil fuels excessively, it is because our economic system needs them to.

Presumably if green economics is to have the sustainability impact intended, it should apply to a broad segment of the population. If this is so, and everyone does as E Magazine suggested and significantly cuts back on buying cars, etc., what would be the investment fund into which investment fund will grow in seven figures? Corporate capitalism is just not built to work this way. If people slowed down spending, sales revenues would decline, which would push down corporate earnings, and eventually stock prices would decline, business loans would go into default, business investment would disappear, and the economy would crumble into a crisis and recession. Retirement funds would be wiped out, banks would fail, and working people would lose jobs. Having people spend like mad in order to maximize profits is not just some nefarious plan cooked up by greedy corporations, it is vital to keeping the capitalist system alive.

Years ago, *Business Week*, seeing that capitalism and sustainability are incompatible reported that, "The sweet notion that making a company environmentally friendly can be not just cost-effective but profitable is going up in smoke." The project of transforming capitalist business enterprise into an institution that is both environmentally friendly and showing robust returns to investors is at cross purposes. In the face of that corporate executives invariably weigh in on the side of investors. "We do," executives stress after all, "have a fiduciary responsibility to our shareholders."[20]

This fiduciary responsibility is sovereign in the corporate capitalist world. If the three Es are like a three-legged stool in which the "do well" leg is much longer than the other two "do good" legs, it is virtually impossible for a corporation to cut down to match. Corporate executives are most likely to give a salute to sustainable practices, but if they cannot result in bottom line returns to shareholders, there will be trouble. In Veblenian terms, the Interests, including activist shareholders, institutional investors, and their attorneys will take action against management. It's not that these people don't care about sustainability or fighting against climate change. Rather, they see corporations for what they are: legal and financial entities designed to make money for investors.

This takes us back to the concept of throughput articulated by Herman Daly over four decades ago. Doing well in the world of corporate hegemony means making money—the accumulation of financial wealth. In terms of throughput, this means putting money into the input side as an investment, and watching it grow on the output side as a return. Such monetary growth exists in a parallel universe to material growth. Money invested is used to buy material resources, which are used to produce material goods and services. Investors want to see money grow not because they are just fascinated by bigger numbers, but because of what those bigger numbers can buy. In the E Magazine example, what is the point of having the million dollars if there is nothing to buy with it.

The corporation is an institution created to serve the purpose of endlessly accruing and accumulating financial wealth for investors. Over centuries this purpose has evolved into a contractual mandate—a structure of contractual obligations in which managers of corporations are locked into a fiduciary responsibility to their shareholders to make sure robust investor profits are realized. In the corporate hegemony, institutional investors, fund managers, and the general public expect publicly traded corporations to live up to this mandate. As they do, they accelerate the process of throughput: producing financial growth with more sales of output and effluents on one side while sucking in more energy and other resources on the other side.

Financial growth is the ultimate taskmaster. Recognizing this problem of finance-driven throughput, investment fund manager and green economics advocate Woody Tasch calls for "slow money." He advocates for slowing down the financial returns frenzy on the output side would, as Daly suggested, give the resource input side a breather and a chance to restore itself. To that end Tasch advocates for models of corporate governance that melds fiduciary responsibility with a slow money principle of asset management that involves natural ecosystem regeneration and the maintenance of biological diversity. In other words, slow money is looking at sustainable throughput by tweaking "to realign shareholder returns—slows them down—with the carrying capacity of the environment."[21] His is a win-win solution like all other green economics advocates, but rather than promoting a "the sky is the limit" version of green capitalism, the ecological restoration as the constraining factor. The result for Tasch would be to do less harm with a compromise model.

His aspiration, it would appear, is to find some middle ground between a genuine commitment to reaching our goal of ecological permanence and the practical concerns of generating profits for investors. He writes, "We must be critical but not too critical of the environmental and governance-related failings of mature corporations. We must be critical but not too critical of the environmental and governance-related failings of start-up companies that explicitly embrace the triple bottom line."[22]

Financialization of the Natural Ecosystem

Tasch inadvertently raises a deeper issue. His slow money model is predicated on envisioning natural ecosystems restoration as "asset management." Slow money, full cost pricing, and green taxes—the darlings of green economics—all involve the ontological transformation of everything under the sun as a financial artifact. To see topsoil regeneration, hydrologic cycles, and reabsorption of carbon in biomass as "asset management" is a salient example of corporate cultural hegemony. An old growth forest is not a living ecosystem as much as it is a collection of assets to be managed. In the culture bewitched by "modern notions of entrepreneurship and fiduciary responsibility" such assets inevitably take the form of a derivative. The regenerative capacity of the world becomes an income earning asset with a future income stream that can be discounted to present value and traded on market exchanges.

Moreover, since nature is refashioned into a derivative, once it is traded on the open market, it will be subject to the efficient market hypothesis, which for neoliberals means the market price of nature is true and efficient price because the open market does not lie.

The Food and Agriculture Organization of the United Nations (FAO) is captured by the same metaphysics of financialization. On their full-cost accounting website, it contends that to achieve a neoliberal market approach to sustainability "ecosystem services or health must be given a monetary value." Recognizing the troubling tone of this message, added a qualifier "The ultimate purpose is not to monetize nature or people, but rather to translate invisible resources (such as intellectual, human, social and natural assets that are not captured in historic financial accounts) into a common currency for strategic decision-making on impact and dependencies that affect overall value creation." To that end, the FAO turns to the Natural Capital Protocol that was established in 2016 for methodology "developing a universal framework for true-cost accounting to better inform decision-makers in governments, businesses and farms."[23]

The Natural Capital Protocol is maintained by the Natural Capital Coalition, which is made up of businesses, government, and NGOs that strive to standardize methods for natural capital accounting and enable its valuation and reporting in business. The protocol was originally developed at the University of Cambridge Institute for Sustainability Leadership (CISL). Then was launched in 2012 to bring together stakeholders including businesses, government, and non-governmental organizations to help businesses improve their decision-making. From the outset, the ultimate goal of the protocol was obvious: to transform nature into a capital asset and call it natural capital. From there the way is paved to take the next steps of monetizing, commodifying, and financializing the natural ecosystem. Again, financialization is a means to end. The end is money-making.

This was revealed in the protocol development process during which about eighty business engagement partners (BEP) including large multinationals such as Shell, Dow Chemical, and Nestle were consulted on the need for such a protocol. The surveys were compiled into a report titled, "The Natural Capital Protocol: Feedback Report from Business

Engagement Partner Interviews." Though there was some disagreement among the BEPs, businesses involved, the majority agreed that valuing natural ecosystems as financial capital is important, either in monetary terms or in some other valuation method.[24] Using monetized valuation of natural ecosystems allows companies to perform cost-benefit analyses and risk. They can measure in financial terms the cost of depleting a natural resource reserve against the benefit of the profits made from doing so. If true-cost accounting is applied in these cases, then a more accurate market solution is derived.

Dow Chemical, a rapacious consumer of water, is showcased in the report. The aim was to apply a risk-based approach to understanding water scarcity, and to enable the company to consider water in a similar way to that which they would typically consider and cost other forms of capital (e.g. labour, gas, etc.). Corporate management then is asked to imagine that given the true-cost of water and thus operating on a need to use much less water because of the higher cost. This stands as a kind of incentivization to lead the corporation to actively seek out mitigation measures leading to valuable savings as well as conserving water. A win-win.

The corporate BEPs were circumspect, however, as they were still aware of their fiduciary responsibilities. In those terms they were unambiguous, "The Protocol Should help a company unlock new sources of value through its application. If the Protocol can clearly demonstrate, through compelling case studies, the commercial benefits of implementation, Boards are likely to accelerate uptake."[25] By unlocking new sources of value, they mean new opportunities for investment and money-making. The further noted in the report that businesses would be particularly if the methodology demonstrates "a strong business case and implications for competitive advantage from application of the Protocol was important for its adoption."[26] The United Nations FAO echoed these sentiments, "Increasingly, companies seek to understand the non-financial factors that improve risk management and unlock new opportunities, investors are interested to secure stronger returns on their investments."[27] Though expressed somewhat euphemistically, the aim of the Protocol is revealed—natural ecosystems are emerging markets.

The corporate sphere loathes being included in a critical narrative regarding the relentlessness of its pursuit of profit, yet it falls so easily into the narrative. Whether we call it corporate capitalism, natural capitalism, or green capitalism it is capitalism nonetheless; and the relentlessness of capitalism is its most prominent characteristic and is the key to its long-term survival.

The Drawdown Showdown

In a final showdown with the stubborn menace of climate change, Paul Hawken presses on with his most impressive work to date immodestly titled, *Drawdown: The Most Comprehensive Plan Ever Proposed to Reverse Global Warming* (2017). *Drawdown* is a veritable catalog of a very comprehensive array of ways the world can decarbon its atmosphere. The book is a collaboration among dozens of scientists, engineers, economists, financial analysts, journalists, and activists, and others involved in the endgame battle in the unwinnable war against climate change. It focuses on science, technology, and established practices with anecdotes for projects ranging from the usual action plans of ramping up wind, solar, geothermal, nuclear, biomass, and recycling. It also includes projects for reduced food waste, dietary changes, empowering women, silvopasture, reforestation, farmland restoration, architecture, and the list goes on.

With each of the eighty possible decarbon action items, there are compelling photographs and a figure for the amount of total atmospheric carbon dioxide would be reduced if implemented and maintained on through the year 2050. There is also a number for net cost of the action item, which is the total cost to "purchase, install, and operate it over thirty years."[28] The cost is factored into a net cost or net savings figure that is also listed with each item, "By comparing this to what we typically would spend on food, fuel for cars, heating and cooling for our homes, etc., we determined the net costs or savings from investing in a given solution."[29]

Take a look at *Drawdown's* analysis of energy, which has been our main focus here (Table 12.1). Taking all their green energy initiatives

Table 12.1 Energy, drawdown, costs, and savings

Action item	CO_2 reduction	Net cost (x billions)	Net savings (x billions)
Wind Turbines	98.7	1797.77	7699.57
Solar	72.4	1651.95	8895.32
Rooftop Solar	24.6	453.14	3457.63
Geothermal	16.6	155.48	1024.34
Nuclear	16.1	0.88	1713.4
Wave and Tidal	9.2	411.84	-1004.7
Methane Digesters	10.3	3671.42	2527.23
Biomass	7.5	402.31	519.35
Solar Water	6.08	2.99	773.65
In Stream Hydro	4	202.53	568.36
Cogeneration	3.97	279.25	566.93
Waste to Energy	1.1	36	19.82
Micro Wind	0.2	36.12	19.9
Energy Total	**270.74**	**$9,101.68**	**$26,780.80**
Drawdown Total	**1051.01**	**$27,405.68**	**$73,874.52**

Source Data compiled from *Drawdown* (2017), pp. 221–225

together there would be a total carbon reduction of 270.74 gigatons (billion tons). As of now, this figure would remove about one-quarter of the otherwise 1000 plus gigatons we are currently on track to contribute over the 30 years.[30] The authors conclude that the 1051 gigaton reduction would be enough to mitigate the cataclysmic effects of anthropogenic climate change and they are hopeful.

But there are some serious problems with their presentation. The IPCC produced a number of different scenarios given different parameters set in their climate model simulations. The scenarios, called Representative Concentration Pathways (RCPs), and project cumulative emissions of CO_2 into the atmosphere over the span of the twenty-first century. The projections show a wide range: from 510 to 7005 of cumulative carbon dioxide emissions concentrated between 2012 and 2100.[31] The generally accepted figure to mitigate the worst affects of climate change would be to keep global warming below 2 degrees centigrade. To achieve that, humans must not emit more than 469 billion tons, which we are on track to exceed over the next 25 years or less.[32]

Given the most optimistic RCP, this might be possible, but if any of the other RCP scenarios play out, there is not a chance.

In the drawdown total, taking every possible solution they have catalogued and given the rosiest RCP projection, they suggest that this might be possible with a reduction of over a thousand billion tons in thirty years. They do not share how they derive these figures and they seem highly speculative given that the IPCC contends that "There is insufficient knowledge to quantify how much CO_2 emissions could be partially offset by CDR [carbon dioxide removal] on a century timescale."[33] Say that the authors know some things the IPCC does not and assume that it is possible to know, even to get to that 1000 ton carbon dioxide removal figure, it would require a net capital investment of over $9 trillion and that would have to be put to work immediately. This is the devil in the details.

$9 trillion is 11% of the current gross world product and income. Nowhere in *Drawdown's* comprehensive plan is it discussed how this investment in green capital would happen or through which institutions. There are anecdotal references to for-profit companies that invest in things like solar or wind energy infrastructure. These companies, under corporate capitalism, would be expecting financial returns and may or may not be incentivized to do it. So if it were possible to scale out an additional $9 trillion for green infrastructure investments, and using a standard long-term equity growth number of 7% as the return, the green capitalism investment sector would need to start generating $630 billion in annual profits to make them financially viable. And until that infrastructure is fully implemented, this growth would be rooted in a carbon-based system.

This is the catch 22. The carbon economy would have to keep growing over the next few decades in order to generate the capital it would need to build the infrastructure in order to stop being a carbon economy. We would have to destroy ourselves to get the means to stop destroying ourselves. Had these investment projects began four decades ago when global warming became a hot political and media topic, it might have been possible. That didn't happen because corporate capitalism did not want it to happen. Now it is too late thanks in part to Paul Hawken who throughout those decades kept telling everyone that the growth imperative of capitalism is somehow compatible with sustainability. The Foreword to Drawdown begins with, "sometimes, when a concept or institution reaches its logical conclusion, the world looks at the results and cries: 'Never again.' For really bad ideas—from totalitarianism to fossil fuel dependence—saying 'never again' isn't enough. Humanity needs other, better ideas to take their place."[34] Apparently it has never occurred to them that corporate hegemony, with its endless need for growth, wealth accumulation, consumerism, and a rapacious appetite for energy has been one of those bad ideas, unless it is included in the category of totalitarianism.

Notes

1. At the time, the standard measure of national output was gross national product (GNP).
2. Willis Harman, "The Role of Corporations," in Paul Ekins (ed.), *The Living Economy: A New Economics in the Making* (New York, NY: Routledge, 1986), p. 344.
3. Ibid., p. 347.
4. Ibid., p. 349.
5. Theordore Roszak, *The Making of a Counter Culture: Reflections on the Technocratic Society and Its Youthful Opposition* (New York, NY: Anchor Books, 1969), p. 124.
6. Herbert Marcuse, "Values in Humanism," *Center Magazine,* June 1968, p. 14. http://www.worldcat.org/title/report-to-the-center-for-the-study-of-democratic-institutions/centerreport.
7. Marcuse, *One-Dimensional Man* (Boston, MA: Beacon Press, 1964), pp. 84–85.
8. Herman Daly, *Steady-State Economics* (Washington, DC: Island Press, 2nd ed., 1991).
9. *The Living Economy*, p. 14.
10. James Gustave Speth, *Bridge at the End of the World* (New Haven, CT: Yale University Press, 2009), p. 12.
11. Nathaniel Rich, "Losing Earth," *The New York Times Magazine*, August 1, 2018, p. 64.
12. *The Living Economy*, p. 14.
13. Paul Hawken, *The Ecology of Commerce* (New York, NY: Harper, 1993), p. 3.

14. Ibid., pp. 13–15.
15. Frances Cairncross, *Costing the Earth: The Challenge for Governments, the Opportunities for Business* (Cambridge, MA: Harvard University Press, 1993), pp. xi–xiii.
16. Ibid.
17. Allan Thein Durning and Yoram Bauman, *Tax Shift*, (Seattle, WA: Northwest Environment Watch, 1998), pp. 5-6.
18. Ibid., p. 6.
19. Editors of E Magazine, *Green Living: The E Magazine Handbook for Living Lightly on the Earth* (New York, NY: Plume, 2005), p. 109.
20. "Little Green Lies," *Bloomberg Business Week*, October 29, 2007, pp. 45–52.
21. Woody Tasch, *Slow Money: Investing as if Food, Farms, and Fertility Mattered* (Vermont: Chelsea Green, 2008) p. 48.
22. Ibid., p. 48.
23. Food and Agriculture Organization of the United Nations, "Sustainability Pathways: Full-Cost Accounting," at http://www.fao.org/nr/sustainability/full-cost-accounting/en/.
24. "The Natural Capital Protocol: Feedback Report from Business Engagement Partner Interviews," June 2015, p. 10, posted at https://naturalcapitalcoalition.org/wp-content/uploads/2016/07/Natural_Capital_Coalition_Business_Engagement_Partner_Interview_Report.pdf.
25. Ibid., p. 12.
26. Ibid., p. 18.
27. See "Sustainable Pathways."
28. Paul Hawken, ed., *Drawdown: The Most Comprehensive Plan Ever Proposed to Reverse Global Warming* (New York, NY: Penguin, 2017), p. xiv.
29. Ibid.
30. IPCC, "Climate Change 2013; The Physical Science Basis," at https://www.ipcc.ch/pdf/assessment-report/ar5/wg1/WGIAR5_SPM_brochure_en.pdf.
31. Ibid., p. 25.
32. Kelly Levin, "World's Carbon Budget to Be Spent in Three Decades," World Resources Institute, September 27, 2013. http://www.wri.org/blog/2013/09/world%E2%80%99s-carbon-budget-be-spent-three-decades.

33. IPCC, Climate Change 2013, p. 27.
34. *Drawdown*, p. ix.

References

Cairncross, Frances. *Costing the Earth: The Challenge for Governments, the Opportunities for Business* (Cambridge, MA: Harvard University Press, 1993).

Daly, Herman. *Steady-State Economics* (Washington, DC: Island Press, 2nd ed., 1991).

Durning, Allan Thein, and Yoram Bauman. *Tax Shift* (Seattle, WA: Northwest Environment Watch, 1998).

Editors of E Magazine's. *Green Living: The E Magazine Handbook for Living Lightly on the Earth* (New York, NY: Plume, 2005).

Ekins, Paul, ed. *The Living Economy: A New Economics in the Making* (New York, NY: Routledge, 1986).

Food and Agriculture Organization of the United Nations. "Sustainability Pathways: Full-Cost Accounting," at http://www.fao.org/nr/sustainability/full-cost-accounting/en/.

Hawken, Paul. *The Ecology of Commerce* (New York, NY: Harper, 1993).

Hawken, Paul, ed. *Drawdown: The Most Comprehensive Plan Ever Proposed to Reverse Global Warming* (New York, NY: Penguin, 2017).

International Panel on Climate Change. "Climate Change 2013; The Physical Science Basis," at https://www.ipcc.ch/pdf/assessment-report/ar5/wg1/WGIAR5_SPM_brochure_en.pdf.

Levin, Kelly. "World's Carbon Budget to Be Spent in Three Decades," World Resources Institute, September 27, 2013. http://www.wri.org/blog/2013/09/world%E2%80%99s-carbon-budget-be-spent-three-decades.

"Little Green Lies." *Bloomberg Business Week*, October 29, 2007.

Marcuse, Herbert. *One-Dimensional Man* (Boston, MA: Beacon Press, 1964).

Marcuse, Herbert. "Values in Humanism," *Center Magazine,* June 1968. http://www.worldcat.org/title/report-to-the-center-for-the-study-of-democratic-institutions/centerreport.

Natural Capital Coalition. "The Natural Capital Protocol: Feedback Report from Business Engagement Partner Interviews," June 2015, https://naturalcapitalcoalition.org/wp-content/uploads/2016/07/Natural_Capital_Coalition_Business_Engagement_Partner_Interview_Report.pdf.

Rich, Nathaniel. "Losing Earth," *The New York Times Magazine*, August 1, 2018.

Roszak, Theordore. *The Making of a Counter Culture: Reflections on the Technocratic Society and Its Youthful Opposition* (New York, NY: Anchor Books, 1969).

Speth, James Gustave. *Bridge at the End of the World* (New Haven, CT: Yale University Press, 2009).

Tasch, Woody. *Slow Money: Investing as if Food, Farms, and Fertility Mattered* (Vermont: Chelsea Green, 2008).

13
Conclusion

As Veblen was preparing to put down his writing pen for the last time, he cautioned his future readers about what we are losing as a society. For Veblen and many other progressives at the turn of the twentieth century there was much reason to be hopeful about the future. The intellectual and technological developments of the age provided hope that humankind was finally climbing out of the darkness of ignorance and poverty. He attested to the steady progress of scientific development, technological marvels, and the potential for human living standards to be elevated by virtue of advancing industrial development. He also saw such promise stemming from creative human instincts. Craftsmanship and industrial technology flowed naturally from a human instinct to better provide for our species. In the Deweyan sense, an instinct for social provisioning.

But Veblen was dispassionate. He observed the development of industry and its impact on human society with the objectivity of an entomologist examining a certain species of insect in its habitat. As it is with institutional economists, in general, Veblen's view was holistic and evolutionary. Everything is connected to everything else, and everything is changing. Nothing is independent or self-sufficient, and nothing is

J. Magnuson, *Financing the Apocalypse*,
Palgrave Insights into Apocalypse Economics,
https://doi.org/10.1007/978-3-030-04720-7_13

static. With this view, he concluded that, for better or worse, the defining characteristic of the whole of modern human life under industrial capitalism was what he called, "the machine process."[1] In his conception, the machine process was not just a bunch of machines, trucks, and assembly lines cranking out goods for consumption. It included those things, but it was something much more comprehensive. Veblen writes, "No one of the mechanical processes carried on by the use of a given outfit of appliances is independent of other processes going on elsewhere."[2] For example, a bakery needs pans and ovens to bake bread. Pan and oven manufacturers need tin, steel, copper to make their goods, which are produced in factories, that need more machines and tools, and so on. Each draws upon and presupposes the proper working of many other processes of a similarly mechanical character. None of the mechanical industries is self-sufficing. Each follows some and precedes other processes in an endless sequence."[3] Engineers, metallurgists, chemists, navigators, and scientists "have been drawn into, and have become integral factors, in it."[4] Workers' entire lives were subsumed into the concert of industry as were entire communities. In other words, the machine process was an entire socioeconomic system in which everything was pulled into a mighty vortex of industry. Moreover, it was rapidly evolving.

As the machine process evolved it created more standardization and uniformity in kind, style, grade, and gauge. The more aspects of economic life that were pulled into heavy industry, the more it impacted the way people live and think. Each new development stirs changes in the rest of the machine process, which further changes habits of thought and action of people. Consumer habits were continually adapting to fall in line with the machine process, "As regards the mass of civilized mankind, the idiosyncrasies of the individual consumers are required to conform to the uniform gradations imposed upon consumable goods by the comprehensive mechanical processes of industry. 'Local color,' it is said, is falling into the abeyance in modern life, and where it is still found it tends to assert itself and unites of the standard gauge."[5]

Comprehensive and powerful as the system came to be, it was vulnerable. If one cog in the machine breaks down, or what Veblen refers to as a "maladjustment," the whole system is put in jeopardy.[6] Thus efficiency, reliability, and standardization were not just characteristics of the system, they became increasingly mandatory to prevent chaos. "So much is clear, that the keeping of the balance in the comprehensive machine process of industry is a matter the gravest urgency..."[7] The need to maintain order is crucial and this gives importance to social institutions, which are, if anything, the means by which people maintain social order. Thus, he then extended his holistic view to include economic institutions—corporations—on the business side of things,

> It is by business transactions that the balance of working relations between the several industrial units is maintained or restored, adjusted and readjusted... It therefore rests with the business men to make or mar the running adjustments of industry. The larger and more close-knit and more delicately balanced the industrial system... the larger and more far-reaching will be the effect of each business move in this field.[8]

In other words, from Veblen's view, the industrial revolution created a habitat or ecosystem in which the corporation found a niche and spread like an invasive species. It was the evolution of the industrial system that created a systemic requirement of corporate institutions take and maintain control. The larger and more complex the industrial system, the larger became the corporations at the helm. But for Veblen, this is where the trouble began.

Veblen saw corporations as institutions controlled by the Interests—the corporate class—who have taken control of the economic system for their own "pecuniary" interests; that is, out of greed. He described the separation of share ownership from actual creative work as an inherent aspect of the corporation as an institution as a system of absentee ownership. He described a business arrangement in which a person can own and enjoy the profits of a business by owning stocks without working for or even seeing the business one owns. Veblen's absentee owner is a capitalist who receives money income from owning and not from working. He writes, "Safe and sane business men would go in for incorporation only on a good prospect of getting a little something for nothing..."[9]

Pecuniary interests split apart from social provisioning and became the dominant force with the institutionalization of capital under the power of corporations. Others at Veblen's time were also seeing these institutional developments with alarm. An English contemporary of Veblen, Richard Tawney, observed the rising corporate domination of attitudes in Western society. Tawney writes, "…the quality in modern societies… consists in the assumption, accepted by most reformers with hardly less naïveté than by the defenders of the established order, that the attainment of material riches is the supreme object of human endeavor."[10] The only measure of social wellbeing was monetary gain and social provisioning was relegated as something of minor significance.

Veblen described a kind of economic ecosystem that has evolved out of the industrial revolution. It was a habitat most conducive for a corporation to grow and thrive like an invasive species. In this corporate ecosystem, everything was being transformed into a commodity or security. Although this system has been evolving for over a century, it blossomed and consolidated into a global colossus during the Greenspan Era. During the Greenspan Era, the percentage of the total assets controlled by financial companies grew rapidly as did their share of corporate profits. In Veblenian terms, financialization during the Greenspan Era constitutes a kind of economic derangement. Derangement in this case signifies that economic institutions have become pathological as they are increasingly directing economic activity to serve the avarice of the corporate class with a certain disregard for social or environmental wellbeing. Although this has always been characteristic of the capitalist mode of production for centuries, what is a unique emergent property of the Greenspan Era is that the corporation has evolved into such a place of power and control, it has taken on a life of its own. It has evolved from a business model of capitalism to an institution that forms its own rules, sets its own political agenda, and creates its own culture and ideology. What was once a capitalist society that used a corporation as a means to its own ends, is now a corporate society that has its own means to pursue its own ends. A corporate society is incompatible with the notion of a commonwealth.

For Morris Berman Americans have never been able to reconcile the discord between the political and economic conditions in America and the notion of a commonwealth. He writes, "… material acquisition and technological innovation were druglike substitutes for a commonwealth, a truly human way of life, that Americans had largely rejected from early on." He sees that in its earliest years America had been torn between that of a land destined for unrepentant acquisitiveness on the one hand and that of a nobler commonwealth for the collective good on the other. Samuel Adams, one of America's "Founding Fathers," saw that the former was gaining traction and grieved that the United States was on its way to become "…more avaricious than any other nation that ever existed." In the struggle for America's soul, the hustlers—a kind of caricature of greed, aggression, and delusion—won out, but not without criticism.[11]

Thorstein Veblen launched a scathing critique of the hustler society that America had become. He lampooned the wealthy segments of America's population as they ostentatiously displayed their affluence by flaunting their ownership of expensive consumer goods. The various accoutrements of the so-called good life signified the winners in the hustlers' game like trophies. Following Veblen have been generations of dissident American intellectuals who lament how their country had become a soulless swamp of corporate commercialism. People seeking to live with a sense of dignity in the States find that there are few choices left to them that have not been consumed by corporate interests. American life, according to dissident Randolph Bourne, has become rudimentary and uninspired and rephrasing Marx and Engels, Bourne writes, "The world has nothing to lose but its chains—and its own soul to gain."[12]

The American Dream is a delusive construct that perpetuates institutionalized and acculturated greed. It also keeps the population perpetually enslaved to the ever-changing fads of consumerism, or in Berman's terms, enslaved to the hustler's life. C. Wright Mills, chronicled the troubling phenomenon of the feverish striving among the population to clone themselves after those in already established structures of power within their political, military, and economic institutions. Mills and others warned about the social pathology that will result from having widespread covetousness become a cultural norm—a nation of hungry ghosts becoming violent. Yet, like other cogent warnings such as the dangers of climate change, Mills's were largely and consistently ignored, as were Veblen's, Ayre's, Dugger's and so many who look candidly at our institutions.

The institutionalist vision gives us a clue as to why changing course is so difficult. difficult to change? This would require that people in significant numbers question their habits and values and culture, which have been marinating in a corporate sauce for a long time. From the very beginning, Samuel Adams saw in the early American culture a peculiar habit of always running headlong into the mad grab for riches, and this habit has long become deeply ingrained. It is like an addiction complete with cognitive dissonance, and it very hard for addicts to imagine themselves free from their addictions, particularly ones that have been around for over two centuries. On this, Berman writes, "…if the American Dream is really about unlimited abundance, and if we are addicted to that as a goal, then alternatives to that way of life are simply too scary to contemplate. Try telling a full-blown alcoholic to put down that glass of Scotch… addiction has a certain 'systemic' pattern to it that is typically not self-corrective. Both capitalism and alcoholism are characterized by cycles of increasing dysfunction, 'runaway,' and breakdown, and the system can do this for a fairly long time."[13] That is until the physical constraints of the planet pull the plug.

It is no doubt bitter medicine for Americans and others who suffer from these same afflictions to see their consumerist and pecuniary lifestyles in this way. But if we could, we would see that our addiction, like all addictions, is taking us down a path toward self-destruction—apocalypse. Ken Jones sees this through an activist Buddhist lens,

> As it is with individual lives, so it is with institutions, societies, and cultures: They may be swept into ruin by karmic and other tangled conditionality even though they have the objective means to avert their fate and more than enough warning of it. The actors are driven by addictive behavior and a kind of tunnel vision that is ultimately self-destructive. And when the majority is locked into mutually affirming karma it may be particularly difficult for even a well-informed minority to achieve a change of direction.[14]

In a perfect circle of pathology, the mad grab for money leaves us astray from our moral center and socially and spiritually malnourished, so in a vain attempts to fill that emptiness we turn to consumer goods and the means to which, of course, is money. The more we grab for money, the more we feel the need to have things to show for the effort, which leads to more grabbing and more greed.

There is no convincing reason why all of us should not be compelled to take a hard, critical look at ourselves along with our values, mythology, and shibboleths. But we are unlikely to do this as long as we can continue to be lulled into a state of somnambulant apathy with financial market bubbles and technological gadgetry that hustle up a collective delusion of progress. Such apathy is hinged to a notion of birthright and entitlement—a Faustian deal, perhaps, made with the promise that we will forever and ever be riding that elevator of prosperity that is rigged to always go in the upward direction and powered by an oligarchy of corporate institutions.

As we step back and take the long view of all this, we can see a system that is doomed to be swinging through one crisis of instability after another. Financial market instability has a history of repetition stretching back hundreds of years from the tulip bulb mania in the seventeenth century, to the government bond and debt privatization in England and France in the eighteenth century, to various stock market crashes and banking meltdowns everywhere in the capitalist world during the nineteenth and twentieth centuries, and now to numerous worldwide financial meltdowns marked the turn of the twenty-first century. These events are as the take off with irrational euphoria of easy riches and end with ruin and the destruction of people's livelihoods. The structure of these events are always basically the same as they open with greed, then the greed turns to fear, fear turns to panic, panic turns to amnesia, and amnesia turns to back greed all over again. What is coming ahead is another round like some many before. The only difference is the unbelievable scale and speed to which the pathology has grown. And because the structure of our financial systems remains fundamentally unchanged, this is inevitable and it raises the pressing question as to whether our countries are able to withstand another major crisis, bailout, debt bubble and so on. Or, will the system crack under such pressure and collapse. Such a collapse would most certainly give rise to a depression, the magnitude of which we have yet seen. When we combine this with the other crises of climate change, polarization of wealth, and resource depletion, the future of humanity looks bleak. Unless there is a substantial change in course, which seems unlikely at this point, the apocalyptic endgame is near.

If it were possible to free the mindset and expectations associated with this doomed system, it will become much easier for us to imagine ourselves evolving into an economically and ecologically healthier society. When we are no longer burdened by the cultural baggage associated with a system that is psychotically trying to achieve infinite growth on a finite planet, we will be able to more effectively explore the possibilities for consciously evolving toward new and healthier ways of living. As Schumacher taught us, this developmental process cannot happen without insight and wisdom, without which we are certain to remain trapped in a destructive society that is fraught with cynical self-aggrandizing consumption habits, greed, and ultimately violence and despair. The crises we face stem not only from how we act in the world, but also from how we perceive the world. Bringing this vision into action and real change is no small matter and will be a process that will take time and enormous effort. And though it may even appear impossible from where we are standing now, I would venture to say that it is not nearly as impossible as trying to survive another few decades in the economy of business as usual.

Notes

1. Thorstein Veblen, *The Theory of Business Enterprise* (New York, NY: Mentor Books, 1904), p. 9.
2. Ibid., p. 10.
3. Ibid.
4. Ibid., p. 9.
5. Ibid., p. 12.
6. Ibid., p. 14.
7. Ibid., p. 15.

8. Ibid.
9. Thorstein Veblen, *Absentee Ownership, Business Enterprise in Recent Times: The Case of America* (New Brunswick, NJ: Transaction Publishers, 1997 [1923]), p. 84.
10. R.H. Tawney, *Religion and the Rise of Capitalism* (New York, NY: Harcourt Brace Jovanovich, 1954 [1926]), p. 235.
11. Morris Berman, *Why America Failed*, p. 24.
12. Randolph Bourne, "Trans-national America" in Olaf Hansen, *The Radical Will: Randolph Borne Selected Writings, 1911–1918* (New York, NY: Urizen Books, 1977), p. 264.
13. Morris Berman, *Why America Failed*, p. 66.
14. Jones, *The New Social Face of Buddhism*, p. 27.

Appendix

Stock Market Bubble

The Standard & Poor's Index representing a broad segment of the corporate sphere shows stocks inflated significantly above the long-term trend. If the markets were to return to trend, which is popularly referred to as a correction, this would mean a collapse—about a 1000-point drop or roughly 39% (Fig. A.1).

The Housing Market Bubble

The Case Shiller U.S. Housing Market Index representing 20 major metropolitan areas, shows housing prices significantly above the long-term trend. If the markets were to return to trend with a correction, this would mean the markets would tank showing a fall in the index from its current level of 204 to collapse to about 160, or roughly 22% (Fig. A.2).

J. Magnuson, *Financing the Apocalypse*,
Palgrave Insights into Apocalypse Economics,
https://doi.org/10.1007/978-3-030-04720-7

Figure A.1 S&P 500 Index, 1980–2018 (*Source* S&P 500 Historical data, https://www.google.com/search?q=s%26p500+historical+chart&rlz=1C1CHBF_enUS798US798&oq=s%26P500+hi&aqs=chrome.3.0j69i57j0l4.10349j0j8&sourceid=chrome&ie=UTF-8. Google and the Google logo are registered trademarks of Google Inc., used with permission)

The Federal Reserve Asset Bubble

To rescue Wall Street from its troubles, the Federal Reserve embarked on a buying spree of Mortgage-backed securities, government debt, and other securities. Its holdings of assets soared from about $800 billion in 2007 to nearly $4.5 trillion a decade later. To do this it created about $3.5 trillion dollars out of thin air. If the Fed were to try to unwind its holdings of these assets and return to trend, it would have to reverse that process and dump about $3 trillion of these back on the markets. Such a move would crash the market and precipitate a global financial meltdown (Fig. A.3).

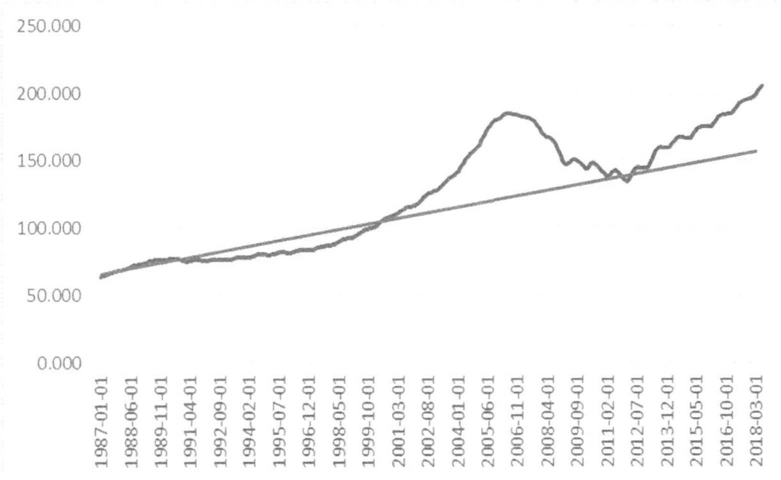

Figure A.2 S&P Case-Shiller U.S. National Home Price Index, 1987–2018 (*Source* Federal Reserve Bank of St. Louis and Standard and Poors, S&P/Case-Shiller U.S. National Home Price Index, https://fred.stlouisfed.org/series/CSUSHPINSA)

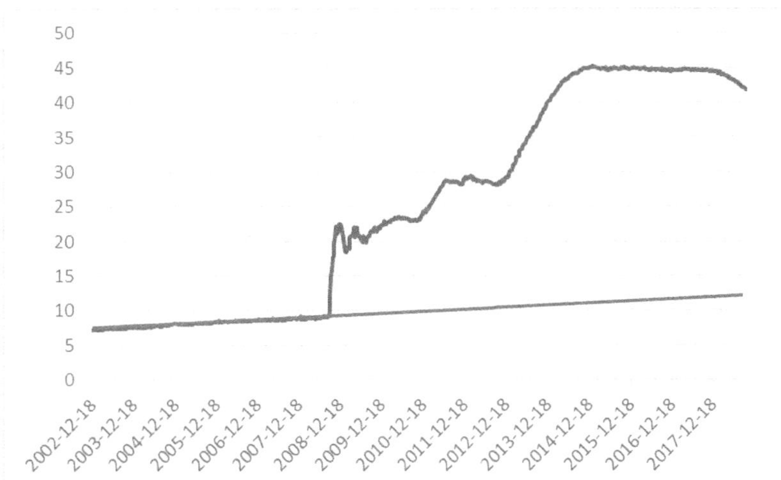

Figure A.3 Federal Reserve Total Assets (x trillion) (*Source* St. Louis Federal Reserve, https://fred.stlouisfed.org/graph/?id=WALCL,TLAACBW027SBOG,#0)

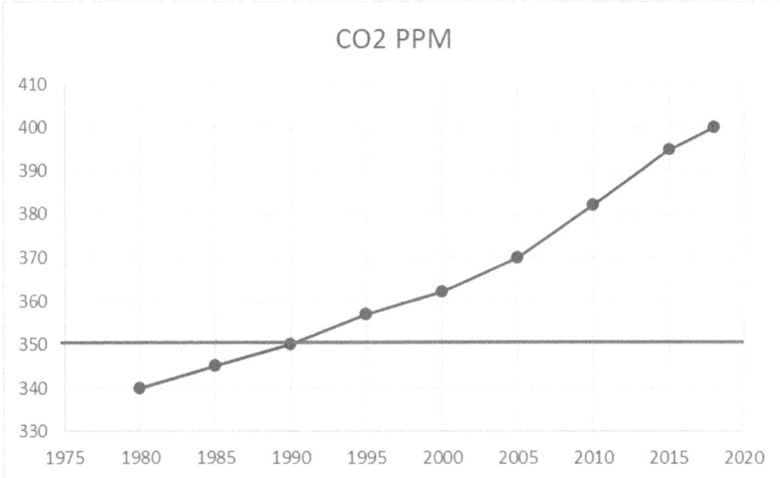

Figure A.4 Atmospheric carbon dioxide, 1975–2018 (parts per million) (*Source* National Oceanic and Atmospheric Administration, Climate Change: CO_2Breaks Record in 2017, https://www.climate.gov/news-features/understanding-climate/climate-change-atmospheric-carbon-dioxide)

The Carbon Dioxide Bubble

According to scientist James Hansen, it is estimated that the world can limit the worst effects of climate change by bringing the concentration of atmospheric carbon dioxide to below 350 parts per million from its current levels of over 400. This number was considered the key to avoiding the climate change "tipping point" beyond which the global climate condition moves from stable to unstable. Humans have already past that point and there is no turning back (Fig. A.4).

The Inequality Bubble

The Gini Index is a measurement of income distribution (see Chapter 6). The higher the index number, the more unequal the distribution of income becomes for the population. The long-term trend is for an

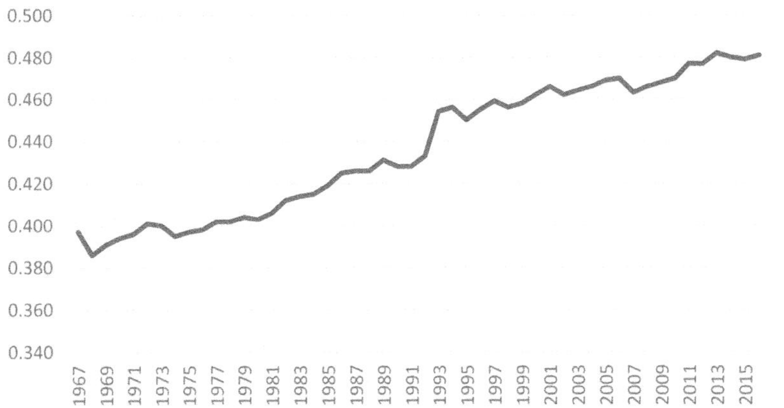

Figure A.5 Gini Index for the United States, 1967–2015 (*Source* Federal Reserve District Bank of St. Louis, https://fred.stlouisfed.org/graph/?graph_id=212325&updated=2000 and Luxembourg income study, https://www.lisadatacenter.org/our-data/lis-database/)

increasingly wide chasm of separating the wealthy from the rest of the population. Given the current political climate, the trend will continue and shows no sign of ever returning to a condition of equitable income distribution. This trend is certain to cause social instability at some point (Fig. A.5).

Index

J. Magnuson, *Financing the Apocalypse*, Palgrave Insights into Apocalypse Economics, https://doi.org/10.1007/978-3-030-04720-7

Printed by Printforce, the Netherlands